Diary of a Shipping Clerk
VOLUME 2

Diary of a Shipping Clerk
VOLUME 2

David Miles-Hanschell

DIARY OF A SHIPPING CLERK ~ Volume 2
by David Miles-Hanschell

First published 2023

Copyright © David Miles-Hanschell 2023

The right of David Miles-Hanschell to be identified as
the author of this work has been asserted by him
in accordance with the Copyright, Designs
and Patents Act 1988.

All rights reserved.
No part of this book may be reproduced in any form
or by any electronic or mechanical means, including information
storage and retrieval systems, without written permission from
the author, except for the use of brief quotations in a book review.

Copyedited by Northern Editorial
Cover design by Red Axe Design
Book interior by Eleanor Abraham

Typeset in Adobe Garamond Pro and Proxima Nova

Diary of a Shipping Clerk Vol 2 Print: 978-1-7391426-2-9

Diary of a Shipping Clerk Vol 2 ebook: 978-1-7391426-3-6

Contents

Dedication	6
Introduction	7
Chapter Nine – Another Long Day at Grange Dock	9
Chapter Ten – I Embark on a New Career	25
Chapter Eleven – I Meet the Secret Millionaire and Travel Far Further	125
Chapter Twelve – The Trip To Bluefields, Costa Caribena, Nicaragua, Meso-America	247
Note to End Volume Two	287

Dedication

To Marion, Amy, David and Johanna –
who bore the cost without complaint – and all
those who made the shipments a reality.

Introduction

On 7 September 2004, Hurricane Ivan caused severe destruction to Grenada. I became aware of the extent of the devastation through a report given to me by a parent of one of the students in my P4/5 class. The letter describing Hurricane Ivan's devastation had a profound impact on me. It marked the beginning of a transformative journey, with my determination to assist the people of Grenada becoming the focus of my waking life.

In this volume, my work continues. I attempt to ship unwanted, fit-for-purpose school equipment – otherwise headed for landfill – to parts of the world with a dire need for it.

The following entries in this volume also show how this aspiring Shipping Clerk set about formalising my efforts – to create a non-governmental organisation. Its primary purpose was to advance education through supplying schools and colleges in disadvantaged communities in any part of the world with surplus-to-requirement educational resources.

In order to achieve this—

- I maintained contact with the key individuals in the world of logistics who had made it possible for me to deliver, during the period 2005–7, four ocean freight container loads of resources to Hurricane-Ivan-devastated schools in Grenada, West Indies;
- I approached individuals in Scottish Local Authority responsible for implementing the Private Finance Initiative to determine from them whether it was possible to acquire resources prior to their disposal into landfill;
- the Surplus Educational Supplies Foundation became a registered Scottish Charity and limited company and became an active member of the Edinburgh Chamber of Commerce.

David Miles-Hanschell

Chapter Nine

Another Long Day at Grange Dock

Friday 23/05/2008

7:15 a.m. I am on the train at Wemyss Bay Station – there goes the whistle. Generators humming. Now in motion. I am up the rails once more. As I cycled up the Mount Stuart road I decided not to leave my bike behind. I met Alistair, yacht-master, as I sat on my perch in the ferry boat café, he kindly invited me to join him and Ann, his wife, for coffee. Chat. They were curious as to where I was going.

I long for genuine interest and support, but I have to take the consequence of 'sailing' solo. *'They have been in institutions all their life,'* said AM with disdain, referring to teachers in response to my comment about teachers and their attitude to uncertainty, innovation, social enterprise, and lack of initiative. True enough, and I hope it is not too late for me having inadvertently escaped – a previous life. I have no hard feelings. Well, just more than a little regret that my career ended so abruptly in a manner I could never have envisaged. Embittered? No, that's too strong a word. I just wish it had not come to an end in the manner it had, a year before I was officially able to retire from teaching. My career had been more than just that: it was a vocation from the start. The first day, when I was directed by the school's principal, Sister John Hugh, the first thing she said to me was, *'David, you just go into that classroom, and if you have any problems just call me.'* I walked into a class of children at the Oxford Street Elementary School in Halifax, Nova Scotia, Canada in the autumn of 1969.

I met Kenny, HGV driver with John MacKirdy Haulage Ltd, who came over to speak to me, and then Martin, who asked,

'*Where are you going now?*' I told him that I was on my way over to the Duncan Adams Transport Ltd yard at Grange Dock to put a coat of paint on my next container shipment of educational resources to Grenada, West Indies. '*You might as well come back on the next boat from Wemyss Bay.*'

8:25 a.m. I pushed my bicycle up from Central Station. I am now in Queen Street Station aboard the train for Falkirk Grahamston. I am out of my comfort zone and en route for 'fame and fortune'.

9:07 a.m. I just passed the opposition, Central Demolition Ltd, at Bonnybridge.

9:10 a.m. Camelon. I alight here for the Forth Valley Sensory Centre. It is raining heavily: a grey morning.

9:20 a.m. I have pushed the bike around to Antonio's Deli, where I have asked directions to Economy Autopaints and have been told that it is just down the road, so I am going to stop here for a wee pause that relieves, sustains, and refreshes. I have spoken to a friendly lady who is kneading a pile of dough with raisins. There are pensioners like me in here for a coffee.

9:30 a.m. I sit here, looking out across the busy main road in Falkirk town centre, munching away at the other half of my bacon roll.

11 a.m. Now I must get along to Economy Autopaints, where I was last year to purchase paint for the 40-foot ocean freight container CRXU4103197, my third container purchase, which was delivered to the Fife Warehousing Company Ltd, Hayfield Industrial Estate, Kirkcaldy in early 2007.

I have been up and down the street trying to find a cashpoint. The proprietor's paint mixers tell me they now have a

Friday 23/05/2008

tropical-green, metallic, URP auto paint. What's next? I told them that I paid cash here in April 2007 for two 5-litre tins and that they had given one of them free, which cuts no ice. I stand at the counter and wait to see what they will come up with.

A gentleman returns, stirring a mixture of paint in a styrofoam cup. The paint is a unique shade of aquamarine green. *'That will be fine, there will not be another box painted that colour anywhere, that's for sure,'* I said. Sign behind the counter: It is illegal to sell a spray paint device to anyone under the age of 16. There is a wee dug, a schnauzer, on the floor asleep on a piece of towel.

I load one of the tins into a saddlebag and the other into my haversack, and set off to cycle along the Forth and Clyde Canal to Grange Dock.

12:45 p.m. I am sitting in the reception of Duncan Adams Transport Ltd. *'Are you ready to start?'* asks Eric. *'Yes, I have brought my boiler suit with me.' 'Would you like a cup of tea?'* he asks. *'Yes, please, with a big lump of sugar, thank you, Eric,'* I reply.

I have just cycled in beside the canal from Falkirk – into an industrial park with ginormous Asda warehouses (Walmart Inc.) and out onto a very busy main road, around two roundabouts, and into Grange Dock. I stopped at the Forth Ports Plc security gate and showed my passport, which I made sure to have with me this time, as photo ID was required.

2 p.m. Allan, the big container forklift box shifter, showed me where the container was and has kindly moved the containers that were on top of mine, and beside it, so I can get in to paint it. Good of him. There is a breeze from off the North Sea moving up under the Firth of Forth Bridge (which I walked across early one morning in July 1974).

Here I am back at Duncan Adams Transport Ltd yard. I dragged three pallets and stacked them so I can climb up onto the top of container CRXU4103197, which I purchased from Freight Container Services (Scotland) Ltd way back in early 2007 and had loaded with chairs and tables, which we had salvaged from Kennoway Primary School, Fife, with the crucial assistance of the Fife Warehousing Co Ltd and a team of volunteers.

2:15 p.m. I struggle into my well-used blue boiler suit, don the rubber gloves and get started to make this 'box', a 40-foot dry ocean freight container, mine.

9:15 p.m. I am sitting on a stool in La Gondola, Chippie of the Year, Grangemouth Mall, trying to digest a fish supper and swally twa cokes. I left the Duncan Adams Transport yard at 8:45 p.m. There was not a soul about as I swung the heavy gates shut, aware of the trust and responsibility given that I might remain on the premises.

I cycled out of the dock and handed in my pass to Forth Ports' security at the North Shore gate. The guard remarked on the paint on my face. It's great to be on my bike: a sense of accomplishment, for I had set out in fear and trembling earlier, and now I am well and truly immersed in this yard. My own work. Beautiful afternoon. Doos for company, flying around the stacks of boxes. I am at peace with myself and the world. I feel whole. Magic!

I managed to persevere with the task in hand that I had set myself. I put one lick of paint on the east-facing side of the container, which had been poorly loaded with chairs and tables last year. The 36 boxes of library books donated by Morningside Library in Edinburgh, and brought out pro bono by Bishop's Move Removals Ltd, are not in the container and must be in storage somewhere in the yard.

Now I will go and find a place to stay for the night. First stop, the hotel in Grangemouth where I stayed last year when painting TRIU5079422, which was my second purchase from Freight Container Services (Scotland) Ltd.

Saturday 24/05/2008

10:19 p.m. Room 35, booked into the hotel by Stewart. '*You tell a good story. I know where you are coming from,*' he said. Chatting to Stewart at the cosy bar along with some of the other residents, I could easily have downed a pint, but I must keep my mind clear. I am going to have a shower.

11:40 p.m. I am sitting on the edge of the bed recording the passage of this day. I am back again in this hotel. Check diary – last time here was April 2007.

I stepped out after a shower, in clean underwear: small luxuries that I do not take for granted. I still have paint on my fingers. I went along to the payphones in the mall to call Marion. Oh, you prat! I had forgotten to bring my specs – couldn't see the digits – so it was back to my room to collect them. We chatted. All is well on the home front. The cost of leaving home comforts, company, and being here on my own: isolation. I stopped off at La Gondola chippie, which was not very busy, and bought myself a vanilla wafer, which I have just scoffed. Brushed my teeth. There is a fresh, light breeze blowing outside. A mild evening.

I am going to read *The 7 Habits of Highly Effective People. Powerful Lessons in Personal Change* by Stephen Covey. I bought *The Big Issue* from a vendor outside Queen Street Station and, as I walked out through Central Station pushing the bike a young lad handed me the morning's business supplement from *The Daily Telegraph*. I certainly shan't be reading all that before I shut my eyes.

Saturday 24/05/2008

1:35 a.m. As you can see, I am now wide awake. Physically knackered. I am exhausted and I am unable to sleep; the bed is very uncomfortable. My hamstring muscles at the back of my thighs had tightened up and I was unable to straighten my legs, and for a while I couldn't sit up. This is the time of day when I get assailed with negative thoughts.

What is the point of all this expense and effort? The container that I painted last year is nowhere near full and it looks as if some of the tables and chairs that it contained have been removed. I'll need to bring container MAEU6085656 (up at Mossend, Coatbridge container base with John G Russell Ltd depot), down here, and take some of the tables out – proper secondary school furniture, good stuff collected from the former Academy, earmarked for GBBS way back in March 2007 – and move them into CRXU4103197, which leaves on 9 June. Why hasn't the gift of library books been loaded into it? I will have to settle my situation and tacit support from Duncan Adams Transport Ltd, bring all of my containers together into one place, empty them, and inventory all educational resources. For that I will need a large industrial unit warehouse, similar to Unit 3, Food and Business Centre, Glenrothes, which had been loaned temporarily to me by Fife Council's Assets and Facilities Management early this year; this facility would need to be in a central belt location. I would have them surveyed to ensure that they are seaworthy and painted with the SESF logo. I will need to create an identity presence: a marketing trademark logo.

Make arrangements to meet individuals who share my vision, with whom I can work and collaborate to realise the objectives of my foundation.

2:46 p.m. I am writing this in brilliant sunshine. A soft breeze is blowing in from somewhere. I am looking at the water moving under the Wemyss Bay ferry platform pier bridge, and sitting on the galvanised railings at the end of the ferry car park. I have not long come off the 1:50 p.m. train from Central Station.

What of today? I had breakfast at the hotel. 'Home away from home,' in jest you mean. This establishment brought back memories of my many months sojourn in Lindsay House Hostel, East

Saturday 24/05/2008

A Duncan Adams Transport vehicle.

Another Long Day at Grange Dock

Kilbride 1984–1985, where I made friends from all over the world. I was served breakfast at the former residence by Surjit from Gujarat in the Punjab. I watched him from the other side of the serving hatch as he plucked two rashers of bacon, one sausage, and a spoonful of tinned tomatoes on to a plate and stuck them into a microwave, while I spooned a helping of Alpen and a crushed Weetabix into a bowl, poured some milk, and walked over to a solitary breakfast resident, who appeared to come from the locality.

'*May I join you?*' I asked, sat down not waiting for his reply, and then fired off another enquiry in my 'hail fellow, well met' manner. '*Could you tell me the easiest way for a cyclist to get from Grangemouth to Falkirk, which avoids the main road?*' He mumbled a reply, which I did not hear and remained silent for the rest of our joint repast. I would need to ask directions once more. I later chatted to Surjit, who told me he visits India regularly, and has a diploma in hotel keeping. Firm handshake. Speaks Hindi and he tells me that he has read the Bhagavad Gita. We exchange business cards.

I went back upstairs and after brushing my teeth returned the room key and cycled out of town, around the roundabout and into Grange Dock, showed my fotie ID, and got back to work. I met Allan who drives the box lifter. A skilled helpful worker, as they all are in this very busy trucking depot. '*Hello, old yin!*' says young Kenneth, cheerily. I just met him when I went to beg Iain for some paint thinner. He is one of the truck-garage machine-shop mechanic's apprentices. I first met Kenneth on Saturday, 9 December 2006 in Inverkeithen town centre, the morning he came through with George, HGV driver, who brought the 40-foot curtain-sider to me, as I stood in front of the Volunteer Arms pub on Inverkeithen main street, to collect the first load of educational resources from Inverkeithen Primary School and who, bless him, had returned the following Saturday, this time with George and the young Callum, to collect yet another container load of educational resources. It was good to see him again. Kenneth tells me that he is not attending day release any more, but intends to continue his apprenticeship in the depot's machine shop and truck garage.

3 p.m. The ferry is approaching Rothesay Bay on this full-of-beauty afternoon, with sunlight dappling the pond calm Firth of Clyde. I will try and take up some more of this scribble later.

Monday 26/05/2008

7:10 a.m. I am sitting once more in a carriage at Wemyss Bay Station bound for Glasgow Central Station. The sun is shining brightly through the glass roof panels of this station platform, refurbished over many months – a Victorian architectural and engineering marvel. I came across on the MV *Bute* and I introduced myself to Callum, who is usually with a number of other regulars at this time, and who was sitting on a stool across from where I am usually perched. He tells me that diesel fuel is costing him £100 per week. There are no John MacKirdy Haulage Ltd drivers this morning. I wonder why?

I treated myself to a white coffee and a roll and sausage, and then went up on deck and stayed there, facing the breeze coming off the braes above Skelmorelie, sunlight dazzling the watta, my mind clear, looking all around me at the magnificent scenery. Inadequate words, but will do for now; a small sigh escapes my throat, because here I am once again heading across the central belt of Scotland to Grange Dock to complete the painting of CRXU4103197. I had better move my bicycle from the doorway before the train stops at Inverkip Station.

8:20 a.m. Queen Street Station, Glasgow. I am bound for Falkirk Grahamston. There was little traffic on the streets of Glasgow this morning because of the bank holiday. As I was pushing the bike through Central Station I was accosted by a familiar face, one of the fellow travellers in days past from Wemyss Bay *'Are you David?'* asks the stranger as we get off the train. *'Who are you?'* I think to myself. *'You travel with Jim, don't you?'* he asks, with a look of surprise on his face. *'Yes I used too. I have not seen him for a while,'* I reply. *'He's retired and he's not been well,'* he said. Jim was chief purchaser with Rolls Royce at Hillington, and after retirement returned to full-time employment to work for the Glasgow City Council project team that brought a Cowlairs-built steam locomotive back from Durban, South Africa, as an emblem for the next Commonwealth Games. And he had hoped that the Big Green place should be awarded the venue for the Commonwealth Games. I will try and get in touch with him.

I am trying to keep up this conversation in motion as the two of us walk out of the crowded station. *'You remember Jim introduced us on a journey last year?'* he said. *'I do recall meeting you. You had mentioned that a colleague of yours was passionate about relief work and was sending resources out to Africa,'* I said. *'Aye, I did that, but not any mair, but one of my mates is going out tae Malawi on business. Cheerio,'* he said.

The next stop is Springburn.

10:36 a.m. Sunshine out of a clear blue sky on the page of this jotter. I am back in one of my life's classrooms. A strong breeze is blowing dust up around the Maersk, P&O, Ned Lloyd and Interpol (Barbados) big boxes. I have just eaten my sandwiches and swallowed cold green tea. I have arrived at Duncan Adams Transport Ltd, Grange Dock depot, having cycled from Falkirk Grahamston along the busy main road intae Grangemouth. Alan the Forklift has kindly moved my container, of which I am about to paint the other side.

I have just seen a John G Russell Transport Ltd transporter come slowly past me. I signalled to the driver to stop, which he did, and I asked him if he would give Mark at their Mossend depot my regards. Ya cheeky sod. Stop yer havering and get back tae wuk.

4:35 p.m. I paused in my labouring to speak to Slowek, HGV driver from Poland. I have run out of paint. I still have a quarter of the top surface of the box to complete; it's a slow process, with a small roller. The sun has been shining down on us all afternoon. I made a mistake of not thinning the first tin of paint. Live and learn. Every day is a school day.

7:55 p.m. Back on the MV *Bute* heading across the watta under a cloudless sky bursting with sunlight. Before I cycled out of the yard, I went across to the office to let them know that I would be off the premises. Eric looked up from his desk. *'Are you going home tonight?'* he asked. *'Yes, Eric. I'll see you all again tomorrow. I still have a part of the top half of the container to complete,'* I replied. I cycled out of the depot and out of Grange Dock. I cycled up the busy Grangemouth road recalling the time when Eric kindly whizzed me up the same road in his Porsche to the Falkirk Station two years ago, Saturday, 16 December 2006 – his words to me as I climbed out were: *'You find the shipping lines, David, and we will deliver your containers to any port in the United Kingdom.'* Wow, that support sure was to get me off the ground and on to another level.

I pushed the bike up the long, steep hill to Falkirk High Street Station to catch the Queen Street Glasgow Express. I headed home. I had a long wait in Central to get the 6:50 p.m. Wemyss Bay train. No pains, no gain. It's back again tomorrow. *Are you serious?* Yes. I will have to wait and see if I can get another tin of that mixture and colour Caribbean Sea aquamarine, and find out where the 36 boxes of Morningside library books are. I am tired.

Another Long Day at Grange Dock

Tuesday 27/05/2008

7:15 a.m. I am now back on the train for Central Station. On the way over I chatted to Ally, digital artisan from Baillieston. Ally runs his own IT firm, which he started after having been made redundant from the National Engineering Laboratory at East Kilbride. 'I worked for the civil service for 14 years,' he tells me. He came in on the cusp of the Digital Revolution and is currently riding the digital wave. What's the next development in the Digital Revolution? He kindly repaired and determined which Apple McIntosh computers that I had salvaged from the Argyll and Bute Council skips were working. These computers went in several container shipments to Hurricane Ivan (2004) devastated schools: Grand Roy Government School in July 2005, and St Paul's Government School in August 2007.

Ally bought me a coffee.

7:20 a.m. The train is moving off from the IBM station platform where a skeleton staff remain at that massive Spango Valley plant, now lying virtually empty but for outsourcers. I am journeying to DAT Ltd Grange Dock yard to complete the painting of the first shipment of educational resources to the Grenada Boys' Secondary School. It will be the fourth container shipment so far. First stop will be Economy Autopaints in Falkirk to see if I can get enough of that special mix to finish the job.

The white flowers on hawthorn bushes are dripping white purity on both sides of the railway track; the yellow flowers of broom have nae prickles, unlike the gorse – watch your pinkies. It is a fresh beginning to a new day. I am brand new every day once I get off on the right side of the bed and foot. There is a pink-flowering hawthorn bush, almost a tree, which I have never seen before growing alone on the main street, on down to the canal in Falkirk. '*See yuz later,*' a man says to a group of his fellow travellers as he got off the train at Whinhill some way back down the line.

Tuesday 27/05/2008

8:34 a.m. I am rolling, rocking, roistering, and swaying my way towards Falkirk Grahamston. I had barely managed to board this train in the nick of time. Swarms of commuters. It is dry, cool, and cloudy. I take a note of Ritchies Plant Training, in Springburn, for the day when I will learn how to drive a forklift truck. The Logistics Man. I catch a glimpse of gridlocked traffic on the M8 to my left. Magpies in flight.

12:09 p.m. I have tried to remove the dried mud and dust from the base girders of the container prior to putting on a coat of red oxide paint. This fresh beautiful morning, I collected the big tin of paint from the 'New Perch', with garden toolshed beneath, constructed not a few years ago with the help of Dan, Robert, Johanna and David.

The sun is rising over Skelmorelie. Now, over here on the East Coast, it is cloudy with a strong breeze blowing up the Firth of Forth. I purchased another two one-half litre tins of the special mixture paint from Economy Autopaints in Falkirk, and cycled along the Firth and Clyde Canal. I saw swans, with their young, grey, furry cygnets, on the grassy bank. I was cycling through the Asda/Walmart industrial estate/park out on the busy main road and pulled up beside the snack bar trailer just off the roundabout into Grange Dock. '*What wid yuh like, son?*' he asked with a smile. '*Whatever you got?*' I said nonchalantly, not feeling too great, with twinges of sharp migraine pain up behind my right eyeball socket. I swallowed two painkillers. Sweet coffee and two rolls, wan wi sausage, the other black puddin' and a squeeze of broon sauce, should fix it.

I stopped in at Duncan Adams Transport Ltd reception, as must all visitors to their yard. '*You are late,*' says Eric with good humour. I like and respect this man. '*I've only got two wheels,*' I reply. *Get back tae wuk.* A wee pause before I do. I munch my special sardine-mix paste sandwiches first and eat an apple. Get my priorities right, and look after the inner man. Ye cannae fight on an empty stomach. It's nice to be chillin' inside my property – the sale of some of the BS&T shares, which I have turned into a tangible asset.

1:30 p.m. I have climbed down from the top of the container. I had borrowed a ladder from the warehouse. The sun occasionally makes its way through a heavy bank of thick, grey cloud to brighten my determined efforts, otherwise it has been a cool and windy afternoon. Earlier today, I met Leo from Holland who works for Pentalver Transport Ltd (a Maersk subsidiary), up from Southampton. He is a reefer refrigeration-container technician electrician. Leo worked previously for CMA and he knows some of the people that I have become friendly with over the telephone in that Southampton Port city office. I asked him to give my regards to Stuart, his present company's chief executive, and if he would tell him that, if it were possible, I wished to purchase another dry ocean freight container. He is forthcoming, informative, and offered me another pair of gloves.

I am going to finish the other half of the sandwich that I made last night before I tackle the last little stretch above. Onward and upward.

6:45 p.m. I am sitting in another train in Central Station bound for Wemyss Bay. I managed somehow to just keep on going on with the slow process of painting, having to apply it with a small roller. The Duncan Adams Transport Ltd warehousemen had kindly lent me, once more, a ladder which I roped to the container and it sure beat stacking pallets on top of each other. Later they lent me a shovel, which I used to tidy up in front of TRIU5079422, which had been loaded with fit-for-purpose educational resources from the former Inverkeithen Primary School on Saturday, 16 December 2006, which I had painted last year and which is now looking slightly worse for wear. It was windy and overcast, but thankfully remained dry all day long. I tidied up

Tuesday 27/05/2008

with feelings of accomplishment, achievement, and immense satisfaction, now that ex-Chronos CRXU4103197 looks a lot better than when I found it. It will look good on Caribbean shores.

I got out of my overalls, and closed the doors thinking that it would still be there at the depot later in the week, for there was still much space left to load more good cargo. I went over to reception and gave Duncan Adams an SESF file with newspaper items, where his firm gets a mention for assisting the initiative, and a letter that I had written to him early this morning, before leaving home, in which I expressed my appreciation for the assistance, advice and encouragement his firm Duncan Adams Transport Ltd had given to me over two years now, and that I did not take their goodwill towards my charitable initiative for granted and was grateful for all the help I had received. *'Here comes the man of the moment. Were you working?'* asked Duncan with a smile when I handed him my letter of thanks for all his firm's help to me. He, along with everyone in the yard, has made me feel welcome from the first day. I told him that I had been working, but didn't tell him I was whacked. I told him that I been preparing another argosy shipment: a treasured, big box of educational resources.

I cycled out onto the busy main road from Grangemouth to Falkirk, negotiating the two roundabouts, bristling with a *noli me tangere nemo me impune lacessit*, 'dare you hit me and you are in trouble', attitude to those motorists who appeared not to give a fig for my safety, and acknowledging with *'Good on yuh!'* hand signals for those considerate souls who slowed down, conscious of my welfare. I stopped in at the Falkirk Tesco to purchase a more agreeable smell and sprayed my nether regions and pushed my bike up the long, steep hill into couthy residential Falkirk and along to Falkirk High Station.

I missed the 4:50 p.m. from Glasgow Central Station because I had to purchase a return ticket. I called Marion to let her know I was on my way home and treated myself to a Cornish pasty and a bottle of M&S orange juice in Central Station. I am tired out. I reflect that for me, now, at long last, at this late hour, it's all about personal responsibility, inner direction, and autonomy. But it has come at a price: *'Be it on your own head, David,'* were the words my Church of Scotland minister said to me all those years ago, when I set out of that comfort zone of secure employment with the intention of joining the Sahara Desert Mission in the Niger Republic.

Chapter Ten

I Embark on a New Career

Wednesday 28/05/2008

6:44 a.m. MV *Bute* is sailing under grey skies against a strong north-easterly breeze. I am off today to meet Jane of the Cranfield Trust for a 10 a.m. meeting at the Edinburgh Sheraton Hotel, and later Adam of the *Edinburgh Evening News*. I am sitting here on my usual perch, slowly sipping a frothy-topped white coffee. No guarantees and no presumptions. I will take it as it comes. I have many plans, dreams, visions, and nebulous ideas swirling around in my mind, however, what matters most is that I am ready to meet all that is in the storehouse of adventure with a positive attitude.

7:12 a.m. I am sitting in the carriage of the train for Central. '*You look smart today,*' said Robert the joiner. '*Thank you, Robert. You wouldn't by any chance happen to know of a quantity surveyor that I could speak to, regarding giving me quote for a tender to uplift educational resources from a secondary school due to be demolished, would you?*' I asked. He gives me the name of someone.

8:20 a.m. I hoofed it up smartly from Central to Queen Street Station, bought a return ticket to Auld Reekie Lums, hurried round to Platform 6 and we were awa.

2:15 p.m. On the train back to Glasgow. I boarded at Haymarket, where I bought a small mocha coffee, a Fresh Bite tuna mayonnaise sandwich, and a packet of McVitie's mini cheese biscuits. I'm sitting facing backwards, not by choice as I prefer to sit facing the direction I'm heading, so I shall resume this scrawled aide memoire later.

2:30 p.m. '*We are now approaching Falkirk. The next stop is Croy,*' she said. I have managed to switch seats. It is raining, with thick, grey clouds overhead.

Roll it back: while I was scribbling on the way out of Queen Street Station this morning, the conductor looked at my ticket and told me that I was on the wrong train. Am I heading in the wrong direction? I can only travel with the light and knowledge that I have. There have been many wrong turnings and dead ends in my life's journey – mishaps, blunders etc. – and no doubt there will be many more before I leave the premises. The train was going to Oban, where I worked for part of the summer of 1974 as a kitchen porter for the Inglis family in their restaurant, McTavish's Kitchen.

I remained cool calm and collected. '*You'll get aff at Dalmuir. Walk up over the bridge and ye'll get the train back to low-level Queen Street, another gentleman has made the same mistake as yourself,*' said the helpful conductor. I rushed out the carriage, up over the bridge and back down the line and, as fast as my spindly legs could carry me, up the stairs and chased him round to Platform 2 to board the Edinburgh shuttle at 9:15 a.m. Gavin, who also got on the wrong train, is travelling first class and I joined him for coffee and paid the extra £4 difference to shoot the breeze with him. He described our boarding the wrong train journey as tears, rips, and breaks in the tapestry, when interesting things, unintended consequences, can sometimes happen. I got a taxi after a long wait at the rank from Haymarket up to the Sheraton Hotel and was let off at the rear entrance. I was disoriented.

I apologised to Jane, the Cranfield Trust volunteer, who was having tea in the café, for being late for the appointment. I feel like a teapot. I shan't use the Glaswegian equivalent of a naff idjit. She had been waiting for some time for me to show up. I did not get off to a good start with this opportunity to give a good impression. I gave my elevator pitch and tried to articulate the kind of help, expertise, and business skills I needed. She tells me that I need funding to research the intended market for the large quantities of fit-for-purpose educational resources that I had collected, a strategy, and a business plan. All sound advice. Fair enough, I knew that much myself. I thanked her for taking the trouble to see me and bid her au revoir.

I crossed Festival Square and went into the Edinburgh Chamber of Commerce conference centre and meeting room for coffee. I decided to call Gillian the marketing manager, who I had met last June at a Chamber speed networking session, who had told me then that her firm would consider doing some signage gratis on one of my containers. She told me that I was welcome to visit their firm to discuss this generous offer, so I jumped into another taxi for Granton on the other side of the city. I was glad that I heeded Marion's advice before departure this morning, that I need not take my bike as it is not always the most convenient means of transport in a metropolis congested by cars.

3:40 p.m. Heading homeward. I am sitting on yet another train platform, Platform 10, Central Station. I have not long hoofed it from Burness Solicitors on Bothwell Street. *'There are over two hundred of us at Burness,'* said the young Graham, to me as we headed up in the lift. I had a brief meeting with Stephen about the intended offer from the local housing association regarding the removal of reusable educational resources that remained in the former high school. I am to contact him as soon as they indicate their offer to me in writing. I found him welcoming and brisk. *'Once you have got the paperwork, it will provide the template for other offers,'* he said. Why do I enmesh myself unnecessarily in legal arrangements, when my word is sufficient? I was bedazzled by the business world and expected more of a guiding hand.

Last night I called Neil of Thorpe Kilworth based in Corby,

whose charity supports education in South Africa, and who impressed me once when he told me he was calling from his chauffeur-driven car. Contact: Bonnybridge Demolition Ltd and other demolition firms. Find out what educational resources they will let me have prior to the school building's destruction. Educational resources that can be sold to generate funds for the Surplus Educational Supplies Foundation. What is the going rate for collection of educational resources from schools? What do these demolition firms charge councils to crush resources prior to demolishing the school buildings and delivering crushed material to landfill sites? What is the rate for disposal of this 'WASTE' at the landfill site? Where can I obtain these numbers? Can SESF salvage these resources before they are destroyed, for less than what the demolition firms charge councils, and sell some of these resources to make a profit? I can provide a service to educational resource impoverished institutions in the developing world. Is anyone in Scotland selling surplus educational resources that have been salvaged from the school system? How do I go about selling educational resources that have been salvaged by SESF.

Marketing, contracts, the tendering process, of which I haven't a clue; everything from these surplus schools has got go somewhere, but surely not crushing and dumping into landfill fit-for-purpose educational resources?

Thursday 29/05/2008

8:35 a.m. Home. Johanna has left for school. Bless her. A little sunshine is beginning to break through the rain clouds overhead. I have just written thank-you letters to Cranfield Trust projects manager Iain, their representative in Romsey Hampshire, and to Jane. Methinks I am too much of a scrapheap challenge contestant for their MBA ilk.

10:05 a.m. Wrote to Eric to let him know of the Lofthus Signs

Ltd offer to paint signage on the side of my next shipment to Grenada. Alastair called to let me know he had more empty cardboard boxes, which I will set off to collect in a minute.

Friday 30/05/2008

11:30 a.m. Home. I am back from the dentist. I cycled on up the road to see John MacKirdy Haulage Ltd and they have kindly said they will take boxes over to the DTA Ltd Grange Dock depot before 9 September. I stopped off at The Bike Shed. '*I've told Liam that the next time Davie comes in here to give him a new helmet and you are to put that one in the bin,*' said David the proprietor. Kindness. And I am addicted to it.

I am now going upstairs to box my accumulated teaching resources for the pending shipment to the Grenada Boys' Secondary School.

Tuesday 03/06/2008

8:45 p.m. Home. I have the recurring sharp pain behind my right eye and tingling numbness in my left hand, so I swallowed two painkillers – co-codamol. Johanna, bless her, bids me goodbye and is off to school. I had a shower and am thankful for creature comforts. I am not feeling too good. I am awaiting a number of phone calls from John MacKirdy Haulage Ltd to confirm delivery next week. I hope to get the boxes at the Caribbean Hurricane Relief Depot across to CRXU4103197 before it leaves for Grenada Boys' Secondary School.

Word has come from Louise at W. Knight Watson Ltd, freight forwarders in Grangemouth, regarding their tariff and that of Maersk for expediting the shipment. The Glasgow Freight Club is Eric's circle of lion's den movers and shakers in the logistics industry, and he had said he would speak to their secretary about the possibility of me making a pitch for support at one of their gatherings. I am now going to lie down and see if I can beat this affliction.

12 p.m. I got a call from Tom Walker container surveyor to see how I was? I was humbled given that he was going through the mill at Stobhill Hospital. I didn't tell him my head was still throbbing.

Monday 16/06/2008

5:45 a.m. I am sitting in the cab of a John MacKirdy Haulage Ltd transporter on the Loch Dunvegan ferry, which is now moving slowly over to Colintraive en route to Grange Dock.

8:15 a.m. Kenny has just dropped me off at DAT Ltd's depot, Grange Dock, Port of Grangemouth. I went into reception where I met Duncan Adams, CEO, who said it was okay for Kenny to drive round to my container to drop off the two palleted loads of boxes. I then asked a helpful warehouseman if he would come round with his forklift and take them off the curtain-sider. '*Nae bother*,' he said.

I have donned my fluorescent bib, which Eric gave me last year when he took me through the busy open-plan office and said '*That will stop ye frae being knocked doon.*' Here comes Allan driving a mini forklift. '*Yer back again, my man,*' he says to me cheerily, on his usually serious face. I managed to load CRXU4103197 with more boxes. I chapped Duncan Adams' office window to say goodbye and he responded with a wave of his hand. I walked out of Grange Dock and around into Grangemouth town centre and along up the main road to W. Knight Watson Ltd, and left a note for Louise. I got a taxi to Falkirk High Station, train to Glasgow Queen Street and walked across town to Central Station. I bought *The Big Issue* and gave the time of day to a young soul hustling for mental health who wanted me to sign up for a direct debit donation. I offered to give her some cash, but not the debit.

Monday 23/06/2008

3:45 p.m. Home. I have not long walked out from Rothesay town. On the way I met someone who asked me where I had been. I remember Jimmy Spencer, my Oban friend and mentor, saying to me over our tea at The Seaman's Mission, summer 1974, '*Davie lad, they are aye watchin' yuh. They want tae know yur bizness.*'

So far a braw day. Migraine hit me again in Port Glasgow Station as I was awaiting the train for Wemyss Bay. I am feeling a lot better now. I went to the bank on my return and deposited the cheque of £500 donation from Jerry and his travel agency firm Just Grenada. Later I wrote him a thank-you letter. Message to call Gemma, journalist, *Edinburgh Evening News*. Thanks and thanks again to: John MacKirdy Haulier Ltd, Rothesay, Isle of Bute; Kenny, HGV professional driver; Allan of Adams Transport Ltd, box lift, forklift driver.

Monday 23/06/2008

6:35 a.m. The sun is shining out of a washed-clean clear blue sky. It is a beautiful day. I am sitting here on my bar stool in the cafeteria area of the MV *Bute* en route to Grange Dock to meet with Lofthus Signs Ltd signage technicians Kenny and team, who are going to do the signage on CRXU4103197. I have the bike with me today; it's worth the effort. I am now officially 'retired' from the teaching profession with a pension. I went to a 'little presentation' at Argyle House in Dunoon on Friday 20th. Carol, Head of Service Pre-5 and Primary Education, gave my efforts for this charitable initiative some recognition and presented me with a silver-plated quaich. Another chapter has formally come to an end in my safari, in this narrative of my life's journey, and a new one has begun.

(*Nine more years of inner-directed work lay in the future, since Hurricane Ivan devastated Grenada, West Indies, on 7 September 2004.*)

I Embark on a New Career

I had to wait at Forth Ports Plc security gate, Grange Dock, from 10 a.m. to 11:15 a.m. Confusion and delay. Ben and Michael of Lofthus Signs Ltd had been waiting for me to arrive at the other end of the docks. Fortunately, I met George, HGV driver, coming into the dock (who on Saturday 9 December 2006 had brought the container CRXU4103197 up to Inverkeithen). '*David,*' he said, as he wound down the window of the cab. It felt good at that moment of desperation to be remembered and recognised. '*Can I use your phone, George?*' I asked. '*Certainly,*' he replied, at which point he pulled his transporter over to a lay-by on the other side of the Forth Ports security gate and he dialled Lofthus for me. What a man! I spoke to Kenny of Lofthus Signs, who reassured me that his team had done the job and were on their way out. Relieved! *Hang in there, boy. Ye cannae' jack it in at this stage of the game. All's well.*

While waiting at the gate I saw a Crust's vending machine coming out of the dock, which I hailed, and the good lady from whom I had purchased a roll and chicken soup months ago kindly stopped. I purchased an order of the same purvey, which was to sustain the inner man for a wee while.

The sun is shining on the page as I sit here in a Sea Land container. Earlier, Allan the big box forklift driver had lent me his bolt cutters to cut the seal on TRIU5079422, which I opened. After my sandwiches and a bottle of Irn-Bru, I began to transfer educational resources into CRXU4103197, which, at Inverkeithen Primary School, we – janitor Frank, HGV driver George, Kenneth, Callum and myself – had hurriedly had to load on that Saturday morning. Another hurdle that we had to overcome in this ongoing, never-ending saga of inner-directed social entrepreneurship. '*Take a break, you are working for yourself and others in your own time. You are beholden to none,*' I said aloud.

I cycled back out from Grangemouth main road, round the hazardous roundabouts, and back along the Firth and Clyde Canal to Falkirk Grahamston Station where I had a long wait. By the time I got back to Glasgow I had missed the ferry connection. It has been another braw day.

9:55 p.m. Home. The Grove, Kilbarchan, Renfrewshire. My Morrison Mum is giving me hospitality.

Tuesday 24/06/2008

8:55 a.m. I am crossing the watta. Heading home. It is overcast and damp. '*Well, what next?*' as Eric would ask. One step forward at a time. He did say, when I mentioned to him about his offer to bring the work of my charity social enterprise initiative project before his circle of business friends in Glasgow, that he would bring it up again before the committee.

I still have to move more school furniture (35 infant tubular-metal chairs, all in good condition, rectangular Formica-topped tables, and 7 filing cabinets etc.) into the spaces that remain in CRXU4103197 before it leaves Grange Dock for Grenada.

(But I should have done it there and then, I was to later discover, as the container was collected several days later and removed to the Port of Grangemouth for shipment.)

Putting off what can be done now is a big mistake, not one which I will make next time. I will probably head back over to Grange Dock tomorrow to complete the load of remaining resources.

Wednesday 25/06/2008

7:10 a.m. I cycled in the drizzle. I am now back on the train for Central Station, en route for Grange Dock. There goes the whistle – a hiss and moving forward, with a rattle and a clank.

I EMBARK ON A NEW CAREER

Thursday 26/06/2008

6:25 a.m. I awoke with an ache behind my right eyeball. '*Not on the bike today? Just you lie down for 20 minutes,*' said Marion. Bless her. I managed to pick myself up and cycled in, parked the bike, withdrew some coppers and posted correspondence. I have just met Pepito, Caledonian MacBrayne ferry purser steward, who comes from the Democratic Republic of the Congo. I was blethering to him and his colleague Frank on the way home yesterday afternoon. There were 1920s Fairlie bespoke-built yachts in the inner harbour and the two masters anchored out in Rothesay Bay. I am on my way over to Edinburgh to attend another Social Enterprise Academy course seminar on 'self-leadership' given by Karen Darke. It is a brand-new day and I am continuing to strive ever upwards. I edit the words of my story.

11 a.m. I am sitting in a comfortable swivel chair in the Edinburgh Conference Centre hub foyer with a cup of coffee and taking the opportunity to complete my brief diary account for 25 June 2008. The taxi driver, a former pupil of Victoria Primary School in Newhaven where I did a practice teaching stint in the spring of 1975 while on the Post Graduate Certificate Education course at Moray House College of Education, has not long dropped me off. I hailed him in a downpour while in Raeburn Place, along from Stockbridge Market, where I had bought some flowers and comestibles from Peckhams for Gillian and workmates at Lofthus Signs Ltd. A small token of appreciation of all their practical help and encouragement.

I took this opportunity to return the Ben Green signage technician's tape measure that Allan the forklift driver had given to me yesterday morning as I was frantically scurrying around the DAT Ltd yard looking for CRXU4103197, which he told me, to my dismay, had been picked up and taken down to Forth Ports export yard. So that trip had been for nothing. Oh well, no point

Thursday 26/06/2008

in complaining. I went and spoke to Mick in the office, who said to me, '*You'll die doing this work.*' Not a cheery prediction: if you think that's the case, I had better burn out than rust out in my opinion. Hard lines, Cyril, for I had been looking forward to shifting the remaining resources out of TRIU597942. Just move on and away from that failure to act on my intuition.

After leaving Duncan Adams and his gallus team, I then cycled along to Forth Ports Plc office and spoke to Liz at the reception desk who was very helpful and suggested I speak to Derek at their office further along the road into Grange Dock. I then had to pedal back along to the security gate to collect another pass, having lost the one they had given me earlier that morning.

Hurdles and yet more hurdles to clamber over. Difficulties to overcome. Perseverance. There's naething else fur it. I left a message for Derek asking if it were possible that a photograph could be taken of the container with the Lofthus signage banner.

It was a grey humid morning. I cycled back out of the dock, around the roundabout, into the town centre, and up to Mandal House of W. Knight Watson Ltd to meet Gary the freight forwarder, to make a slight murmur of complaint regarding the unnecessary and premature removal of my container. I then biked out of Grangemouth, past Finn Forest, Syngenta etc., stopped off at Asda (part of the Walmart Inc family) and up to the Firth of Forth Canal towpath, and back to Falkirk Grahamston railway station where I had the chance to scoff my tuna paste sandwiches and quaff 500 ml of Irn-Bru.

Present tense. I have just met John, a marketing adviser with the Edinburgh Chamber of Commerce, of which I am a member, who I had met in one of the Chamber's meetings. He had mentioned that he would be in contact with someone who might be able to assist my social enterprise. So far, nothing. Chatting. I have not had the chance to enjoy my coffee. I am sitting here alone, in my striped shirt, tie, best trousers and shiny black shoes. Smart. I was told that first impressions last. The rain is off, the sky is blue, and gulls are soaring over Festival Square. I had better get moving.

1:45 p.m. The Social Enterprise Academy, 5 Rose Street, Edinburgh. *'I am Neil, the director,'* he tells me, as I walk through the door. I meet Martin, of Scottish Family Business, who gives me his business card and tells me to get in touch with him. 'The Nature of Social Enterprise' is a short talk. Starter packs are handed out. The speaker talks about transformational change, self-leadership, and self-leadership journeys. She tells the audience to think about their own journey. I do that all the time. Someone said, *'If you want to keep flying don't look down.'* A process of influencing yourself. Zero tolerance of negativity. I will say, 'Amen to that.'

If You Fall by Karen Darke: the speaker at this seminar has overcome severe physical impairment. '*I help businesses to articulate their visions and to implement relevant actions. Achieving social impact. With the right team and the right equipment anything is possible. Don't get stuck in what you are doing,*' she said. An interactive experiential session follows her spiel. I am somewhat bewildered by the jargon. I have enjoyed a light buffet lunch. Another fruitless journey.

Wednesday 02/07/2008

6:10 a.m. I am sitting in the waiting room of the Rothesay Pier Terminal. The ticket seller has just told me that the new bridge is open and when I come off the boat that's the way I'm to go. I have walked in from home. I am on my way over to see representatives of the Homeless World Cup organisation in Edinburgh. I am making another trek across Scotland, trying to overcome my inertia, apathy, lack of confidence, fear, and anxiety. *'Courage brother, do not stumble, there is a star to guide the humble.'*

10:20 a.m. I am in the Loaded Sandwich Bar, corner of Bernard Street and Shore Road, Leith. I have walked from Waverley

Wednesday 02/07/2008

Station. It is a beautiful day. I am sitting at a small table beside a large bay window looking up into a clear blue sky. I continue to move forward. Possibilities? Synergies, what are they? Mutually beneficial connections and relationships. I have found out where their office is, No. 5. Timberbush, round the corner, and I shall go in there in half an hour. Friendly waitress.

12:30 p.m. I have not long had a meeting with Karina, who is the personal assistant to Mel Young, the founder of this charity, and Andy Hook the director of football for the Homeless World Cup. I gave my pitch. This outfit has teams playing to better themselves all over the world: Malawi, Zambia, Rwanda, Nigeria, and Liberia to name a few countries. I believe Scotland won the cup last year. I'll have to wait and see what comes from this meeting.

I jumped onto a No. 16 Silverknowes bus for Pilton. I had my first teaching practice at Silverknowes Primary School with Jean Rennie and her Primary 7 class, and just managed to survive that ordeal having failed the critique of my first lesson, after which, when the class had been dismissed by Mr Finlayson, he said to me, *'That is the worst teaching practice I have ever invigilated and, frankly, I don't think there is much point in you continuing on this course. But you wait here and I shall go and speak to Mr Brodie your head teacher.'* It was not long before he was back. *'Mr Brodie thinks that you are such a clean-cut, well-mannered young man that, against my better judgement, he would like to give you another opportunity, and after the Christmas holiday you will join Mrs Stewart's Primary 5 class.'* My classroom experience at Silverknowes Primary School, Pilton, Edinburgh, improved in that class. Many of the children were from Traveller families. The rest is history.

I am riding on the top deck of the No. 16 back to the city centre, via Granton, Newhaven, and other leafy parts of the suburbs.

I Embark on a New Career

Thursday 03/07/2008

7:15 a.m. The train is rushing through the tunnel towards Inverkip Station. The sun is shining out of a cloudy sky. I met a fellow raised-beach dweller, an escapee from South Africa who was telling me, as we walked up the Wemyss Bay Pier, about the waves of immigrants and refugees from the surrounding countries who, on arrival in the country, are having to live in huge shanty towns on the outskirts of the major cities. She is not hopeful; it is a desperate situation in the Rainbow Nation.

While on the boat munching a roll and sausage piece and quaffing a white coffee, I met Alison. *'Off somewhere? Where are you going all suited up?'* she asks. I tell her what I am about, that I'm off to attend an Edinburgh Chamber of Commerce speed networking session hub, top of the Royal Mile. Nothing ventured nothing gained. I tell her that at last year's session I met David Bruce the general manager of the Bishop's Move, a removal company that this year has collected, pro bono, 36 boxes of library books donated by Morningside Library from the Lothian Region Community Transport unit at the Elizafield Industrial Estate and delivered them to Grange Dock. And in another of those sessions I had met the marketing manager of Lofthus Signs Ltd, whose firm had prepared the signage, again pro bono, for container CRXU4103197, soon to be on its way to the Grenada Boys' Secondary School and that Gillian would assist me in locating a derelict storage premises for SESF at the West Shore Business Centre in Granton.

Then she asks, *'What do you want a quantity surveyor for?'* I tell her that I need someone to determine what might be the resale value of the educational resources that remain in the Lochgilphead High School buildings prior to their demolition, and that the possible sale of them would go towards defraying the cost of collection, storage, and shipment.

Wednesday 16/07/2008

8:30 a.m. I am sitting in Peter's car aboard the Portavadie to Tarbert ferry. We have been chatting about the ways and means that the local housing association and the Surplus Educational Supplies Foundation can best work together to ensure that the fit-for-purpose educational resources that remain in the high school can be salvaged from what were the former high school buildings. I gave him a copy of the Burness solicitor's letter. Thick grey clouds interspersed with small patches of blue.

(I was to discover that a lot of these resources in the school had been vandalised.)

9:20 a.m. Peter has brought us into the car park of the Grey Gull Hotel, Ardrishaig, where he has a meeting. I am to meet him later in front of the post office in Lochgilphead. He has arranged for Tony, an employee of a construction firm who has the keys to the high school, to meet me here shortly.

A recollection. I was brought to Ardrishaig village in early July 1974 by a kind and hospitable couple who, after giving me high tea in their home in Lochgilphead, took me to some friends of theirs who ran a B&B, The Canal House in Ardrishaig, where I rented accommodation for the night. I was on my way back to Prestwick Airport to use my return Air Canada ticket to fly back to Halifax, Nova Scotia.

10:35 a.m. I have been shown around the former high school buildings by Colin the construction company's plumber, who tells me that a lot of the educational resources that were left have already been taken. It is evident that many resources have been taken away and what remains is being wilfully destroyed. He is as upset as I am at this wanton and mindless destruction of what is left; as always I am not to be defeated, I think that there are still resources that can be put to good use, providing my social enterprise/charitable foundation is given the opportunity and financial assistance to fund the uplift of what can still be salvaged, and I am able to obtain storage prior to shipment to deserving recipients.

11:15 a.m. I am now in a local café. Jackie, the reporter and editor of the Argyllshire Advertiser, has not long dropped by to show me a brief article she has written about my efforts and intention to salvage what still remains in the vacated premises of their community's former secondary school. I have had a bacon roll and mug of coffee. There is a pleasant easy-going ambience in this tiny café, where I meet Dan, who tells me that he was a mental health nurse at the hospital, has been retired for 35 years and comes here for lunch every day. We chatted for a while, and then as the café was getting busier I bid them all goodbye.

I went for a stroll and into a small art gallery-cum-shop where I introduced myself, left my business card, and then walked around the block to the tourist board and got a map of the town, along to the Community Centre and there I met a young lad at the front desk. I introduced myself and explained why I was visiting the town and gave him my card. I walked back to the main street and went into the Victoria Hotel for a pot of tea and a biscuit at the bar and blethered some more with the locals.

1:40 p.m. Back to Rothesay with Peter. I journeyed and expanded my horizons in an unfamiliar environment. Self-development.

Saturday 19/07/2008

7:15 a.m. I cycled in and tethered my bike at the Albert Pier railings across from The Bike Shed and then walked up to Guildford Square and along Montague Street, turned right on the Gallowgate, and put my letter with container invoices and puff from the fourth estate about my initiative through the metal roller

Saturday 19/07/2008

door of One 2 One Accountancy Services. I will wait and see if this firm can recover some Value Added Tax. How much? Time will tell. I found the accountant, Lesley, supportive of the work I was engaged in.

I am sitting here on a metal bench in the Rothesay Pier waiting room. I can hear a motor humming away somewhere. I am too early for the eight o'clock boat. It is dry, but humid and overcast with thick, grey clouds. Yachts are out on Rothesay Bay gathering together, there is just enough of a very slight breeze to move them. *'Where are you off to today?'* you may well ask. Wemyss Bay. Train to Central Station and taxi up to Queen Street Station, get a train either to Falkirk High or Falkirk Grahamston, whichever leaves first. Then taxi to Duncan Adams Transport Ltd, Grange Dock depot. There is nothing else for it. The gates to this firm close at midday and I hope to be able to remove school furniture and resources from TRIU5079422 and have it ready to be delivered to Unit 3, Fife Food & Business Centre, Glenrothes, on 23 July. I hope to have a team from Community Services uplifting resources from Units 19/20, Woodgate Way South, Eastfield Industrial Estate, stored there back in March. I can hear Eric's words of advice ringing in my ears, *'You only want to move it once.'*

I have contacted Craig, the manager supervisor, group leader and social modeller, and left a message with Archie, his boss. They will provide a team for this uplift. I have spoken to Valerie in the office of Duncan Adams Transport Ltd and she has told me that the container should arrive sometime around 2 p.m. I make the provisional tentative preparations that are necessary. I do all I can to ensure that arrangements are made and go according to plan. Renwick, the estates surveyor with Fife Council's Assets and Facilities Services, will be on holiday and has told me to get in touch with Dave of the development service, which I have done, and will do again. He will bring the key to Unit 3 on 23 July.

On arrival at reception I was met by Suzanne, who appeared from the office. *'Could I have my banner please?'* I changed into my

I Embark on a New Career

boiler suit, donned the fluorescent jacket, and walked through the yard to find that my container had been boxed in, which meant that there was no way I was going to empty it today.

I did what I could and tied my banner '*Caribbean Hurricane Relief*' to each corner of the outward facing side of container TRIU5079422 and taped the top and bottom halves of it. I got the chance to speak to Allan, the container forklift driver, and asked him if he would move the boxes around for me on Monday – he knocks off at lunch time. So it is back over bright and early next week. I have no other choice but to keep plugging, chipping away at this rock face, since no one else is either interested or will do it for me, that's for certain.

I got the No. 3 bus from Grangemouth to the foot of the road that leads up to Falkirk High Station. The taxi driver this morning tells me that he had been a driver for DAT Ltd and had not found it a happy experience. He went on to tell me that his daughter had won a week's holiday in Barbados and they had not enjoyed their stay at their hotel. The food was terrible.

There is warm sunshine on the page as we roll, rumble, sway and shuggle from side to side towards my adopted city and I am moving forward towards home.

2:45 p.m. I have boarded the train at Platform 13 for Wemyss Bay. There goes the whistle. The doors have shut once more. The sun is shining through the clouds. I did not achieve what I had planned for today, but it was not for nothing that I had made this journey. On my return home I found a letter from Forth Ports Plc with a cheque for £500. I was overcome with gratitude. Why me? My heart sings.

Monday 21/07/2008

8:29 a.m. The sun is shining on me through the windaes of this train bound for Falkirk Grahamston – it's back to DAT Ltd,

Grange Dock. Why you may ask? TRIU5079422 was boxed in on Saturday and there was nothing that I could do about it. '*You are now approaching Springburn,*' he said.

This morning I will be able to remove the school furniture and other good classroom resources that I had loaded way back on Saturday 16 December 2006 into another container ready to be delivered, all being well, on 23 July 2008 to Unit 3 Fife Food and Business Park, Faraday Road, Glenrothes. TRIU5079422 on delivery will be unloaded with educational resources from the former Dunshalt Village Primary School, which were uplifted and stored on these premises back in March. The plan is that this container will be shipped in due course to schools on the islands of Carriacou and Petit Martinique later this year, if I get the vital cooperation from the Government of Grenada that I have sought over many months.

When I was coming over on the boat I met Romilly, who is off to work in Geneva, and who was glad to see me. He was in one of my classes at the Port School and his brother Greg, who I had met yesterday loading their car for his mum's 60th birthday party to be held on the beach at Ettrick Bay, was also friendly. '*They break out of the norm,*' he said, referring to all who had contributed to the success of the Surplus Educational Supplies Foundation, (SCO39331).

The train is now approaching Stepps, where I lodged in the home of John and Nan Tennant from 1975 to 1980. The sun continues to shine out of a pale blue sky.

9:55 a.m. The DAT Ltd yard. There is a crow flying over to Grangemouth under this pale blue sky. Gulls squawking low overhead. A light, cool breeze from the east is blowing across the depot. Here I am again. Any normal human being would have packed it all in by now. No wonder when Louise, freight forwarder at W. Knight Watson Ltd, asked Eric who I was, he said, '*He's a nutter from the West Coast.*' Allan with the box lift has manoeuvred and lifted my recent purchase INBU4923875 (Interpol), to be painted in due course, into a space directly opposite TRIU5079422. It's just as well Pentalver Transport Ltd, Andy in Leeds, had this box delivered on time as there are more educational resources in this container (that was loaded on 16 December 2006) than I had realised.

Get to work. I am having to move these resources twice – mistakes that I made along the way. I learn the hard way. Every day is a school day. Nothing else for it: get stuck in.

12:15 p.m. The sun is cracking the sky and I am going to take a break and eat ma piece. Oh! The van with the nice soul stopped for me as I was walking into Grange Dock along the North Shore Road and I bought a cup of chicken soup and a buttered roll, which I had scoffed before I started shifting this lot. Hopefully it will only be moved again when it is unloaded at the beneficiary. I am knackered.

Later, on my way out from Grange Dock, I stopped at Forth Ports Plc, Carron House office. The receptionist, who tells me that she comes from the Isle of Barra, is welcoming and friendly. Liz, who had suggested to me some weeks ago that I write to Wilson Murray, chief executive officer of Forth Ports Plc, is on holiday.

I then hoofed around to Grangemouth and stopped in at AG Office Supplies Ltd to see Richard, who was not in. AG said she would let him know I had dropped by. I am whacked. I took a taxi back up to Falkirk High Station, train to Queen Street, and walked down Buchanan Street, teeming with humanity, to Central Station where I had a long wait for the Wemyss Bay train. Ferry back to Rothesay. Cycled home.

Wednesday 23/07/2008

5:59 a.m. Rothesay Bay is still, pond calm. Thick, grey clouds overhead. It is humid, close. I am walking past the Craigmore

Wednesday 23/07/2008

Tea Room when a car stops beside me and the driver rolls down the window and offers me a lift. '*You are a gentleman, a player of the bagpipes, and master butcher,*' I said to Alisdair, who had given me a lift years ago when I was walking up the road from Delhi Cottage to Rothesay Primary School to begin a short-lived chapter as newly appointed senior teacher (1990–1991). He had dropped me off at the foot of Bishop Street all those years ago.

I am not feeling too good. My head is sore with a migraine. I will have to stick it out, thole it, en route to Glenrothes New Town. I will need to get a bus from Buchanan Street Bus Station. On arrival I hope to meet a team from the Community Services Criminal Justice Department who will give me a hand to help load the container that will be brought over from Duncan Adams Transport Ltd at Grange Dock. Plans can go awry in a blink of an eye, mine are aye tentative and provisional. Fight on!

6:35 a.m. I am on the boat. I bought a white coffee and a bacon

Community Services team.

roll. I meet Martin, who asks me, '*Where are you going today?*' I tell him, '*Glenrothes.*' '*I remember you telling me, as long as you are getting on,*' he said. A little encouragement from a man of few words. I have swallowed two painkillers. My arms are aching.

8:40 a.m. Taxi up from Central. I am now on the bus for Glenrothes leaving Buchanan Street Bus Station. On ye go pal!

12:45 p.m. Units 19/20, Eastfield Industrial Estate Community Services workshop. I am in the supervisor's office with Norrie, Stan, and Colin. '*Am aff tae Tennereefe with ma mates. Ah've got a croissant and cheese here.*' They are welcoming.

Along with Norrie, Connor, Mark, and myself, we managed to shift most of the resources, mostly chairs and tables, up to the warehouse industrial unit entrance. It would suit Surplus Educational Supplies Foundation (SCO39331) to have something similar for storage, if it were in a more central location between Edinburgh and Glasgow and in a similar, well-maintained condition. This beggar has to take what he has been given. I had not realised that we had uplifted so many educational resources from just the two classrooms of the former Dunshalt Village Primary School back in March. It is an Aladdin's Cave store of 'treasure'. As long as the recipients in Carriacou and Petit Martinique get the benefit of it, all my blood sweat and tears, and the payback effort of these young folk from Community Services, will have been worthwhile.

(*Little did I know then, that the promises made by senior officials in the Government of Grenada were empty.*)

6:55 p.m. Rolling back to Wemyss Bay and I will now roll it back in time to describe briefly some of the highlights of this day.

John, Duncan Adams Transport Ltd HGV driver, from Letham, he tells me, but originally from Airth in Ayrshire, brought me back to Grange Dock from Unit 3 Eastfield Industrial Estate, Glenrothes. After we had unloaded the container, I went in to

Wednesday 23/07/2008

reception and there met Duncan who greeted me. '*Here is the man of the moment,*' he said, with words that made me feel good.

I met Eric before being taken through the big, open-plan office to the company accountant. '*Can I seal the container?*' he asked. '*Yes please, Eric,*' I said. I paid the bill for taking the container to Glenrothes this morning and for bringing it back. '*I'll make it £150 plus VAT. I did say £185,*' he said. '*Thank you very much for that, Eric,*' I said. I then walked out of Grange Dock on the North Shore Road and over to Grangemouth.

It has been a beautiful day this side of Scotland. I waited in the rank on main street for a taxi up to Falkirk High, soon into Queen Street, another taxi to Central, and almost an hour for the train to Wemyss Bay. I started this morning with the help of Norrie, the supervisor social modeller and his clients, Mark and Connor. We moved the educational resources (chairs, trolleys, filing cabinets, tables) from the back of the warehouse to the front roller door of the warehouse so that they could be moved more quickly later into the container when it came, and then we returned to the Community Centre Services Unit 3, Eastfield Industrial Estate, to have some lunch. It was not long before John, the HGV driver, turned up. '*Wi' a little bit of luck,*' he said cheerily. John backed the trailer, expertly, to the entrance of the warehouse and by then another team of clients had arrived, Paul, Kayleigh, Jock and Barrie, and we all got stuck in.

By 3:35 p.m. the container had been fully loaded, all a bit jumbled but all of it top-quality fit-for-purpose educational resources that would be essential in any up-to-date classroom: all of it rescued, salvaged, from the jaws of the crusher, the demolition lorry's skip, and landfill. Another stage in the delivery process journey of this shipment has begun. Norrie handed me the key to Unit 3. Trust. I thanked everyone of the team individually and, to some who wanted it, I gave my website (www.grenadarelief.co.uk).

(*Which was broken up some years later by a digital artisan and rebuilt by one of the good guys, Sam T, now www.haitirelief.org.uk, I was to rise from those ashes once again.*)

I need more business cards. Rachel from the *Fife Free Press and Herald* came by to snap a picture of the team, some of whom understandably did not wish to have their photograph taken. There is still enough space left to fill a quarter of the 40-foot ocean freight container load before container TRIU5079422 is ready to be shipped. I shall need to prepare an inventory and make further arrangements for INBU4923875 to be delivered here within a fortnight, to uplift the resources that remain in Unit 3, as it is going to be let soon. Not having a permanent storage facility is proving to be a barrier to any further progress. I am now deep into a pickle of my own making.

7:17 p.m. I am aboard the train for Wemyss Bay. A breeze is blowing through the open window of the carriage as we head into a pale sunset over the Kilpatrick Hills. This day, all things considered, has gone well. The Community Services supervisors were helpful and hospitable, and their teams were brilliant. I could not have asked for more.

Thursday 31/07/2008

8:35 a.m. '*How old are you?*' asks the taxi driver, who has brought me up to Queen Street Station just now and who, coincidentally, had brought me up to Buchanan Street Bus Station last week, on 23 July. I tell him how old I am. '*Naw, yer not that auld. You are so enthusiastic! Were you successful last week?*' he asks. He lifted my spirit with the recognition and compliment. I am encouraged. '*Yes, thanks to the collaboration of not a few guid folk who made that collection a success. See you again, I hope,*' I said and bid him goodbye.

The train for Edinburgh is now whizzing forward. '*The next stop is Croy.*' Last week, in my absent-minded haste, I had forgotten

Rachel the photographer's ladder and, what was much worse, I had mistakenly dropped my bunch of keys on the floor of the semi-transporter cab and I thought that I had lost them along with the Unit 3 key. What a relief when Valerie, in the Duncan Adams Transport Ltd office, had called home to tell me that John, the HGV driver, had found them on the floor of the artic and thoughtfully left them for me. I am now heading back to Grange Dock to collect these items. I will also confirm arrangements to have INBU492875 delivered tomorrow afternoon. What a relief!

8:40 a.m. Tea and coffee trolley coming up the aisle. I am going to stop scribbling and have a treat. A few more lines. Earlier, Marion dropped me and Johanna off at Paisley Gilmour Street Station.

10:45 a.m. I am making good time so far. There are always pros and cons. I am now back in Central Station, sitting in a carriage for the train to Wemyss Bay. I got the 9:35 a.m. train from Falkirk High Station for Queen Street. On arrival at Falkirk I had taken a taxi to DAT Ltd, Grange Dock. I asked the taxi driver if he would wait for me and went to reception where I met Eric. *'Come and get your keys and ladder, David,'* he said. Bryan, sitting at another desk in the wide, open-plan office, nodded to me to indicate that the container was ready for tomorrow. I will call and confirm later.

While I was waiting for the train on the Falkirk High Station platform, I met Iain, a jazz fan who tells me is taking the Orient Express to Fort William tomorrow. He looks at me and asks, *'Guess how old I am?'* *'Seventy?'* I answer. *'I am 80, and I have been retired for the past 15 years,'* he said. Lucky you.

Friday 01/08/2008

6:40 a.m. Marion has not long dropped me off at the Rothesay Pier head. It is raining heavily out of a thick blanket of misty grey cloud. I am perched once again in the Coffee Cabin of the

I Embark on a New Career

MV *Argyle* en route for Wemyss Bay, Glasgow Central Station, Buchanan Street Bus Station and on to Glenrothes New Town, Kingdom of Fife, to uplift, move, shift, and load the remainder of classroom resources that were left in the Unit 3 warehouse after we had fully loaded TRIU5079422 on 23 July. All being well, container INBU4923875 will be brought through from Grange Dock by 2 p.m. and there will once again be a team from Community Services to help me load it.

I received an email from the principal of Bishop's College, Hillsborough, Carriacou, West Indies, saying that she had spoken to the newly elected Prime Minister of Grenada, Carriacou and Petit Martinique about the plans to deliver two containers of educational resources for their schools. I hope that there will be some financial assistance from this new Grenadian Government to facilitate the delivery of these two 40-foot ocean freight container shipments, otherwise it will not happen; that's the future, now I shall return to my cup of frothy white coffee.

I met Robert the coach builder and local bus driver who lives along the road, he is always friendly, and also Robert the joiner, whose team did a lot of work on the Delhi Cottage roof many years ago and who is travelling to work on a newbuild Private Finance Initiative school in Greenock.

8:40 a.m. '*Will you put your card there please,*' says the bus driver, testily. '*Sorry I have not used my card before,*' I replied, lamely. Pensioners like me want to live and continue learning in this 21st century world of increasing and unstoppable complexity. I got this No. 6 Saint Andrews bus at Platform 6 Buchanan Street Bus Station. The bus is moving up North Hanover Street through the Cowcaddens to Port Dundas on the M8 motorway.

I recall visiting residents of the night shelter back on a Sunday morning in the autumn of 1975 and taking 'my guests' along to attend morning worship at Sandyford Henderson Church, and later for some lunch on me at the café, since demolished, at the

Friday 01/08/2008

corner of Argyle and Sauchiehall Streets. I was eager and committed, a born-again, creating a new life in Scotland and attempting to make a fresh start; a Christian redeeming the years that the locusts had eaten.

I hope I am a little wiser today and cautious about imposing my 'save the world' agenda on others. It is raining heavily, we've just passed Chung Ying Supermarket, which takes me back to the 1950s when my mum did her weekly grocery shop at Kong Tings large grocery store in Curepe, Trinidad. I must stop in there some day and purchase some oriental groceries.

The bus is rattling its way on the motorway, once part of the Firth and Clyde Canal, which when I arrived in the Big Green place in August 1975 was still being filled in. One of the bus windscreen wipers is loose. Cars are bumper-to-bumper on the opposite lane, on my right, into the city. Trucks, artics and trailers are gridlocked, here are some of them: Reliance Custodial Services; Rentokil; Initial Hygiene; Mamoet Transport; Caledonian Wildfoods Specialising in Fungi; Wallace Express; Royal Mail; Maersk; FedEx; Macpherson of Aberlour; Vos Logistics; Freight Route; WH Malcolm Transport Ltd of Brookfield; Carntyne; McCaskill of Stornoway; Stalkers; B. K. G Transport Ltd; Alpine Trucking; Eddie Stobart (Tran, Store, Logistics); Strathclyde Transport Ltd. They are shifting stuff all about the place, and are all jam-packed, bumper-to-bumper, frozen in time, being controlled by the laws of supply and demand. To Let High Quality Industrial unit. Discount Bathrooms. I look towards the Necropolis and the sooty Royal Infirmary: a strange place, to build a hospital beside a graveyard. Victorians were then unaware of infectious microbes on the breeze.

I love the golden chanticleer cockerel on the steeple of Glasgow Cathedral, which is pointing in the direction I am heading, the sight of which always cheers me up. We are now passing Provie, Provan Mill, Provie Easterhouse scheme and urban sprawl industrial parks. My home turf 1975–1982. Massive warehouse-type buildings – all of this up until quite recently, the mid forties and up to mid fifties, was farmland. I get glimpses of greenery on my left, where I once trekked across fields from the mid sixties' Craigend housing scheme, through the much older fifties Garthamloch scheme to the Easterhouse Library, where I would borrow a box of books for my classroom library. Sometimes I was accompanied by a band of fitba players from Sunnyside Primary School (1975–1982) on our way to play a team from Bishoploch Primary School, and at other times I went to visit patients at the Gartloch Mental Hospital on a Sunday, which is recounted in earlier chapters of my journey. On ye go big man, yuh cannae' weaken now, for you have some way to go yet. As someone wisely said, '*If you want to keep on flying, don't look down.*'

(It is just as well that I did not know that morning that I would be self-employed, reliant on my pension and pro bono support in this work of 'logistics' good works, for another nine years.)

9 a.m. Almost that time of day and the bus is in another traffic jam on the outskirts of Cumbernauld. A rush of traffic coming from all directions. Where are these motorists going and what do they do for a living? I ask myself. The bus has stopped under the shopping centre underpass of Cumbernauld town centre. 'Silk Cottage Oriental Buffet. Eat As Much As You Like £5.75'.

9:08 a.m. On the move again. McDonald's, Town Centre East roundabout, Asda 24-Hours Supa Centre, Old Inns. We are now about to head across the Kincardine Bridge, travelling slowly as there are large road works underway.

Grangemouth petrochemical refinery chimneys in the distance are spewing toxic smoke into the Blue Planet commons. The bus has stopped.

9:40 a.m. Village of Kincardine. '*I don't think we will be going*

Friday 01/08/2008

much further with this bus. The window wipers are broken, as you can see. The blades are hauf way aff the wiper blades. Ye wan me tae risk your life as well as mine? We'll get ye goin as soon as we can.' The bus driver's retort to a passenger's querying complaint. So stay put and chill for the time being. I see three drookit craws perched on the rim of a roadside cottage lum. It is continuing to rain heavily.

10:50 a.m. I am now sitting on the top deck of a double-decker bus waiting to leave Dunfermline Bus Station for Glenrothes New Town. Sound of air brakes and we are off and up the road.

11:15 p.m. It is a slow bus. Enjoy the journey, Davey Boy. I am slightly anxious, though, that I won't get there on time. Coming in to Crossgates. 'Fife's First Energy Village.' En route through lots more villages on a grand tour in this charabanc. Is that Benarty Hill over to my left? I could see that summer's day in 1974 as I picked strawberries in a field of Classlochie Farm on the banks of Loch Leven with families of berry pickers from Kinross-shire villages, and from as far away as Dundee. They had travelled by charted bus every day to the Classlochie Farm's berry fields. I have given an account of my time in Gairneybridge in an earlier chapter of this narrative.

11:45 a.m. I arrive at Glenrothes Bus Station. I call Renwick, who is welcoming. He invites me round to his office in Kingdom House. I went up to the 5th floor and into a large open-plan office, with desks positioned according to pecking order, and with magnificent and panoramic views of the Kingdom of Fife. I met Gillian who, from early on, had made this initial collection and temporary storage of educational resources from the former Dunshalt Village Primary School possible. Renwick made me a coffee and introduced me to his colleague Alan, who looked at me in an odd manner as I delivered my elevator pitch. He told me that my story was amazing and indicated vaguely that Fife

Council might consider further arrangements with the Surplus Educational Supplies Foundation regarding their disposal donation of educational resources that were now surplus to their educational systems requirements due to the falling school roll, school closures, and newbuild. They were supportive of my efforts and were pleased that some of these resources were going to be put to further good use. I then went over to the Kingdom Centre and into Greggs the bakers, and stood in the queue for a cup of soup and a tuna fish sandwich.

I met Renwick later, at 1:40 p.m., outside the council buildings and he drove me over to Unit 3. The sun was shining through at last. I donned my boiler suit and at 2 p.m. sharp John the HGV driver came around the corner towing container INBU4923875. Soon after that the Community Service Team arrived with John, Jock, George, Jason, George, David, Colin, and their supervisor. We all got stuck into the work in hand and by 3 p.m. had uplifted the remainder of the surplus-to-requirements educational resources into the container. I thanked each of the Community Services Team individually. John then drove the trailer and container round to Kingdom Avenue, and parked across from Kingdom House. The sun was shining as I crossed the street, went up in the lift into Fife Council's Assets and Facilities Management Services office, and put the Unit 3 key on the desk in front of their boss. Away back to Grange Dock.

I paid the tariff and gave the cheque to DAT Ltd's accountant. I walked out of the dock and over to Grangemouth and got a taxi up to Falkirk High Station, and soon got a train to Queen Street Station. I hailed another cab for Glasgow Central and just managed to board the 4:50 p.m. train at Platform 12 for Wemyss Bay with three minutes to spare. I had run as fast as I could. I saw Amy Elisabeth on the platform at Paisley Gilmour Street Station and we met up again on arrival in Wemyss Bay. Marion and David were there in the car to collect us and we got an order from The Three in One Kebab. A wonderful and successful day.

Wednesday 13/08/2008

11 a.m. I have not long received a telephone call from the housing association to inform me that they have had a funding crisis and, as a consequence, they will be unable to fund the uplift of resources from the former high school. I was disappointed to get this news after all the effort to make arrangements for the uplift of resources and the expense of the solicitor's letter to validate the agreement. I asked the caller if I could still have the fit-for-purpose resources that remained in the buildings.

Thursday 14/08/2008

7 a.m. I left home in a hurry. I had just enough time to park my bike and walk to the ticket office at Rothesay Pier. It is a beautiful morning. There is light shining down on the green hills of the Cowal Peninsula and above Skelmorelie. I am perched on my usual bar stool in front of the Coffee Cabin.

I am now sitting in the front carriage of the train. I had met Rosetta, we were chatting as we walked off the boat together, who has recently settled on the island and has come all the way from South Africa. I am going to see Mark, transport manager of John G Russell Ltd, regarding MAEU6085656, which was loaded with resources, mainly desks and chairs, from the former Rothesay Academy on 3 March. Kenny, HGV driver for MacKirdy Hauliers, was also on the boat this morning and had taken that container up to Russell back in March. I was also chatting briefly to Pepito, the steward, who is always cheerful. He comes from the Democratic Republic of the Congo and has told me that his uncle might like to receive a shipment of fit-for-purpose educational resources. Pepito gave me his address. I am on the way again. One step and one day at a time, as ever, pressing forward.

The next stop is High Street Station. Rumbling through the tunnel. I am rattling like the train itself into the welcome daylight. I had walked up to Queen Street Station from Central – there had been a long queue at the taxi rank. *Use yer legs man!* Next stop is Bellgrove en route for Sunnyside, Coatbridge. I am returning full circle to these parts of my adopted nation, where I settled down and was given an opportunity to make a new life for myself. I have some good memories of teaching years at the primary school in Craigend, Easterhouse from 1975 to 1982 '*Please mind the step while alighting from this train. Change here for stations to Springburn. The next stop is Carntyne,*' he said. I can see the multi-storey tower block at the top end of Duke Street. I lived up a few blocks at 55 Garthland Drive, Dennistoun from 1980 to 1981. I had sublet the flat from friends while they were in Germany.

Heading east. I am passing familiar landmarks on the left and right of the track. Brown McFarlane For Steel. '*Next stop is Shettleston,*' he said. There is a Rowan tree laden with red berries. I am now looking at this area with fresh eyes. The next stop is Garrowhill. I am looking out of the window and I can see the Craigend scheme and the Tardis-like Garthamlock Water Towers. Dookits are smeared with graffiti on a hill just along from Garrowhill Station. The next stop is Easterhouse. Now under the M8 motorway. Adonis Construction. New housing developments. I spot a sparrowhawk, a kestrel perhaps, flying low over a patch of dry grass with what looks like a fieldmouse in its talons. Makes me feel good to see a bit of wildlife: a survivor in this environment. Hard lines mouse.

Central Car Auctions. The next stop is Blairhill: attention 24-hour CCTV in operation. Under power lines and I am relieved to get glimpses of open countryside under a pale light and cloudy sky. Sparse efforts of reafforestation. Little trees. Rosebay willowherb. In a blink, back now into conurbation territory. Next stop is Coatbridge Sunnyside. I was travelling on the Festive Glasgow Orchid? The Summerlee Coal Company, Lamberton. I am now in what was once the industrial, heartland belt of Scotland.

Thursday 14/08/2008

2:45 p.m. Home at the desk. I arrived back safe and sound. I met Raymond, from along the Mount Stuart road, returning on the train from Central Station. We shot the breeze on the train and over on the ferry. My meeting with Mark at John G Russell Ltd in Coatbridge went well. He told me that my container can stay pro bono at Russell Eurocentral Freight Terminal for the time being. I am most grateful. This firm will rail-freight the container MAEU6085656 from Mossend to the Port of Tilbury as and when I need to ship it. Mark said that they can give me a better deal on 40-foot ocean freight containers. He knows Tom Walker, Independent Container Surveyor.

He knows everyone in the yard and on the road. He said that John Russell, chief executive and founder of John G Russell Transport Ltd, and John the managing director were enquiring after me. I was humbled that they had taken an interest in my quixotic initiative; that was a most worthwhile meeting.

On my return home I got a call from Philip of Willmot Dixon Construction Ltd. He called out of the blue to tell me about a council library to be demolished in Southall. The pressure is on. Was I interested in acquiring the bespoke library furniture? *Another opportunity? Into the deep end once more?* are the questions I pose to myself as he is talking to me over the phone. I told him that I would need some form of assistance with the uplift and the temporary storage of these resources prior to their delivery. I don't want to be spoon-fed; it is good of them to get in touch with me out of the blue, but they will need to facilitate the removal of this quality library furniture and shelving that they are offering me prior to the demolition of the building. Philip had come across my efforts for the Surplus Educational Supplies Foundation when he had gone on the web and found an article by Liz, journalist of *The Fife Free Press and Herald,* about the uplift and storage of educational resources from the former Dunshalt Village Primary School (Fife Council) earlier this year. I thanked him for taking the trouble to get in touch with me. I am now going to chill for a wee bit.

I begin to figure out how I am going to organise this removal. Am I up for the challenge? Here is another one on my plate and I won't be beaten. Transport from a library in Southall? I try to find it on a map of London City. I will contact Ealing Borough Council and the Chamber of Commerce in Southall tomorrow. The library furniture could be loaded into a container at site and, providing it was fully loaded, could be shipped to Grenada, West Indies, from the Port of Tilbury. Another shipment of school classroom resources for the Grenada Boys' Secondary School.

I will require temporary storage capacity somewhere close to that port and transport from the library. I will need to purchase another container. I contact Pentalver Transport Ltd in Southampton. What is on offer from the library? A treasure trove of quality fit-for-purpose library shelving. On offer: 13 bays with 5 shelves each; 16 metal shelving units; 16 wooden cubes for storage; kitchen units; and 3 wall shelves. Philip has sent me digital images of the shelving – all good kit.

I get in touch with Frances, the Librarian at Ealing Borough Council Library in Southall. I call Ben of Mundell Transport Ltd in Tarbert, Argyll, who, according to Gary Middleton's Mundell family tree, is a distant cousin. '*Friday is a very busy afternoon. Will you get to the point quickly, please,*' he said. My call to that firm way back in 2006, when I just happened to speak to the right person at the right time that Friday afternoon, was to set me on my way to little fame and loss of a fortune.

Thursday 28/08/2008

11:45 a.m. I am attending the First Port and Social Enterprise Academy course being held at the Springkerse Business Centre, Enterprise House, Stirling.

7:30 p.m. Bus stop. Tillicoultry, Clackmannanshire. Slight breeze blowing in from the west. I thought I would take a short jaunt up

Thursday 28/08/2008

the road. I am now looking straight ahead over this little town to the Ochill Hills escarpment, which is like a massive wall, an embankment pressing down on me. It has been a beautiful sun-filled day, and now late summer afternoon. I found my way this morning by taxi from Stirling train station to the Springkerse Business Park, where I was met at reception by Edna, who was helpful and efficient. I meet lots of new people, which is good for my self-confidence as I continue to reinvent myself. People who, like me, are all aspiring social entrepreneurs, each of whom have come here to draft a credible business plan. Shortly after 4 p.m. I walked from Enterprise House, out of the business park, along the busy road and into the sun setting over Stirling town centre and from there got another taxi out to Cressington B&B, Causewayhead Road, where I met the landlord Alan and booked in to Room 3. I then walked back up the road in the bonny gloamin' sunshine to the new Wallace High School and back along the busy road of motor traffic to Corrieri's Café. I then walked back along Causewayhead Road and got a bus into the bus station.

I was feeling disoriented, at sixes and seven with myself. I then boarded another crowded No. 63 bus on its way to Alloa on a drive through the campus of Stirling University. I got off at Tillicoultry, went into a Spar nearby and bought a *Herald* to get change for the phone box to give Marion a call. The newspaper slipped from my grasp and before I knew it had blown all over the town square; Bean Mark 3 strikes again. I managed to collect most of the sheets out of the shrubberies and returned to the phone box, where I was desperate to answer a call from nature. I asked an approachable passer-by if the Community Centre was open. '*No it is shut, but the betting shop and the pub are open,*' she said. I then strolled down the road to the pub. I could see ripening fields of barley and the Wallace monument stood out in the setting sun.

I called home. Marion and Johanna are at a meeting. I spoke to Amy who told me that Derek Kerr, with a charity in Zambia, had called. I have just managed to speak to him. He works outside of

Lusaka apparently and is currently equipping a 6,000 pupil capacity school. He said that he was interested in collaborating with me and had heard about SESF from a friend in Grangemouth. I told him about the offer of library furniture from Ealing Borough Council Library Services' library in Jubilee Gardens, Southall, that was due for demolition. On my return to my Stirling residence I had a chat with the landlady, who keeps a sweetie shop. I told her about Chantal, the businesswoman chocolatier of Rococo Chocolates.

11:55 p.m. I am tired and I am now trying to prepare an assignment which Jay Lamb, Canal boater on the Union Canal, the course leader for the Social Academy First Port course has requested for tomorrow's class. The class has been so far so good and I was glad to be out of my comfort zone.

The sun has shone brightly on the Ochill Hills and the Carse of Gowrie today. The new St Modan's High School is quite something. A spanking-new school. What happened to the educational resources that were left behind in the former vacated buildings? Say no more. Find out. It is the school break and children of all ages were out on the large pitches in their hundreds. It makes me feel good to see them jumping and fleeing all over the place. Hopeful. Today and tomorrow's world. Go for it chilluns! Move on ever forward. Some of these students, perhaps every single one of them, will appreciate how fortunate and privileged they are, and will take good advantage of the opportunities being offered to them in their new school.

Saturday 30/08/2008

Home. I am down in the dumps today and clutching at straws. I make more phone calls to Grenada: Noel Construction; Grandview Hotel, Carriacou; Roydon's Guest House; De Freitas. The process is a maze, a labyrinth of dead ends that have led

Friday 19/09/2008

nowhere. I can't turn back or quit at this juncture, having accumulated so much surplus school furniture, stored in five 40-foot ocean freight containers. I have to retrace my steps in order to go down another avenue. I stumble on in this way by faith. I wish that things were clear cut, it would be so much easier. My way and your way are different. We are all, however, in the wilderness wasteland, living in the age of precarity, while our 21st Century consumerist humanity is devouring what remains of the Blue Planet's remaining natural resources. I am mining your waste streams, putting to further good use what you have thrown away without thinking.

I call First Containers UK Ltd, Rainham, Essex, because it is near to the Port of Tilbury. I speak to Mitch, a contact given to me by Howard Clack. *'It's a small world in our industry. What is it you want me to do?'* he asks. I tell him that I require somewhere near to the Port of Tilbury so I can park a 40-foot ocean freight container prior to shipment to a secondary school in Grenada. West Indies. I then made what I thought was an innocuous comment, which I cannot remember. *'Are you tyking the piss out of me?'* he asked angrily. *'Definitely not, sir. Why would I want to insult you, I am seeking your help?'*

I had left MSKU6311690, now loaded with the Jubilee Gardens Library shelving, longer than planned. I have now been told that Grenada Boys' Secondary School do not want it! Problems, problems.

Friday 19/09/2008

---

5 p.m. Home. The office. My optic vision has gone all squidged. I have been at this desk since late this morning. I crashed, or rather groped my way through my own lack of energy, state of inertia, and feelings of total inadequacy for the task in order to fulfil the objectives for this project. And then the phone went!

A call from Philip of Willmot Dixon Construction Ltd, which

I Embark on a New Career

lifted me off the bed. He told me that they were all set to demolish the Jubilee Gardens Library on 30 September, and that should I still wish to salvage the library furniture I was to make my own arrangements to have the it uplifted. When I told him that, so far, I had not got the logistics problem solved he seemed confident that I would. '*Sweet talk*' (his phrase) assistance, for that part of the logistics solution.

Sweating. Where next? Ipswich? Tilbury? Where do start? I have not a clue, but I am determined to bring the pieces of this puzzle together. I then made a call to David, general manager of Bishops Move, Pentland Industrial Estate, Edinburgh, who I had met at an Edinburgh Chamber of Commerce speed networking session. He is helpful. Goodwill and pro bono practical support has made my initiative possible and without it I would not have come this far. He told me that he had no contacts in the London and Suffolk area, so he took the time and trouble to give me some telephone numbers from the *A to Z Removers Directory for the United Kingdom* and suggested I give them a call. Brilliant! He has boosted my flagging spirits.

I then called JA Steel & Son Ltd and spoke to Ian, the firm's general manager, who said they would use one of their 18-tonne removal vans to uplift the library furniture. Gratis! '*What goes round, comes around,*' he said. A breakthrough at last. I had gone from the slough of despond this morning, to the mountaintop of exhilaration.

Next piece of the puzzle – I need some container storage. I then called Andy at Pentalver Transport Ltd in Leeds to find out if I can load my container at their storage depot in Ipswich. He said he would find out, and within minutes called me back to tell me that the depot there was too busy for me to load the container, however I can purchase one of their containers from their depot in Tilbury. Change of plan. I called Howard of Freight Container Services (Scotland) Ltd, who is based in Newark, Nottinghamshire, to see if he had any contacts in his business with storage facilities who might let me keep an SESF container, either at Ipswich, near to the Port of Felixstowe, or near to the Port of Tilbury. He is also helpful: he suggested I contact Fraser, the operations manager at Freightliner Ltd in Coatbridge, and gave me the name of Mitch, of First Containers UK Ltd. I called that number again, he answered, and said he would call me back. I would still be waiting. I will badger him once more on Monday 22 September.

I feel a lot better now than I did this morning. I have managed to enlist the help of one firm based in Enfield, Middlesex, who are going to go the second mile to uplift the library furniture and resources from the former Jubilee Gardens Library and, furthermore, are also prepared to deliver them to my container, and all of this free of charge! I have had to learn the hard way that one should never give up, especially in difficult circumstances.

Tuesday 23/09/2008

10:26 a.m. There is sunlight on the page. I am sitting in the cab of a John MacKirdy and Son Ltd artic transporter towing a 40-foot curtain-sider, parked in a yard at the far west end of the Hillington Industrial Estate park complex. Neil is driving, and forklifts are removing pallet loads of empty metal beer kegs from the trailer. I am looking out through the cab window into a clear blue sky. McNair Engineering warehouse is to my left and a B. Mundell Tarbert-Glasgow-Islay curtain-sider is parked over to my left. A distant kinsman who gave me short shrift recently?

My grandmother, Ashie Howatson-Mundell, was my opening line of patter that Friday afternoon, way back in the autumn of 2006, that opened the door into the Scottish road haulage industry. One contact leading to another. The radio is on. I cycled into Rothesay to get the 9 a.m. ferry. I had got a call from Elaine MacKirdy to say that the driver was leaving earlier.

I Embark on a New Career

10:30 a.m. I am now en route for the John G Russell Ltd depot, Gartsherrie Road, Coatbridge.

On arrival at 11 a.m. I went straight to reception, situated on the ground floor of a large modern building. I asked to speak to Mark, who greeted me warmly and introduced me to Graeme. I was then handed over to another young gentleman who took me out into the big yard where I was accompanied by Michael, who told me to go and look for Raymond. A yard much larger than Duncan Adams Transport Ltd at Grange Dock and very busy. The big box forklift driver appeared and kindly took my two pallets of boxes off Neil's curtain-sider and brought them round to MAEU6085656, and I got stuck into loading them. Raymond came by and he helped me to load the boxes that I brought over from the Caribbean Hurricane Relief Depot into the container, which I had loaded on 3 March with a team from Employability Bute. The container has been parked at Russell's since, and it is about time I had it shipped; it's due to go to the Grenada Boys' Secondary School. We will have to wait and see.

Raymond had been expecting me. He tells me that he used to live with his family in a five room apartment on Tillycairn Road, Garthamlock – the late fifties scheme to the east of the newly built late sixties scheme of Craigend, where I spent many a day from 1975 to 1982. He knows the score. A wise head. A real character. He invited me to join him in the Russell lunch room. He shared his lasagne lunch with me and made me cup of tea. I chatted to Alec, the big container forklift driver, as I was about to have another mouthful of lasagne; Raymond has a generous heart. He was assigned by Michael in the transport office to paint over the Maersk decal on the SESF container MAEU6085656. I thanked him for his kindness; he, among others, has helped to make what was, for me, another memorable and wonderful day. I left him painting over the decals, but not the registration numbers on the container. I am now on the train about to leave Sunnyside Coatbridge Station.

Tuesday 30/09/2008

I have not long walked up the Gartsherrie Road from the Russell and Freightliner Eurocentral Freight Terminal, and over the railway bridge, and am now trundling back to Glasgow Queen Street Station. It was a beautiful morning. It is now cloudy and cool, still dry, heading home. *'You go two steps forward and one back,'* he said. Sometimes it is a lot more than just two steps back. I said to myself.

Thursday 25/09/2008.

7 p.m. I am in the Campbell Tartan Room of the Neidpath B&B, Linden Avenue, Stirling, which is along the road from the busy roundabout. I am back in the room. I had got a lift earlier, from the Stirling Business Centre, with a kind soul driving a Mini Cooper. I booked in and then hoofed it up to the castle and back down to another roundabout and over to a KFC for a piece of fried chicken, a portion of stringy French fries and a cup of 7up. I perused *The Scotsman*. I have not long called Marion. I miss them. This is the down side of being away from home. I shall stay put now that I am here. The course day was all about marketing research. *'What does the customer want?'* etc. I am going through the motions and, as per usual, I am out of my comfort zone. *'What are you going to do on Monday?'* I am asked to send a postcard to myself. Daft. It is another beautiful day. I'll wait and see. I live one day at a time. If the need is not the market. What is it then?

Tuesday 30/09/2008

8:26 p.m. Room 11, the hotel near Southall Park, West London. I have just returned to this room which reeks of nicotine. The window remains firmly shut. There is a continuous noise from the sounds of rushing and roaring traffic and the intermittent scream of sirens outside on the main road. The room, otherwise for the stink, appears to be 'clean' and I must be grateful to have found somewhere so easily to spend the night.

Roll it back. This morning Marion travelled with me across the watta. We got the 8:45 a.m. boat and we went in, on arrival at Wemyss Bay, to the always welcoming Sea View Café for a coffee and a fruit slice each to await the 9:45 a.m. train. Marion alighted at Inverkip Station and I at Paisley Gilmour Street to board the bus for Glasgow Airport.

I checked in at Terminal 2 easyJet. Flew out at almost 2 p.m. on an Airbus A319. A bus too high off the ground for my comfort. I arrived at Luton Airport, which is a lot further out from London City than I had expected, and I took another bus to the Luton Rail Link where I bought a train ticket through to Southall. Train to St Pancreas Station – huge station – and from there the underground to Paddington Station and boarded another train for Southall. This is multicultural Britain, big time, man. *Vive la difference mon vieux.*

Beautiful afternoon. I walked from the station into the town centre and through the suburbs of Southall, and found the Jubilee Gardens Branch Library, which had been vacated and moved across the road. The library was now in temporary accommodation in the health centre. I made myself known to the library staff and asked them to pass on my good wishes to Frances and the staff at the main library in Southall, and expressed my appreciation for the donation of library furniture and told them what SESF hoped to do with it.

Ha cha Babu! It is time for a curry, you ragged-trousered peripatetic philanthropist. *What makes you so cheerful, eh?!* As I began to walk back into the town it began to drizzle, and through some helpful Sikhs in an electrical shop on the main road and later, as I plodded on, a young polis lassie at the town crossroads, I was directed to this place of shelter, which will have to do me for the time being. I was booked in by an Irish American. The wee office had pin-ups of El Papa Grande on the walls.

Tuesday 30/09/2008

The Willmot Dixon team, collecting library shelving in Southall.

I Embark on a New Career

(As I write these words I feel as if I am on autopilot, so keep on course, no turning back, just steer straight ahead.)

I then went back out onto the main drag, still drizzling. Back along the bazaar-like main street. Lots of Metropolitan Police about. I found a huge Punjabi family restaurant – The Lahore. There were many meals to choose from. I had a Karahi chicken, a portion of pilau rice and later a mango smoothie. Delicious and filling. I seemed to be the only Caucasian Occidental white man on their premises. I was joined by another diner who told me that he used to live in Pollokshaws. On enquiring where I had come from, he had nothing more to say to me, having satisfied his curiosity. He was well dressed, and appeared prosperous in a hard-man sort of way. I walked back along the crowded main street. I stopped at a phone booth and called Marion. I wished that I could bring her, Amy and Johanna down to the town and, should they have wished, had them rigged out in their choice of all the shalwar kameez, sari, sequined finery, seen in nearly every shop window, all of which were open at this late hour.

I am tired, tomorrow is another day. I have already informed Philip of Willmot Dixon Construction Ltd that I will be at the former Jubilee Gardens Library at 8 a.m. tomorrow morning. I need a pay phone to call Pentalver Transport Ltd, Southampton, to speak to Sam to find out if my container MSKU6311690 has been delivered from their depot to the Port of Tilbury by Premier Freight Services Ltd of Basildon.

He was not in the office, enquiries were made and it has been taken away, and I hope it will now be at First Containers UK Ltd in Rainham. We'll have to wait and see. I am anxious about the amount of shelving, its weight, and the loading here and unloading there of my container in the Rainham depot. One day at a time. Sufficient unto the day is the evil thereof.

Wednesday 01/10/2008

6:40 a.m. I am sitting on a low wall outside the Jubilee Gardens Library, Jubilee Gardens, Ealing suburb, just outside the park gates. The sun is coming up brightly over the other side of the park, and there is a cool breeze at my back blowing in from the west. A car has just pulled up and the driver is getting out and coming over to speak to me, I think it's a journalist from *The Ealing Times*.

It's not. It's one of the team from Willmot Dixon Construction Ltd. It is Steven, their estimator.

1:15 p.m. I am now sitting at a table near the big window in the MacDonald's, Brunsdown, on the main road near Enfield. I have just walked out from JA Steel & Son Ltd's modern removal premises and warehouse in the industrial estate. The sun is shining brightly today. Their removal van did not arrive until 10 a.m., it had got stuck in traffic.

All hands to the shelving: the Willmot Dixon team were brilliant. They took the library shelving apart and helped to load it. They had even thought of providing trolleys and barras, with and without handles. At 10 a.m. Philip and I went off to bring back tea, coffee, and sausage butties for their team. Their public relations person, Stephanie, was snapping away. Joe and Kevin from JK Byrne Construction Ltd had arrived earlier to erect fencing around the demolition site; Kevin comes from Carriacou, West Indies, and stays in Bedford. Joe is from Ireland and tells me he left school at 14. He is well read. Self-taught. His son is with the Territorial Army and is not long back from a tour in Afghanistan.

There were problems, however. It turns out that Dean at Premier Freight Services Ltd in Basildon had not managed to collect my container from Tilbury depot, as had been arranged, and deliver to the depot in Rainham. And they won't be able to carry out this arrangement until next week! I kept my nerve, stayed cool. Kindness and flexibility rules. Philip let me use his mobile to speak to Ian, who is kindness and helpfulness itself. He hasn't a problem with cock ups. *'We have two options, David. We bring the shelving through to us and we'll load your container here in Enfield as and when,'* he said. Ian was speaking to me over Philip's mobile phone. I had not learned how to use one, and had avoided its purchase for some time because of my increasing deafness.

Boyar from Bulgaria gave me a lift in the removal van from Jubilee Gardens. Now for the time being I don't need to make alternative arrangements regarding the loading of my container; thankfully JA Steel & Son Ltd will keep their removal van loaded with the library shelving for the time being, which is a really big favour of them since it will be out of commission for their own use.

1:30 p.m. I had better stop havering and eat my three Mac meal, quaff my Sprite and catch the next train back to London Town. An incredible day in which I received help in abundance.

Thursday 02/10/2008

10:20 a.m. I am perched on another stool in the arrival terminal of Luton Airport. I walked up the hill from Hotel Ibis, where I had spent the night in luxurious accommodation. I am due to fly back to Glasgow via easyJet early this afternoon. I bought myself a latte and *The Times*, now cooling my heels. Before I left Room 124 I called Dean, of Premier Freight Ltd, apparently my container has not been collected! I then called Sam, of Pentalver Transport Ltd, to let him know. I then called Ian, of JA Steel & Son Ltd, to let him know that Premier Freight Ltd would inform them as to when they would deliver my container to their premises, and that I would come back down to help load the library furniture into my container. In theory you should only have to move the stuff once. I then called First Containers UK Ltd and left a message for

Thursday 02/10/2008

Mitch, just to confirm that it would still be okay to deliver my container to his depot, which hopefully would be sometime next week, and park it there until I can ship it from the Port of Tilbury, probably later this year.

'*Once you have checked in, please proceed to departures, where you will find a range of restaurants, shops, and bars.*'

Some reflections. In spite of contingencies, outwith my control: Pentalver Transport Ltd are not releasing my container because Premier Freight Services Ltd are telling me, '*We haven't cleared your cheque yet.*' '*I can't keep my truck in the queue,*' the artic driver said. It is now going to cost me £200 to have the container, on top of its cost to purchase, delivered to Enfield and taken back down to First Containers UK Ltd in Rainham. These people, Ian, Dean, and Sam have been very helpful. I have also made contact with a member of the Asian community in Southall, Councillor Gurnail Singh, who was supportive. I just have to move on.

12:11 p.m. I am sitting on another low wall backed by railings, looking across to the Luton Airport control tower and empty easyJet hangars. I am feeding a small flock of starlings on crinkle chip scraps. They have just flown. A little sunshine a while ago, now a thick blanket of grey cloud. It is a long wait. I have scoffed an M&S cheese and onion sandwich. Jets are taking off and landing. I am now receiving welcome short bursts of sunshine. They don't last. It is now time to go back inside the terminal and begin the process of the flight home. **5:05 p.m.** Paisley Gilmour Street Station, Platform 2. A cool breeze is blowing up the railway line from the south-west. I touched down at Glasgow Airport at 4:15 p.m. and got the bus to Paisley Gilmour Street Station. The sun is now shining out of a cloudy sky. Awaiting the train for Wemyss Bay, heading home.

I EMBARK ON A NEW CAREER

Friday 03/10/2008

2:25 p.m. I am sitting in the Vision Express shop, Eye Care Clinic, Oak Mall, Greenock. I have had my peripheral vision tested and evidence for macular degeneration. '*You get this for free because you are over 65,*' she said. It has been a glorious light-filled day. I got the one o'clock boat, and met Peter, chief executive of Flexi Tech and Professor at The Strathclyde University Business School, who I acknowledge here along with Tish, who introduced me to John G Russell, for which I was most grateful. He has given me an appointment to see him on Monday 6th at 4 p.m. '*You'll have problems if you are trying to run your charity as a business. Come and see me. I will give you my mobile, should I be unable to see you,*' he said.

Thursday 09/10/2008

11:25 a.m. I called Jake, Renfrewshire Community Services Department, to see if I could get some feedback from Archie and Lindsay, the team leaders, about the success, or otherwise, of their teams clients' involvement with the recent SESF uplift of resources from Seaward Street. Their two teams helped transfer resources from the Seward Street industrial units into the two containers at Russells depot, Deanside Road, Hillington back in January of this year.

Friday 10/10/2008

Home. I called Mark at Russell Coatbridge about the container to be delivered to the former Greyfriars Primary School, the old burgh school, in St Andrews. My foundation has been offered the entire contents of this school and I am unable to handle the quantity of educational resources that are coming my way. I have created problems for myself and those closest to me. Mark is busy

Monday 13/10/2008.

and asks me to call him again later. He tells me that he will be away on a computer course and told me to contact John, their general manager, who is based at their Hillington depot.

2:10 p.m. I called John, who is always approachable, and he will try and locate a container for me, and will call me back. I call Neil at Homeless World Cup, a Sir Tom Hunter Foundation funded charity in Edinburgh. I call Archie, manager at Community Services Glenrothes, Fife, about an assessment from them of the Surplus Educational Supplies Foundation contribution to their work, and vice versa. He said he would get back to me. I call Dr Buckmire of the Grenada Cocoa Association (GCA), regarding the import of cocoa and if he could chase up the money SESF was owed from the sale of CRXU4103197. Where is it? I was given his number by Kim of GCA. I keep trying.

Monday 13/10/2008.

5:50 p.m. Home. Scratching a line. I am whacked. I have been working outside in the garden. I was extending the garden bed on the north side of the cottage. I got a call from Sam, who is the High Commissioner for Grenada in London – he tells me that he had someone who wished to purchase my container CRXU4103197. I presume he had been speaking to Claude, chairperson of the Grenada Voluntary Hospital Committee. I received a call from Roy at Roydon's Guest House, Grand Anse, Grenada, where Marion and I had stayed back in July 2006, saying that he had a buyer for the container. '*What is your bottom line?*' he asks. '*Two grand US,*' I reply.

I then told him that I had had a phone call from Sam, the High Commissioner in London. The former tells me that the political party, formerly the Government of Grenada, wishes to purchase it for a constituency office.

I Embark on a New Career

Tuesday 14/10/2008

4:45 p.m. Home. I have returned from the tiny metropolis where I posted a letter to GA Menzies, chief executive of Geo. F. Huggins & Co (GDA) Ltd asking him if his firm would assist SESF in the sale of CRXU4103197, which is currently in the possession of Valentino of Tradship, who so far has not moved, as promised he would, on the sale of my container. Last night Roy, of Roydon's Guest House, said he had a buyer.

While in the town I had stopped off at the One 2 One Accountancy Services office in the Gallowgate to see Lesley, who told me that she had moved on my attempts to recover Value Added Tax. Now, whether HMRC will cut me some slack remains to be seen. Lesley is always welcoming and supportive, as are her very busy staff. I then cycled up and around to the High Street to John MacKirdy Hauliers Ltd to ask the office if they would send SESF their invoice for taking the recent two pallets of boxes across the watta and up to MAEU6085656 at Russells depot Mossend. I intend that somehow or other, whenever possible, SESF should pay its way and not presume on further pro bono support. I try to keep short accounts with whom I do business and try to give my custom to those firms that are supportive of the SESF.

Thursday 23/10/2008.

7:15 a.m. I have just caught the train from Wemyss Bay Station. I am enmeshed, stuck, in a problem of my own creation, having given my word to uplift these resources and I am now unable to fulfil my side of the agreement. I have no choice at the moment but to run with it and play it for all its worth for the time being, as these fantastic school resources become available; to salvage at least a fraction of a fraction of these resources from the waste stream coming from Scotland's education system is a once in a life time opportunity. I am currently receiving marvellous support

Thursday 23/10/2008.

from the Scottish road haulage industry, which has encouraged me to persevere with my initiative.

John of WH Malcolm (Brookfield) Transport Ltd, who is based at their Newhouse depot, has kindly offered the services of his firm to the Surplus Educational Supplies Foundation to collect chalkboards from the Inveralmond Community High School, Livingston. However, I must source an ocean freight container in which to store these resources and have it delivered to their premises.

Yesterday I spent a not unpleasant morning attending a Strathclyde University Alumni lecture given by Ron Gilchrist, who is a worm and compost expert and biologist. Lunch provided. There I met a consultant John Breckenridge of The Scottish Chamber of Commerce, who is self-assured and has done it all; he tells me that he had made chocolate with Terry's and had participated in many other technologically and manufacturing-type related enterprises. *'What you need is a member of the commercial equivalent of the SAS to get your surplus furniture and educational resources sold,'* he said. Fair enough. I'll see if the experts at the Edinburgh Chamber of Commerce can assist SESF. He suggested I contact the commercial attaches of all the different embassies. I need to have specifications, prices, and inventories of all that I have currently on offer, and somewhere to store these resources and my containers. Something I have known for some time. *'You need seed capital,'* he said. *'Yes John, I know I need a lot,'* I said. Back to the present.

2:10 p.m. Conference room, Enterprise House, Springkerse Business Centre. A Social Academy classroom for this afternoon. I am sitting in a rather tedious bookkeeping, cash flow accounting session. At 12:15 p.m. I called John, managing director at Russell Hillington's depot, who told me that he would call me back and will put in place the delivery of two scrapped containers to WH Malcolm Transport Ltd depot at Newhouse. He knows

John Murray and he will contact him and get back to me. He said he would put in place delivery of a container to Greyfriars Primary School in St Andrews.

7:05 p.m. Neidpath B&B, Linden Avenue, Stirling. I am showered and in the lap of luxury. Pine flooring, and Campbell (or is it the Lindsay) tartan decor. I have just called Marion. All's well at home base. I will call again later. I intended to walk back from the Springkerse Business Centre at 4 p.m. but I thought better of it as I was slowly getting soaked with the wind blowing smirry rain into me. I walked around the busy roundabout, over to the shopping mall, and met four bright-faced St Modan's Secondary School pupils.

I asked them if there was a bus into the town and there was – a Park and Ride bus on its way back into the town centre. I went into Millets, and bought a pair of showerproof trousers and a tuke from BHS, and I stopped off at the Lingle Internet Café for a bowl of watery soup and a roll. I read my book, *Shadow Behind the Sun* by Remizzi Sherifi, an account of the horrors her family and community experienced in The Balkans and an account of refugee asylum life in Glasgow. I returned to my comfortable lodgings.

I am grateful. Today I was chatting to Iain from Edinburgh, who is partially sighted. He has his own IT web design company. '*When I first met you, I couldn't understand what you were all about. Now, what I think you are doing is great,*' he said. Those few words of his were an encouragement to me. I met Audrey, from Glasgow, who is doing good work with the marginalised and isolated. She is an art college graduate who let me use her mobile phone at the lunch break to call John at Russell. We will have to wait and see what happens on that front. I am now going to read through the course notes before I turn in.

Monday 27/10/2008

10:40 a.m. Home. I called Ed Ricketts of the London Chamber of Commerce regarding information about the potential market for surplus educational supplies resources worldwide. He is helpful and is to return with figures.

Tuesday 28/10/2008

7:16 a.m. Home. I am making lots of phone calls, attempting to locate a storage depot warehouse, industrial unit, space for my container, that is not too far from the Port of Tilbury.

Thursday 30/10/2008

7:16 a.m. I have just sat down in the railway carriage of the train in Wemyss Bay Station bound for Central Station, Glasgow. There goes the whistle. I came over on the MV *Bute*. I was chatting to Callum, the steward from Stornoway, who was telling me about the work done by the Blythswood charity. '*Where are you off to today?*' he asked me. I told him briefly. '*Are you taking a wage from your charity?*' he asked. '*No I am not,*' I replied. I am off to meet a team from HBOS. '*Don't lend them any money,*' said Steven, my neighbour, who travels every day across the watta. The meeting is being held in the Quaker Meeting House, Victoria Street, up near Edinburgh Castle. I am, as always, travelling expectantly, watchfully, and carefully.

11:45 a.m. The meeting is in progress with Celeste, Jen, John, Sam, and Paul. We stopped for coffee. '*Market, income stream, costs. Define. Quick wins. Focus on these. You will be further down the road.*' More jargon offering me nothing concrete. Get links off sites that are environmentally friendly.

I Embark on a New Career

3:57 p.m. I am sitting in another railway carriage at Platform 10, Waverley Station. *'This train is for Glasgow Queen Street,'* she said. I gave an impassioned pitch, perhaps it was too much so. I was confident but not overly so. The team from HBOS Halifax and Leeds were not as sharp as I expected they would be: all of them young folk on the way up their human-resource ladders. I chatted to Norman from First Port, the sponsor, along with Business in The Community, over scrumptious sandwiches. The purvey served up in the Quaker Meeting House library was excellent. I would have loved to have spent some time looking at the titles and peruse the contents on the shelves. I chatted to Saki, from Leeds, who works in human relations and Colin who works in administration, who is blind, and comes from Merseyside. Celeste, in my team, who is pushy, thrusting, comes from Trinidad via Carriacou and meets another pushy – the auld yin, still on the road, a fellow West Indian Bajan.

I gave them plenty of documentation to work with as a basis for discussion. Paul said I could stick it on my website. I was challenged from all sides and this made it a worthwhile experience for me. We'll see where the contacts, leads, suggestions, and brainstorming leads. I was grateful for another opportunity to develop my speaking skills. It has been a beautiful, crisp winter's day. Views over the Cowgate rooftops to the Pentland Hills always lifts my spirit.

Tuesday 04/11/2008

---

9 a.m. I called the deputy head teacher of Inveralmond Community High School, West Lothian Council, who may assist with the uplift rescue of roll-top blackboards, whiteboards, and chalkboards. I then called Recycling Scotland at the Deanside Industrial Estate down the road from the school – would it be possible to store the chalkboards in their storage centre? I am uncertain of what to do next. I am under pressure.

2:15 p.m. I called Howard for some business advice. He is a businessman. '*It's not easy to make money,*' he said.

Wednesday 05/11/2008

Home. I called Pentalver Transport Ltd and spoke to Tom, who is always helpful. He is going to call me back. There are 10 more boxes of precious children's library books due to be collected before the end of this month from the Morningside Library in Edinburgh. I will now call Jimmy, City of Edinburgh Social Work Community Pay Back Scheme, regarding their uplift

Monday 10/11/2008

10:30 a.m. Home. I call John at the Russell depot in Hillington, who is always willing to give me the time of day. He has every right to tell me to beat it. '*I'll see if there is anything I can come up with,*' he said. '*Thank you John,*' I said.

Tuesday 11/11/2008

11:30 a.m. Home. I called James, of Community Transport, City of Edinburgh. They have come up trumps once more. They will collect the 10 boxes of library books from the Morningside Library. I then called the library and spoke to Lisa to let them know. I then called Robert, HGV driver, who works for himself. '*Can you no call me when am drivin?*' he said. He was not well pleased. I know that I have now become a nuisance to many in the Scottish road haulage and logistics business, but what other choice do I have if I still want to salvage, to further the good use of, at least some of these fit-for-purpose educational resources? I then called Brian of TNT Transport Ltd.

12:12 p.m. David Alexander has just offered to make me a bacon sandwich. I am now speaking to Doreen, CMA/CGM Shipping branch office, West George Street, Glasgow. I am desperately trying to get the container loaded with library shelving brought back up to Scotland. I had made a grave error in assuming that the schools in Grenada would be glad to receive it.

(I should have drawn the line there and then, and cut all ties to any further shipments of educational resources to Grenada, West Indies.)

Wednesday 12/11/2008

6:15 a.m. I am sitting on one of the swivel-type bar stools facing the Coffee Cabin of MV *Bute*. I bid a cheery '*Good morning*' to the two Franks, who are first-class ship stewards. I cycled, as per usual, into Rothesay town. A crisp, calm morning; the moon is like a golden platter which hangs low over Ardmory Road. '*Well, where on earth are you off to today?*' I ask myself.

I am travelling with £700 out of the Surplus Educational Supplies Foundation RBS account, withdrawn yesterday afternoon. I hope to obtain a second third-hand seaworthy 40-foot ocean freight container to park in the playground of Inveralmond Community High School, Livingston, which has now become part of the Interserve Projects Construction Ltd construction yard, into which will be loaded the surplus-to-requirements educational resources from the school classrooms that are being refurbished. Does that answer your question, for that is what I am aiming to achieve this morning. I hope to see Fraser, operations manager at Freightliner Ltd, Coatbridge, to see if they can help me out with the transport of my container in Rainham, Essex, up to Scotland. These steps and plans are provisional.

10:15 a.m. CT Engineering Services Ltd office. I am with Mary, who is their business manager. Frank has just shown me the container, 40-footer GATU4072944, which I hope is in plate: still seaworthy. I was taking their word for it that the container was seaworthy.

11:50 a.m. I am sitting in the swish prefab office. '*That's the container ready, and we'll phone Carson, who will deliver it to Inveralmond Community High School, okay?*' he said. Carson Transport Ltd, Westfield Industrial Estate, Cumbernauld. So far so good. I was brought a cup of coffee. All very helpful.

On arrival I went to the Ravenstock MSG office at the other end of this building, after meeting Benny who directed me to it, where I met Fiona, who took me out to their yard. Stacked containers. She showed me a rusting 20-footer. I had to negotiate; bargaining is not my forte, but I am still teachable. No deal. I returned to the prefab office and the way ahead has opened up.

'*That's lovely. Thank you very much,*' I said.

12:15 p.m. I am in the cab of a Carson Transport Ltd transporter artic, with the young Ross, HGV driver and expert high hab hydraulic lift operator, at the wheel of the artic and trailer, and we are heading east to Inveralmond Community High School via the M8 motorway.

4:50 p.m. I have just sat down in a carriage of the Wemyss Bay train.

Roll it back. Ross and I arrived at the gates of Inveralmond Community High School around 1:45 p.m. Ross waited in the cab while I went to look for Gerry, the site foreman. I met a burly, rude gentleman, who said I needed a hard hat and high-vis jacket. Fair enough. And when I told him my business, he said that my container could not be parked until Friday since a crane was in the way. I ignored him and I went looking for the site manager. '*You are causing us a lot of trouble,*' he said. I don't mean to be a nuisance, but I told him that I had phoned Gerry from Mary's office in Coatbridge this morning to let him know that I was bringing

I Embark on a New Career

the SESF container over, and he had told me that the container could not be lifted off before 4 p.m. I told him that the business manager had negotiated an uplift before 12 noon. I am learning, rather late in life, to hold my ground and be politely assertive.

One of the construction workers who happened to be in the site office of Interserve Projects Ltd, Christopher, construction worker, kindly loaned me his hard hat and eventually I found the man I was looking for, or rather he found me about to knock on the door of the site agent's office. I walked back to the gate and told Ross that he could bring the container into the yard, once the playground and school's parking lot, and I climbed back into the cab. New state-of-the-art hydraulic lifting gear. Ross used a ladder to get on top of the container and hooked four chains to each top corner, climbed back down the ladder and, from a remote-control-type device at his waist, lifted the container off the trailer and on to the ground to precisely where the site manager wanted it placed. '*He's a good driver,*' he said. Ross was kind enough to ask me how I was getting back to Glasgow and I said I would be making my own way home. He was going to offer me a lift, but was heading in the opposite direction. I thought I would let the school administration know that I had brought a 40-foot container over to collect their unwanted educational resources, which I been promised. Christopher had told me that there had already been large quantities of fit-for-purpose resources junked into skips. Oh well, who am I tae blaw against the wind. I met friendly office staff at reception and left some information about the Surplus Educational Supplies Foundation for the depute head teacher, who, Gerry had said to me earlier, was too busy to see me. '*He's in a technical meeting,*' he said. Anyway, I got a word in with the school authorities despite him telling me to shove off.

It has been a beautiful, light-filled crisp day. I waited at the bus stop outside Inveralmond Community High School. At the bus stop I met Robert, who tells me that he comes originally from the Wester Hailes on the outskirts of the city of Edinburgh, and most of his peers from school and his neighbourhood had died of AIDS related illnesses. Robert went on to tell me that he had moved out of Edinburgh to Livingston New Town to give his sons a better life. We chatted away and he told me that he admired what I was doing. Bless him, and all his. I am on a slow bus to Bathgate.

I had another long wait for another slow bus to Falkirk via California, Shieldhill etc. I managed to get off at a stop not far from Falkirk High Station. I puffed up the hill and got the 5:31 p.m. train to Glasgow Queen Station. *'Are yeh tae cheap tae pye for a taxi yursell?'* said the taxi driver, on hearing me ask people standing in the rank behind me if they were heading in the same direction. I am not cheap I was only trying to be considerate; I gave him a fiver, keep the change dude. I had another long wait in Central Station. I called home twice. Grab the present moments.

I am munching on a piping-hot, microwaved Cornish pasty and drinking a coffee. I am anxious as to whether or not I'll make the last ferry sailing of the day. Take it as it comes. I had not intended to purchase another container but given the facts that:

- CT Engineering Services Ltd staff were helpful, with a flexible as opposed to inflexible attitude, as opposed to the other management crowd through the wall I had to deal with;
- I took the decision to take up the former firms offer;
- The container, when it was shown to me by Frank, the CT Engineering Ltd depot container, smelled fine, and looked fine, except for the one pinhole that I could see, which he said they would repair before the container left their yard;
- Mary, the business manager, was prepared to make further arrangements to have the container delivered TODAY! because I represented a 'charity' (I took your advice, Eric, to get a charity, but it did me no good whatsoever in name only), and;
- Furthermore, what clinched the deal was that all of them made me feel welcome.

The transaction was done and dusted. Mary is the owner of the company – a formidable character and business acumen. We had spoken over the phone in days past. She knew a lot of the people I had been dealing with over the past three years. Small world. The company secretary made me a coffee. Bless her. I have taken on more risk, complexity and difficulty.

I am now up to my eyeballs in this initiative, fledgling social enterprise, self-initiated, and self-financed charitable effort and quasi-business. Another step along the high road. There is no way back, only forward and upward.

Thursday 13/11/2008

Home. I called Fraser, accounts manager at Freightliner Ltd, Coatbridge, who is someone who, from the first time I spoke with him, has been very helpful. '*I will speak to the powers that be,*' he said and he will see if they can bring up my container from Rainham to the Eurocentral Freight Terminal. He is a decent and trustworthy man who will help me if he can; I am greatly encouraged by his response and such gracious treatment.

I call DHL Marketing. I can only keep on trying to enlist support and not give up now. I call the broker of Tradship in Grenada, once more: I had called him on 9 November. He tells me that he will hand over the funds from the sale of my container CRXU4103197 to Roy of Roydon's Guest House. He has not remitted the money for the sale. What can I do about it? I call Sandra, chief executive of Rural Transformation, Grenada, and let her know that I am getting nowhere with this individual, who she had recommended to me some weeks ago. She now tells me it is the responsibility of Philip, the acting principal of the Grenada Boys School.

I call the Homeless World Cup charity in Edinburgh and speak to Callum. No joy there either.

Friday 14/11/2008

Home. I call Eric at Duncan Adams Transport Ltd about the possibility of more storage of educational resources in my containers at their Grange Dock depot. He tells me that they are at full capacity, and space to park containers is at a premium. He suggests I contact Falkirk Council. I then call Fraser, accounts manager, Freightliner Ltd, Coatbridge, who tells me that they will assist me in bringing MSKU6311690 up to Scotland to be stored temporarily at their depot in Coatbridge, and I am to send a cheque for £100 to their office, Freightliner Ltd Credit Control, Southampton, who will open a credit line and email the form, which I am to fill in and fax back. BRILLIANT! I am back on the road again. I love it! I am so grateful to him and his firm for this assistance.

'The secret of that spark is no secret, that one should throw oneself with disciplined love into all LIFE'S moments.' I don't know where I got those inspirational words from. *'Are you a do-gooder?'* asked Dr Camrass, a Bridgeton Glasgow GP, when I called him one lunchtime from the Primary School office telephone in the mid seventies. I had asked him if he could assist me in helping a damaged individual afflicted with alcoholism, who I had stopped to help, and who was staggering across Bath Street in front of oncoming traffic one late wind- and rainswept afternoon in August 1975; it was not long after my arrival in No Mean City, where such sights of broken humanity were then commonplace. I strive for the opportunity to do some good for others, providing I am prepared to step out of my comfort zone and overcome my fear of failure and feeling of inadequacy, to meet the needs of other human beings through my efforts of will and inspired constructive action, in collaboration with key players to meet those needs. There is also the personal satisfaction which I experience from working with others to achieve those goals successfully. What more can I say, that will justify my current commitment?

I EMBARK ON A NEW CAREER

Monday 17/11/2008

Home. I call up Robert, the independent haulier who is based in Airdrie, a friend of Martin's, regarding information on a possible location for storage of the container that is to be brought up from England and a buyer for my containers. He, as a rule, usually gives me the time of day, and suggests I contact Sweeney Kincaid Ltd, a firm of auctioneers in the Hillington Industrial Estate complex.

I call the Prince's Trust and speak to Jane. I am to call again tomorrow to speak to Nancy or Margaret. I call Falkirk District Council and I speak with Jennifer in their Education Property office, and ask them to call me back. I call Falkirk College of Further Education to speak to personal assistant Pauline. I speak to Crawford, who was at a meeting earlier when I called the property executive with Falkirk District Council, and who was interested in my pitch. I then call the INEOS office at Grangemouth, at what was once the BP petrochemical refinery across the way from Grange Dock, at the suggestion of Richard who I had met some months ago, who has an office supplies company in the town. He suggested I speak to Allan – another problem to solve.

I am now sweating over the logistics of the collecting and storage of educational resources from Greyfriars Primary School in St Andrews, formerly the old burgh school, which the Saint Andrews Preservation Trust hope to acquire. Once more the pressure is on. At this point many would say, '*I told you so. You are totally out of your depth. You have taken on the collection and storage of surplus-to-requirements educational resources that you are no longer equipped to cope with. And it is entirely your own fault, because you have given Council Education Department authorities the impression that you, aka Surplus Educational Supplies Foundation, had the logistics capacity to manage the salvage of them.*' The truth hurts, but I am still confronted with the problem and I must solve it. I shall not give up! I often find encouragement in the words of the following quotation, '*Every great cause is born from repeated failures and imperfect achievements,*' (Maria Montessori).

I try to contact Neil Logue, who told me to persevere. Later, I was contacted by Claire of Squirrel Storage Ltd in Livingston, a contact given to me by Sarah, someone I had met at my first Edinburgh Chamber of Commerce speed networking session in 2007. This firm is offering me some storage space for the educational resources being salvaged from Inveralmond Community High School, but is not suitable for the time being. I thank them for this generous offer of support and will get back to them soon as possible.

Wednesday 19/11/2008

Home. Crawford of Falkirk District Council, who is offering the Surplus Educational Supplies Foundation the resources in the former Grangemouth High School, called. He will call me back on Friday.

Thursday 20/11/2008

Home. I contact Archie, the community services manager, Criminal Justice Department Unit in Glenrothes New Town, regarding assistance with the uplift, inventory, and storage of the educational resources at the former Greyfriars Primary School in St Andrews.

2:30 p.m. I speak to Archie, who tells me, '*David, it will be the same as last time.*' That is good news. Community Services will supply teams and transport. I gave him the Fife Council Assets surveyor's telephone number and he will inform her of this collection. I then called her to tell her that Community Services were prepared, yet once again, to step into the breach to offer their support to the Surplus Educational Supplies Foundation and I gave her the Community Services telephone number.

4:45 p.m. John of WH Malcolm Transport Ltd, Newhouse depot, called me to see if I had managed to deal with the collection of chalkboards and other assorted classroom resources from Inveralmond Community High School. I told him about what I had done. I thanked him for taking the trouble and I am humbled by his continuing support. Bless him and all his team at Malcolm teams in Newhouse and Linwood.

Monday 24/11/2008

7:45 a.m. Home. I have sent emails to the facilities and assets management surveyor, Fife Council, who have agreed to let SESF have some temporary storage for the educational resources from the former Greyfriars Primary School in Saint Andrews in one of their Food Resource and Business Centre units, and to Archie, senior projects officer, Community Service Criminal Justice Department, who have kindly offered SESF some of their teams to help uplift and load educational resources from this school into a container, which will be delivered.

I am now going to work on the presentation of my business plan. I hope to make this presentation to the Social Enterprise Academy Dragon's Den panel at the Enterprise Centre, Stirling at 9:30 a.m. on the 27th and 28th.

9:30 a.m. I call the depute head teacher, ICHS, Livingston. Someone in the school's office tells me, '*He's in a contractors meeting at the moment.*' I had called him to find out whether or not an inventory was being taken of the resources that were being loaded into GATU4072944 and, if not, could one be taken. I left a message and apparently an inventory was being taken and I confirmed this by speaking to Gerry, the Interserve Projects Ltd manager.

Thursday 27/11/2008

10:15 a.m. I call Murdo of the Edinburgh Chamber of Commerce. We spoke briefly. He seems positive and will follow up my query as to if a market exists for surplus school resources in the developing world. I then sent him an email. I have not received a reply. Research the market for fit-for-purpose, surplus to requirements, educational resources.

3:45 p.m. I am kept waiting to speak to His Excellency the High Commissioner for Grenada. I have had no reply to my email of 11 November. I am on a hiding to nothing and should have realised that many months ago.

Tuesday 25/11/2008

Home. *'Have a chat with Matt,'* suggested Douglas, Property Acquisition, Tesco, regarding their massive warehouse on the M8 between Glasgow and Edinburgh. I do, and speak to Matthew, Asset Management, who is helpful.

I have learned today that Community Service Glenrothes will collect the educational resources being stored in the former Greyfriars Primary School on 3 December and 5 December. These resources will be stored in Unit 9 of the Food and Business Park, Glenrothes. Archie and Craig, Community Services, will supervise the uplift and they do not require my presence and are happy to do the uplift with their teams. I am so grateful to them both for their no-nonsense, efficient response to my request for assistance and, not least, a big thank you to you both, and to all the young folk on your teams,

Thursday 27/11/2008

7:10 a.m. The whistle blows. Something kicks into electromechanical movement. I boarded the train at Wemyss Bay Station. Marion dropped me off. I walked across the new inner harbour bridge. I greeted the MacKirdy HGV driver and John the harbour master. Here I am once more on the move again. I am travelling to attend the final two days of the Social Enterprise Academy course to practise my executive summary delivery, today, and present it tomorrow. Journeying mercies to and from Stirling.

I have stayed the course so far. I can but try. This one and only over-the-top nutter from the West Coast must receive some form of funding and further pro bono assistance if the Surplus Educational Supplies Foundation is going to continue to survive.

My elevator pitch:
1. An introduction. This what I am going to tell them: tell them what you are going to tell them – how the Surplus Educational Supplies Foundation started and why.
2. Tell them it.
3. Tell them what you told them.
4. Tell them a little story; be humorous, self-deprecating, which won't be too difficult, and keep smiling, don't use my accents: remember all the work I have done.

Friday 28/11/2008

12:10 p.m. Home. I did give my elevator pitch at 10:30 a.m. I was not tongue-tied. I said what I was about to say, I said it, and managed to answer questions from the panel. I stood up, spoke up, sat down, and shut up.

Monday 01/12/2008

3:50 p.m. Home. This morning I called Matthew, Tesco surveyor, affable but not delivering. I sent off an application to Enterprise Europe Scotland. I have been speaking to Sam at the Grenada High Commission in London, two floors down the corridor from Her Excellency the High Commissioner, who has gone to dinner.

Wednesday 03/12/2008

10:55 a.m. Home. I called Renwick to confirm the uplift arrangements from Greyfriars Primary School. He told me that Archie, the community services supervisor, has the keys to Unit 9 of the Food and Business Centre. *'All we are doing is moving council property, from one place to another,'* he said. Encouraging letters came from the schools in Grenada, who were the beneficiaries of the shipments of educational resources.

Write to: Bill, community service manager, and to Stephen, executive director of Social Work Service, Fife Council, to express my appreciation for enabling SESF to salvage some educational resources.

Thursday 04/12/2008

Home. I have just spoken to Archie, who has told me that their Community Service Teams have successfully collected the educational resources from Greyfriars Primary School in Saint Andrews. I am incredibly grateful for his help and all associated with the valuable work being done by Community Services, to which my foundation is making a small contribution.

Friday 05/12/2008

12:39 p.m. Home. I called ESA McIntosh, Kirkcaldy, and Forbo, Kirkcaldy regarding storage space. No joy. And I called Gertrude the education officer for Carriacou. I spoke to Gertrude and sent an email. *'Allison, senior administrative officer, Ministry of Education, is on holiday at the moment,'* said Rholda, principal, Bishops College, Hillsborough, Carriacou.

I keep on trying to contact these people, but my gut feeling is that they are not interested, or as they say in Scotland, *'Ah cannae be bothered.'*

(Sadly that was also the prevailing attitude of Grenada government officials and their representatives in the United Kingdom.)

Monday 08/12/2008

11:45 a.m. Home. I receive a call from Brian at Clydeport Ocean Terminal, Greenock Peel Ports office, who will approach his senior management team to see whether they will let me have some storage space for my containers. I await a reply.

I call the Sierra Leone High Commission in London and the Belize High Commission in London.

Thursday 11/12/2008

Home. I called Mick of the Don McMath Foundation, Gambia, West Africa and Mae Schools for The Gambia. I called Paula, Belmont Estate, Grenada.

3 p.m. I called Rob of Forth Ports Plc, Property, regarding storage. I left a message. He kindly called me back and told me that he would speak to Operations. No deal. At least I tried. Nothing ventured, nothing gained. I then called the Scottish Development International and spoke to Lorraine.

Tuesday 16/12/2008

1:22 p.m. Home. I spoke to Matthew, Tesco Property, regarding storage in their Dundee warehouse. A possibility. He will send me an email. I am still waiting.

Saturday 03/01/2009

4:05 p.m. Home. I called Walter, chairman of the Grenada Port Authority, to see if he can assist me in the recovery of my container

CRXU4103197. He sounded helpful. '*You know that Grenadians tell you what you want to hear.*' You had been warned.

Thursday 22/01/2009

1:35 p.m. Home. I am very tired. I am not feeling too good. I am preoccupied with the problem of delivering seven 40-foot ocean containers of fit-for-purpose, surplus to requirements, educational resources, stored at a number of locations all over Scotland, to deserving beneficiaries. And if those seven 40-foot ocean freight containers loaded with resources were not enough – the recently acquired resources from the former Grey Friars Primary School in St Andrews, which are being stored temporarily in Unit 9 Glenrothes Food and Business Centre.

This morning I called ESA McIntosh in Kirkcaldy and I spoke to Adam about whether their firm in Kirkcaldy would provide storage and publicity. He said they could give me the latter in their next in-house newsletter. I called Knight Watson and spoke to Louise, who heard me out. I had sent her an email about my need to temporarily store the contents of two 40-foot ocean freight containers over at Duncan Adams Transport Ltd, Grange Dock. Where do I go from here?

I then called John, business adviser at the Edinburgh Chamber of Commerce, and left a message.

Friday 23/01/2009

Home. I called Findel (a big firm supplying educational resources worldwide, based in Cheshire) to speak to Perry, and spoke to Sophia in the Nottingham office, and then Scott. I'll keep chasing them. Grippit. They are not giving anything away. '*You need to have an agent,*' he tells me.

12:20 p.m. I am giving it another go. I am not going to go and lie down just yet. I called another firm, who tell me, '*We put the laboratory equipment in the skip, because it is contaminated.*' I call Forbo, Nairn, and they put me onto Thomas Mitchell Homes Ltd, who now have their warehouse in Kirkcaldy. I speak to Naomi and I send her an email.

11:15 p.m. Home. I pause for a scribble, to reflect and attempt to recollect the highlights of my efforts – all day spent mainly in front of a monitor, contacting different organisations over the telephone.

I received a call from Ian of Masterton Demolition Ltd, Falkirk, to ask me whether SESF was interested in acquiring the educational resources from a secondary school in the Grangemouth area, which I presume to be Grangemouth High School and which their firm was scheduled to demolish in two weeks. I told him that I needed storage space, since I could no longer rely on pro bono support to store my containers and the labour to uplift the educational resources from the school buildings. I sent him an email with information about the Surplus Educational Supplies Foundation initiative. I also mentioned that I would contact the Community Services Criminal Justice Department office in Falkirk to see if they would provide my charitable foundation with a team to assist in the inventory, removal, and loading of the surplus-to-requirements educational resources.

I contacted the Sierra Leone High Commission and, at long last, after many telephone calls, I spoke with one of their counsellors who had spoken earlier with Florence Bangali. He told me that his government was very interested in acquiring educational resources. I sent him an email: wait and see what happens.

Later I spoke with Gertrude, education officer, Carriacou, West Indies. Another very expensive long-distance transatlantic telephone call. Can her Ministry of Education show some commitment regarding the delivery, awaiting shipment, of the two 40-foot ocean freight container-loads of educational resources that were uplifted in July 2008 from the Dunshalt Village Primary School, and which were specifically earmarked for schools on the island?

Saturday 24/01/2009

4:15 p.m. I have just called Valentino of Tradship Grenada, who had been recommended to me way back in July 2006.

I told him that I wished the return of my container. He told me that Roy of Roydon's Guest House was to call him on Monday and come and collect it. I then called Roy, who said he would do just that. I leave the matter in his hands. He, as always, is helpful – the opposite of the former Grenadian.

Wednesday 28/01/2009

11:20 a.m. Home. I called the Sierra Leone High Commission to speak with Counsellor Bangali. She is interested but no commitment.

5 p.m. Spoke to Paul, Delmas Shipping Ltd, Liverpool, about the tariff to Freetown. He will send me a quote.

Thursday 29/01/2009

10:35 a.m. Home. I have a pain behind my right eye and feel not up to par. I am making more telephone calls in spite of the acute discomfort. I contact the West African Business Association. I speak with Tony, who gives me the name of David, a banking consultant, who I am unable to contact.

2:10 p.m. Vanessa of Christian African Relief Trust, Huddersfield, called to tell me that they have delivered the Surplus Educational Supplies Foundation gift of a 40-foot container of educational resources to Benin. I call Ian, the demolition contractor, but he does not return my calls or reply to my emails. I call the Scottish Enterprise office in Glasgow and speak to Pamela, who is very helpful, and her interest in what I am doing encourages me to press on. I call Kathrin, Community Services in Dunoon, about a contact for the Falkirk area and leave a message. I end up calling Archie of Community Services in Glenrothes. He is always positive and encouraging, and gives me the names of Mary and Sharon, and their manager Susan, at Community Service Falkirk.

Friday 30/01/2009

10:20 a.m. Home. I speak with Kathrin at Community Services in Dunoon. She is positive and encourages me to keep on with my project, and was the first person on the Isle of Bute who, in June 2005, encouraged me to do whatever I could to continue to salvage fit-for-purpose educational resources and deliver them wherever they were most needed. She will speak to her supervisor about the contribution that the Surplus Educational Supplies Foundation can make to the rehabilitation, renewal and personal development of their clients, and about my foundation's work with their teams.

I send an email and call Crawford, Falkirk Council Property. He is on holiday – back on Monday. I call Sierra Leone High Commission and speak to Florence. They have received my correspondence addressed to His Excellency Chabolah. '*We shall discuss it today,*' she said. I call Demolition Man and left a message.

I got off my bed in weakness, determined to keep plugging away.

11 a.m. I called Archie, Community Services Fife, who is very helpful and gave me the Falkirk area contact, who I am to call on Monday. He suggests I contact Gordon Brown and Douglas Alexander and gave me the telephone number of Jim, who is a political fixer in London and who has privileged access to the Labour Party.

I received an email from David, Commercial Manager of Willmot Dixon Construction Ltd, asking me to get in touch. He tells me to call him in June regarding the possibility of acquiring educational resources from schools in Barnet. Philip of that firm had passed on my contact. I am also to contact Chris about resources available from a school in Hackney, East London. Logistics is the key to it.

I call the office of the Grenada Chamber of Commerce to obtain contact with Heather of Bacolet Developments about the sale of SESF container CRXU4103197, assuming I will ever be able to recover it. I can but try.

Tuesday 03/02/2009

9 a.m. Home. I called Neil, of Thorpe Kilworth, and spoke to his personal assistant, Mary, and left a message; I spoke with David of Fife Enterprise Business Gateway; I spoke to Carolyn of Social Enterprise, Fife Council, who is interested and made an appointment for 12 February. I posted a copy of the executive summary of my business plan to her. See where that leads.

12:30 p.m. Finally, after numerous phone calls, I get to speak with the Sierra Leone High Commission in London, who tells me that he is off to Greece and will contact me on his return. He comes from the Kono region of that West African country. *'It's where dey have dimonds,'* he said. I will need Customs Duty Waiver Papers.

Contact Sierra Leone Book Trust, Goderich Warehouses, Freetown. *'You will need a clearing agency, Sallieu Turay is de man yuh want,'* he tells me. Contact executive director of SALBOT.

Wednesday 04/02/2009

2:45 p.m. Home. I received a call from Mark. At first I thought it was Mott, the Grenada USA expatriate cocoa farmer, calling from the parish of St Andrew, Grenada. Mark Green has called me out of the blue. '*We are building the best school in Sierra Leone!*'

He refers me to their charity, A Call to Business (ATCB). They wish to acquire surplus-to-requirements educational resources. He is involved with Terry, who had told him to contact me. Interestingly, this afternoon I received a reply to the email I had sent to the Chief Education Officer, Julian, in the Ministry of Education, Grenada expressing support for the SESF initiative, but no commitment to reciprocate action. I am becoming tired of persisting with my efforts in that direction; the Government of Grenada, could quite easily facilitate the delivery of shipments.

I received an email response to my query to the Christian African Relief Trust from Vanessa, who I had spoken to yesterday. She tells me that they wish to acquire the two 40-foot container loads of educational resources that I currently have stored at Duncan Adams Transport Ltd yard at Grange Dock (MAEU7412692 and SEAU4272551) and will deliver their own container to uplift the contents, but not until 13 March. Christian African Relief Trust (CART) appear to be doing good work in Ghana. This charity was recommended to me by Tim at the Red Cross in Glasgow.

Thursday 05/02/2009

12:20 p.m. Home. I have been tidying up outside. The sun is shining and I am feeling better. A call from Sanjay. Work beckons, we have an appointment for tomorrow.

12:30 p.m. Home. I am not feeling too good. I have no energy, however, I persevere. I call Crawford, Falkirk Council, who has offered SESF the educational resources in another three schools

Monday 09/02/2009.

that are due for demolition. He mentioned Denny High School. No reply from Masterton Demolition Ltd.

5 p.m. Home. I called David, general manager of Bishop's Move Ltd, who I had met at an Edinburgh Chamber of Commerce speed networking session last year. They will collect the 10 boxes of books from the Morningside Library, held in the Community Transport storage Unit 4C in the Elizafield, Bonnington Industrial Estate, Newhaven, and deliver to Duncan Adams Transport Ltd depot Grange Dock. This is really good of them; these offers of pro bono support keep the Surplus Educational Supplies Foundation afloat, and me from sinking beneath the waves.

I then called Jimmy at Community Transport in Edinburgh to let him know that these boxes will be collected at long last. Later this afternoon I received a call from Barbara, whose charity is based in a Derbyshire village and who are building a school in Bangbutt Village in Sierra Leone. Another encouragement to continue with my work. I contacted Delmas UK, Princes Dock, Liverpool. I also contacted Paul who had replied 29 January with a quote.

Monday 09/02/2009.

Home. I receive a call from Vanessa of the Christian African Relief Trust to let me know that a transport company will be delivering a container to DAT Ltd Grange Dock on 27 February to uplift the educational resources from SEAU4272551 and MAEU7412692.

I send emails to Eric and Bryan in the office at Duncan Adams Transport Ltd to let them know, and ask if it is possible to have these containers parked somewhere in the yard where they can be unloaded. This would cause problems.

(At this point I was becoming overwhelmed by the process I had initiated several years ago.)

I Embark on a New Career

Wednesday 11/02/2009

9:45 a.m. Home. I receive a call from Carolyn, business adviser, Social Enterprise Start Up Economic Regeneration and Partnerships, Development Services, Fife Council about my executive summary, which I had sent on Monday. She said that their Social Enterprise Fund could not deliver on funding and it did not run to the £50,000 figure I had quoted. I told her that, though funding was necessary for SESF to continue its relief work, what I expected from her organisation was: some joined-up thinking about the vast quantities of fit-for-purpose, surplus to requirements, educational resources being dumped into landfill, the brilliant cooperation from the Community Service Criminal Justice Department, and the rehabilitation opportunities that the Surplus Educational Supplies Foundation can offer their clients; council facilities and asset management industrial unit availability of work space for refurbishment of educational resources prior to shipment; and her own Economic and Development Services.

(Fast forward to March 2017. Brake The Cycle Community Payback Order scheme in Edinburgh. The recycling project, which took old unwanted bicycles and renovated them. Over a hundred bikes were shipped as part of an SESF shipment of educational resources to a school to being built in Dame Marie, South West Region, Republic of Haiti.)

I called Demba, SLHC, in London. I am told that he is at a conference and will be in the office next week.

Thursday 12/02/2009

4:20 p.m. Home. I have been on my back all day, reading. I have no energy. It is grey and wet outside. One minute I am down and out, and the next minute I am airborne.

Friday 13/02/2009

A few moments ago, I thought I had better check and see if there had been any messages on 1571. Crawford, Falkirk District Council, had called at 11:28 a.m. I must have fallen asleep. I am to meet him tomorrow at the former Denny High School. '*I have arranged access to the school. Give me a wee phone call and we'll set up a time and we'll confirm the details,*' he said.

I am encouraged to continue with the project. I have called him and confirmed that I intend to meet him tomorrow.

Friday 13/02/2009

11:10 a.m. The Town Bakery, which is just along from the crossroads, Denny, Stirlingshire. I am ensconced with a cheese roll and a cup of tea. I have just walked up the main road along from what was the former Denny High School. I got there around 9:45 a.m. by bus from Buchanan Street Bus Station. I walked across the snowy fitba park and was welcomed at the door by a tall gentleman – a member of staff, who was civil to me. He took me into the main building and told reception who I was and I was taken up another flight of stairs and along a corridor and into a staff room, where there was a meeting in progress, and was ushered back outside into the corridor. Crawford came out to meet me and took me on a tour of the now-empty school buildings. There are good quality desks and chairs in the classrooms. Most of the technical equipment in the technical department has gone. There I met the principal technical teacher and depute rector, Bill, who accompanied us around his technical department and former classrooms.

It's a dreich wet morning. I had made good time and I will now have my tea break. I need to contact Mary at Falkirk Community Services by 23 February to arrange for work teams to assist with the removal and loading of resources, and arrange for a 40-foot container to be delivered on the same day.

5:15 p.m. Home. I returned without Marion's digital camera. I had engaged a party of Somalis on the bus from Denny on the journey back to Glasgow. I would not have expected them to take it out of my haversack while my attention was drawn to some of them in conversation. I am a right mug. A big down, but that is my only explanation. I'm sure I put it back in my bag after using it to take some digitals on my tour round the high school. On the other hand I could have left it behind, if so, no disrespect intended.

Monday 16/02/2009

10:35 a.m. Home. I called Mary, Community Services Falkirk Area, regarding collection from the former Denny High School buildings. She will contact Crawford Campbell at Falkirk Central. She is okay about the press involvement. I called Robert about storage and he is to call me back.

I called the Sierra Leone High Commission, spoke to the Head of Chancery, and sent emails to His Excellency Melvin Chalobah, and counsellor Sahr P Demba. I have made numerous phone calls to the elusive. It is now almost 12 p.m. I have a heavy cold and cough and am not feeling too great. I press on until I hear from Community Services Falkirk and SLHC. I will have to wait and see. Pamela at Business Gateway sent me an email with helpful leads. I send a recorded delivery letter to Philip, Director General for Education Scottish Executive, which had blocked my email. Await a reply.

Friday 20/02/2009

9:30 a.m. Home. I call Mark at John G Russell Transport Ltd, Coatbridge. '*Leave it with me. Hold on a minute,*' he said. I received a call from Robin, S&R Services Ltd, Huddersfield. '*Ask Eric to put CART'S container on the floor,*' he said.

I am now to contact Eric to find out when he will have my

Saturday 21/02/2009

containers SEAU4272551 and MAEU7412692 in place for me to unload contents into CART's container.

5:30 p.m. I spoke to Karen at Freightliner Ltd, who is always helpful. I call Rosetta, principal of St George's Anglican Junior School in Grenada. Later, I contact Carson Transport Ltd in Cumbernauld and speak to John.

I have applied to the Glasgow Freight Club for membership. No response from them. *'Hoo de yeh think you are, Mr Big Head? You made all that effort and expense for what? To get a reward in Heaven?'*

(No, I was not looking for a reward in Heaven. I just wanted to make a success out of the things, projects, and this initiative, that I considered to be especially worthwhile here on the Blue Planet while my strength remained.)

Saturday 21/02/2009

10:35 a.m. Home. I am preoccupied with the collection, unloading, loading, and delivery of fit-for-purpose, surplus to requirements, educational resources to schools in the impoverished developing world. 'I will have to do some fancy footwork,' she said.

I have just called the Christian African Relief Trust in Huddersfield and spoken to Vanessa, their mover and shaker. I told her that I did not think it necessary to empty my two freight containers over at Duncan Adams Transport Ltd, Grange Dock. I suggested that the two containers could be delivered to Huddersfield as they were, since I would donate these two 40-foot ocean freight containers and contents to their charity.

11 a.m. I called Duncan Adams Transport Ltd and spoke to Bryan in the office about shifting the two containers to where they could be unloaded. I told him that there may be a change of plan and I wanted those two containers off my hands, doing some good, given that I could no longer expect to store them indefinitely at their depot. And furthermore, I did not think I could unload and load these containers on my own. I have no energy because of the current state of my health. Eric's words of warning kept on ringing in my ears. '*You only want to move it once, David.*'

Bryan said he would speak to Eric on Monday morning.

Sunday 22/02/2009

Home. CART are willing to accept the gift of one of the containers. And 10 boxes of library books for container MAEU741269.

1:40 p.m. I received an email from Vanessa of the Christian African Relief Trust regarding collection of the educational resources and school furniture on 27 February, for CART Warehouse and Shop, Huddersfield. I am to contact Robin who is their freight forwarder in Huddersfield regarding transport.

Monday 23/02/2009

9:30 a.m. Home. Mary from Falkirk Community Services called and gave me the name of the person she suggested I contact, who is their supervisor, to arrange the uplift of resources from Denny High School. I reluctantly had to inform her that it would be unlikely that my foundation would be able to uplift these resources. I experienced a great sense of failure of having to let go of the two 40-foot ocean freight containers, which I had purchased at my family's expense. I can't win them all.

11:10 a.m. I call Jim, supervisor, Community Services Falkirk area. '*You liaise with us when you can.*' His positive response made me feel a little better. I then called Crawford and left a message. I have had to cancel the uplift and collection of educational resources from the former Denny High School.

Wednesday 25/02/2009

11:25 a.m. Home. I am about to cycle into Rothesay town to fax the invoice, proof to CART of my purchase of MAEU7412692, from Print Point. I had called Robin regarding his email.

I am making light of this radical change of plans as the edifice of what I have worked so hard for crumbles around me.

12:20 p.m. Mission accomplished. CART do not have a fax machine. I posted the invoice with my best wishes. I am now going to go for a long stroll up and over Canada Hill, around past Loch Ascog, and back up the shore road.

2:45 p.m. Back from my jaunt. I met Ninian, a Port School parent from former days, who is building houses in the Eastlands Park, once an open field below Canada Hill. '*You look well*,' he said. I am still climbing.

Tuesday 24/02/2009.

10:30 a.m. Home. I call Robin, who deals with DAT Ltd on behalf of CART. It is a small world. I told him to negotiate whatever he thinks best and he told me that they are shipping the container from the Port of Grangemouth to Africa '*Ah'm stuck intae summat. Give me four minutes and I'll call you*,' he said.

11 a.m. '*I am awfully sorry, but for insurance purposes we cannot let you have the resources in Grangemouth High School. You know how it is these days*,' said Ian, who has just called.

Wednesday 25/02/2009

6:45 a.m. Aboard the MV *Argyle*. Generators, motors, electromechanical devices are humming over my head. I am on my usual perch in front of the Coffee Cabin Café 'For all your journey's needs.' Postcard foties of Bonnie Magic Scotland by Colin of Scotland. Where are you off to today?

I left home at 5:55 a.m. On the bike and out on the damp, streetlight-lit road. Fresh morning. I will write my own script for a new day, freewheeling round the Craignethan corner with no hands on the handlebars. There is no one about. I am not showing off. The sheer pleasure I get from riding the old bike: I feel free, unburdened, birds are singing telling me, once more, that spring is here.

I parked the bike at the new railing at the new pier where I met Kenny, who once did a teaching practice at the Port School. I have vague memories of him. He now has an honours degree in Gaelic Studies, he tells me, and is on his way to Cape Breton, Nova Scotia, Canada: Nova Scotia, 1963–1971, Halifax City to be precise, which was my stamping ground. Good on him. '*I think I might live there,*' he said.

I met Graeme the painter, now tier-up of the ferries. '*You look smart,*' he tells me. And later I meet Alasdair, the butcher, with whom I exchange a few words. I am en route to Edinburgh, where I hope to get my money's worth from my exorbitant membership fee of that city's Chamber of Commerce, to attend a 'Social Enterprise Meets Business' conference, which is being held at the Grosvenor Hilton. I can but keep on trying to associate in a milieu where I hope to become acquainted with at least two individuals who I can persuade to become directors of the Surplus Educational Supplies Foundation (SCO39331).

7:25 a.m. The train has just passed the IBM station, where I can see below that Whiteinch Demolition Ltd is in the process of demolishing the entire IBM manufacturing facility; capitalism is 'creative destruction.' What a waste of accessible storage space, which I could so easily take sustainable advantage of right now.

Thursday 26/02/2009

9:30 a.m. Home. I am replying to Carolynn, Social Fife Council Enterprise.

3 p.m. I am hardly moving today. I have overpowering feelings of oppression: my mood swings. No energy. I feel miserable. However, there is a ray of sunshine. I have received an email from Sanjay, who I met yesterday afternoon at the Grosvenor Hilton ECC conference, who says he would like to come on board SESF. I replied and said that I welcome working with him, especially with his background in the business, commercial, and charity sector; he has read through my executive summary/business plan and he is of the view that there is potential for development. Damned with faint praise.

I contact Lesley of One 2 One Accountancy Services in the town, who has kindly offered to chase up, pro bono, some VAT refund for SESF. She told me to see Donna, who works with her, tomorrow. I need to provide SESF accounts for the Office of the Scottish Charities Regulator.

Monday 02/03/2009.

9:30 a.m. Home. I donned my boiler suit to go outside and begin power-washing the slabs. I will give it a miss until the rain stops. I have a pain behind my eye and numbness down my right arm. I swallowed two Kepak tablets. I now do not feel like doing very much. I am going to chill out. Listening to Radio 4. I have no energy.

11 a.m. I have just spoken to Matthew, Tesco surveyor. They will let me have temporary use of part of their Baird Street warehouse in Dundee. We'll have to wait and see what happens. I called Pete, Dundee Council Environmental Services, who will be helpful. He offered to shift resources on a Saturday morning and offered me hospitality the next time I am over there. Unmerited kindness, which has kept me afloat from day one. Contact Community Services Dundee. Wait till I have got the premises.

2 p.m. I called Sahr P Demba at the Sierra Leone High Commission. I never seem to be able to make contact with him. Why do I persist?

2:50 p.m. I have just come back indoors. I have been sorting through wood that came from the old floor – pulling and straightening nails is my favourite activity. It is now pouring cats and dogs. Drookit.

3:22 p.m. I have been speaking to Terry of the Call To Business charity: he is non-committal. He said that Mark of the same outfit was out in Sierra Leone and will be returning to the United Kingdom with the teacher who is responsible for the school that they are building. He told me that they will come up to Scotland to look at the educational resources that are stored in Unit 9 Food Park, Glenrothes, and take their pick.

To do: obtain public liability insurance; make arrangements to have the containers delivered to the Tesco warehouse Dundee, Baird Street depot; contact *The Evening Telegraph* and post DC Thomson PR and publicity.

I called Matthew. Spoke to Linda at the caravan park in Dundee, who has links with the Samaritans, and who will me back; called Kathrin, Community Services Dunoon.

Friday 06/03/2009

11:45 a.m. I am in the foyer of the Millennium Hotel, George Square, Glasgow. After browsing in Borders Books, I walked up here and I am waiting for Sanjay, a possible business adviser. I am

Monday 09/03/2009

seeking advice and support from him. A help, up a notch. We'll see. I have an open mind. It was only last week that I set out for the 'Social Enterprise Meets Business' Edinburgh Chamber of Commerce conference, and was hoping to meet someone who could, possibly, assist SESF in the next phase, stage of development. And here I am besuited un homme d'affaire in good faith.

9:45 p.m. Home. Safe. The meeting with Sanjay was constructive and bodes well.

Monday 09/03/2009

11:25 a.m. Home. I have received an email from Sanjay with the minutes of our meeting of 6 March and 'Back to Basics' with a to-do list from him.

I call Terry, who represents the charity that is building a school in Sierra Leone. Mark returns from Sierra Leone today and will contact me as to when the teacher of the school, which ACTB are building, wants to come and have a look at the educational resources being stored at the Glenrothes unit. Call Renwick, estate surveyor, Fife Council Facilities Assets Management Services, to let him know that I will be contacting him to find out when it will be convenient for him to show the party from the Sierra Leone charity, and myself, the educational resources in storage at the Food Centre industrial unit.

4:55 p.m. I have just returned through wind, rain, and sleet, going and coming to Rothesay town on an errand to fax a copy of a letter that was sent to Philip, Director of Education, Portcullis House, Glasgow, in my email of 4 March, which was blocked because of an inappropriate word! A registered letter, which was not received. So, helpful Stephen in the aforesaid office gave me the fax number. I battled the elements once more to Print Point where Matthew and Karen faxed the letter, which was received.

I now await a reply from 'The Directorate'. I called Gerry, Interserve Projects Manager at Inveralmond Community High School, who assures me that an inventory is being kept. '*Your container is filling up nicely,*' he said.

For tomorrow: post details to John, freight forwarder, who is now with RH Freight Services Ltd, Atlantic Terminal Port of Liverpool, regarding the SESF container. I am trying to find out why this 40-foot container has gone missing in Grenada. Proof of my purchase etc.; send email with Geest quote to Grenada High Commissioner Elizabeth, also to Paula, manager marketing at Belmont Estate; contact Claire, area manager Squirrel Storage Ltd, about possible storage.

Tuesday 10/03/2009

8:30 a.m. Home. Clear blue sky above my head. The sun is shining. Still cold.

2:20 p.m. I am just back from having walked along the Mount Stuart road, past what was Ascog Church, and up the Loch Road and into town. I stopped off at the Victoria Hotel for a bowl of soup and a pot of tea and over to get my hair cut. There was welcome sunshine most of the way; it's now cooling down and beginning to get cloudy. I feel better for making the effort.

I've just tried to contact the Minister of Education and Human Resources in Grenada. '*Hold on a minute, de Ministah in cabinet right now, she'll kall yuh.*' Don't hold your breath. I still waitin' pun she. I keep on waiting on her, perhaps my persevering spirit will have achieved something of value for someone somewhere: there are no guarantees of that.

I called Palestinian Solidarity Campaign. I called George the HGV driver, who may be able to pick up the container and deliver.

4 p.m. I called Philip, acting principal of the Grenada Boys'

Secondary School. I asked him if he had been able to do anything about finding out where my container CRXU4103197 had gone. '*Ah'll kall him foh yuh,*' he said. I persist with the Surplus Educational Supplies Foundation rather than drawing a line under any further donations to that place and saying to myself, '*Enough is enough.*' If I quit what else is there for me to do around here on this little island?

Wednesday 11/03/2009

9:05 a.m. Home. Raining out of grey skies. I have sent an email to International Trace Adviser at Scottish Enterprise. I contact Blythswood Charity in Evanton, in the Highlands. I have contacted them before and they never replied: a Christian charity to whom I had sent an email a while back.

I am going to put the rest of the soup on the boil. It is still dreich out of doors. I am going to head up and over Canada Hill. I don't feel much like it, but I will feel better afterwards. A call to Business Charity regarding the SESF donation/shipment to their school in Sierra Leone.

Thursday 12/03/2009

10:25 a.m. Home. I am moving forward ever so slowly. Showery rain and grey clouds. I am looking for warmth and sunlight. I called the High Commission for Sierra Leone in London. '*May I speak with Sahr, please?*' '*He is not in the office. He's on his way,*' she said. '*Why don't you give up on these people?*' I ask myself.

I called the Grenada Ports Authority. I spoke to a gentleman in the Port Manager's office, who at least gave me the time of day. I then called the Bel Air Children's Home in Calliste, St George's, which Marion and I visited in July 2006. I spoke with Allendra, the manager, and mentioned the fact that the principal of the Calliste Government School, their feeder school, had promised way back in 2007 to write a letter acknowledging the donation of the contents of a 40-foot container of educational resources collected from two primary schools in Kirkcaldy, Scotland by my foundation. A letter which I could pass on to the editor of the *Fife Free Press* in that town. I am still waiting!

Now 12:22 p.m. I am going to stretch my legs.

5 p.m. I have just spoken to the Head of Chancery SLHC, Florence, about the proposed SESF shipment of educational resources to schools in Sierra Leone. She tells me that she has written to the Ministry of Education in Freetown and awaits a reply. She has told me to write a letter to her saying what they would like to have written to the Scottish Executive. I told her that when the charity 'A Call to Business' indicate their firm commitment to acquire surplus educational resources from Scottish schools, I will get in touch with the Sierra Leone High Commission.

'*The future of work consists of learning a living,*' (Marshall McLuhan). Which is what I am trying to do.

Friday 13/03/2009

9:22 a.m. Home. I am trying again. I can only climb up and out from under the pickle that I have created for myself.

10:45 a.m. I have just called the High Commissioner for the Tri-Island Nation State of Grenada, Petit Martinique and Carriacou. I am looking into whether or not their Ministry of Education wishes to support the delivery/shipment of educational resources to Carriacou and Petit Martinique.

'*A healthy doctor creates a natural resentment in a broken patient,*' (Isaiah Berlin).

Monday 16/03/2009

5:45 p.m. Home. I called Spice Isle Retreaders Ltd, Frequente, St George, Grenada, to speak to Azam. I spoke to Zaid, his son, who gave me the telephone number of Salim, his brother, who is on the directorate of the Grenada Chamber of Industry and Commerce, to see if he could chase up his fellow Chamber of Commerce member Valentino, who has failed to either sell or return my 40-foot ocean freight container CRXU4103197. Zaid sounded helpful.

7:05 p.m. Home. I have spent most of the day reading Capitalism and Slavery by Eric Williams. I am about to send Salim an email having done the dishes.

8:05 p.m. That's another email sent to Salim, let's see what happens next, and that's Johanna making mellow music on the saxophone, bless her! For tomorrow: see Lesley at One 2 One Accountancy Services.

Tuesday 17/03/2009

11 a.m. Home. I have been sitting out of doors having done some chores: washed the kitchen floor, cleaned the toilets and the shower, and I am now going to finish putting together a book case. The sun is shining brightly, as you may have guessed.

2:10 p.m. Home. It is clouding over. I have returned from the town. *'Is that you retired now?'* he asked me out of the blue. I did not reply. *'Are you enjoying your retirement?'* asked the Solitary Soul of whom there are many in this island; he, over the years, has always been enquiring after the Port School. *'It's behind me now,'* I reply.

Wednesday 18/03/2009

3:20 p.m. I have just boarded the train at Kirkcaldy Station, for Edinburgh Haymarket, where I bought myself a treat: a bottle of Orangina and, unintentionally, a packet of Walker's Chilli and Chocolate crisps.

It is a beautiful and glorious day of full-on sunshine, which is streaming through the plate-glass carriage window as the train winds its way through the Kingdom of Fife. I am moving through Burntisland, and just passed the yard of Burntisland Fabrications, Dalgety, Aberlour.

Roll it back: I walked through the town park from Adam Smith College, past the massive bronze War Memorial – there were hundreds of names and more names. On arrival at the college this morning I set up my stand and met a lot of individuals and listened to what they had to say, and I had the chance to explain what the Surplus Educational Supplies Foundation was about. I received some good suggestions: see their Business School for students as a potential source of SESF board members? I gave a copy of my executive summary to a young lad, Stewart, who works for the Fife Council Procurement Service. I asked him to acknowledge its source if they use it. I was asked to give an interview about my initiative. I think it was worth making the effort coming across fae the West Coast and I expressed my personal appreciation to the organisers of the conference for being given the opportunity to attend.

The Firth of Forth is shimmering calm on my left. Shipping is moving up and down the Forth. There are freshly ploughed fields on my right. The train is streaking past Aberlour Station.

3:35 p.m. Inverkeithen. Full circle once more. I first arrived here early one morning in July, in the summer of 1974, having walked across the Firth of Forth Bridge. '*G-D's providence is my inheritance.*' – the first text that caught my eye, which was chiselled

Thursday 19/03/2009

into the front door lintel of a cottage as I walked up the hill from North Queensferry.

Thursday 19/03/2009

10:09 a.m. Home. The sun is shining brightly and I am going to work outside wi' ma wee hauns. Hip hip hooray!

11:23 a.m. I just chilled. Warmed myself in the sunshine. I am about to contact Whiteinch Demolition Ltd regarding possible sponsorship of containers to Carriacou. Interested in publicity and public relations. '*Mr Beattie and Mr Barclay have your message,*' she said.

12:30 p.m. I have replied to a call from Billy, the janitor extraordinaire at St Andrew's Primary School, who has informed me that the school wished to 'donate', chuck my way, some more materials stored in their dunny.

This afternoon I posted an evaluation form to the Social Enterprise Day Conference, which was held at the Adam Smith College. I learned when I cycled into town that VAT recovery funds were debited to the SESF charity account on 6 March. I had gone into One 2 One Accountancy Services and met Lesley coming out of Summerfield, and she told me that she is not sending me an invoice for the work her firm have carried out to recover some VAT for my Scottish Registered Charity (SCO39331). I have been greatly privileged to receive pro bono assistance from this local business.

7:54 p.m. Home. I have just switched off the computer. I replied to Sanjay's email action list. He has given me good advice regarding approaching MBA students; okay, it's over to him and his skillbase in that sector for the time being. '*The future's already here; it just isn't evenly distributed,*' William Gibson.

I Embark on a New Career

Friday 20/03/2009

12:29 p.m. Home. I have come indoors from working out the back of the cottage: emptying the compost bin (I have a huge crop of worm)s; tidying up; raking up dead leaves; and sorting the interior of the shed. I am keeping busy. I stink of rotting organic matter. I shall have a shower, a luxury which I never take for granted.

I called Whiteinch Demolition Ltd. They will call me. I can only try. If you don't ask you don't get. What is it that you want from them? Will they sponsor the two 40-foot ocean freight containers for Carriacou and the two teams of Community Services clients who loaded them?

Monday 23/03/2009

9:05 a.m. Home. The sun is trying to break through thick, damp, grey clouds that hang low over Rothesay Bay. I'm trying to get started. I am going up to St Andrew's Primary School. *'A lot of school bits and pieces we want to get rid of,'* said Billy the janitor. And much else. I have no room to store the stuff, and decline his offer. I called J&J Denholm Ltd in Glasgow. I wrote a letter to their company chairman John, and to Maersk, Logistics Division, and left messages. I spoke to Ray at Denholm Bahr Ltd and to Michael Beveridge's secretary, Carolyn about funding.

4:12 p.m. Home. Raindrops are bouncing off the skylight window.

Friday 27/03/2009

5:25 p.m. Home. I set off this morning with David Alexander. Amy drove us into Rothesay to get the 8 o'clock boat. We got the train up to Glasgow Central Station. He to shop, and me to visit the People's Palace in Glasgow Green. I knew I would not have long there as we had agreed to meet outside Borders Books

Friday 27/03/2009

on Buchanan Street at midday, so I got a taxi – an extravagance. As I was leaving the station I bumped into David D, who was on the Social Enterprise Academy course last year. Brief chat, he was on his way to meet Sanjay: it is a small world in the Blue Planet Global Village. I found the People's Palace shut until 11 a.m. so I had a coffee in the café among the tropical flora, beneath the big glasshouse, and learned that they did not have any exhibits about the Sugar Lords: cultural amnesia, Glesgae disnae wan tae know aboot their trade in slaves. I have just finished reading *Blood Legacy. Reckoning With A Family's Story of Slavery* by Alex Renton.

(Just to let you know, dear reader, that I am typing this diary during days of lockdown, late 2021.)

(Tuesday 25/01/2022. Bring on the present moments, but I must complete my editing of these pages of The Diary of a Shipping Clerk, *whatever else is gonie happen tae me.)*
Return to the past:

I walked back up to London Road and headed back to the Trongate and got me another taxi to the Mitchell Library, never having been there before. What a treat that place is! Up to Level 2, The Glasgow Room. The helpful librarian disappeared into the stacks and returned with two small volumes. I got some information. I was looking for illustrations. I could have spent more time.

I walked back up to Bath Street to meet David Alexander as arranged. We then walked across town and George Square, and up to Chung Ying Supermarket in Cowcaddens where we purchased some groceries, and went back the way we came. Just as we were about to walk into Borders Books I bumped into David, fellow social entrepreneur, once more. Coincidence? Then he chased after me to mention following up with the headmaster of James Gillespie High School in Edinburgh, who he had told me about before.

David Alexander and I had tuna fish sandwiches and beverages that cheer, but do not inebriate. Train back to Wemyss Bay. Home safely.

'Why not go out on a limb? That's where the fruit is,' Will Rogers

'There are victories of the SOUL and SPIRIT. Sometimes, even if you lose; you win.' Elie Wiesel.

I love these quotes which lift my spirit.

Thursday 2/04/2009

10:35 p.m. Home A beautiful 'summer in spring' day. The sun shone brightly. I worked out of doors. I made David Alexander brunch and we sat on the deck; I remained sitting there, and I heard a chaffinch singing in the branches above my head. I made a step for the deck and just lost myself in the inner-directed pleasure of pottering and tidying round the back of what was once the blacksmith's bothy.

Wednesday 08/04/2009

11:12 a.m. I have just called Terry at the ACTB charity about the resources that SESF has available to deliver to their school in Sierra Leone. He said that Mark, who is the project manager, was to get in touch and he feels that ACTB are letting me down. I said not to bother; Terry may come up to Scotland to have a look at the educational resources that had been uplifted from the former Greyfriars Primary School in St Andrew's in a Glenrothes, Fife Council Facilities and Asset Management, industrial unit.

I told him about the West Indian island revolution, rebellion on my island of Barbados, and the freed slaves that were repatriated from Barbados to Sierra Leone. Connections. I'm connected to everything and to everyone in some way or another. Terry asked me if I would send him the booklet *Bussa. The 1816 Barbados Revolution. Rewriting History* by Professor Sir Hilary Beckles, the illustrious Barbados historian, Department of History, Cave Hill.

He was recently awarded an honorary doctorate from Glasgow University.

(I posted the letter and booklet to Terry, which he never acknowledged. Why am I such a nice guy?)

I collected calendars from Bute Naturally. I met a dear soul from Port Bannatyne, who said I did not look a day over a hundred. I gave a calendar to Brian B, Andy W, Richard the postmaster, the garden centre family, John MacKirdy Ltd and Margaret R.

Supporters all. I will call David at British Chamber Shipping next week and Algy: and why him you may well ask? He is a gold and diamond miner in West Africa, who might be willing to make a few introductions on behalf of the Surplus Educational Supplies Foundation to officials in Sierra Leone Government offices.

Thursday 09/04/2009

4:50 p.m. Home. I sent an email to Algy, at the suggestion of his receptionists, to see whether he or his firm can assist SESF with the delivery of educational resources to Sierra Leone, and negotiate with the bureaucracy.

(You are so naïve. Could Cluff Gold Ltd provide a way through? You have such high hopes. I was to get nowhere with that outfit.)

Wednesday 15/04/2009

5:10 p.m. Home. I have just received a call from Sandra, librarian at Morningside Library in Edinburgh, to say that they had another 20 boxes of books for SESF. I told her I would contact Jimmy at Edinburgh Community Transport, Granton, to see if they would be willing, yet once again, to uplift and store temporarily this wonderful donation of books until I can have them delivered out to Duncan Adams Transport Ltd at Grange Dock. Sandra said they had collected 10 boxes of books earlier this year.

Earlier today I called RBS Rothesay to learn that funds from the sale of the 40-foot ocean freight container CRXU4103197 had been transferred from Grenada into the SESF account. Perseverance pays. Thank you Spice Isle Retreaders Ltd and Salim.

I was out at Stirling Yacht Services Ltd, The Boat Yard, Port Bannatyne, this morning tidying up the Caribbean Hurricane Relief Depot, SESF 'headquarters', and made a good start. Wind blowing in from the north-east. A beautiful day. I took apart the shelving. I am making preparations to ship out fae the Port.

Thursday 16/04/2009

Home. I collected my bicycle from The Bike Shed; David did not charge me for repairing the puncture. A supporter for certain from early days. I went back out to the boatyard. Tidied the depot. *'Catch a man a fish feed him for a day. Teach him to fish and feed him for life.'*

Friday 17/04/2009

8:55 a.m. Home. Email from Mark to contact Caroline at Clackmannanshire Council. David will let her know that I called. I was speaking to the janitor of Alva Academy, which has moved into new premises.

10:42 a.m. I have just tidied the tool box. It is windy and cold out of doors. Called John, who is now at RH Freight Services Ltd, Liverpool, to let him know they have found CRXU4103197 and I got some funds back on it. I called the Morningside Library to let them know that Edinburgh Community Transport will soon come to collect their next donation of 20 boxes of library books. I wrote a letter to His Excellency, Sierra Leone High Commission for the United Kingdom, Counsellor Sahr P. Demba and Head of Chancery, Florence Bangali Ministry of Foreign Affairs and International Cooperation, Freetown, Sierra Leone.

'Why do you think it takes so much international assistance to achieve anything better for our country? Because we Sierra Leoneans only care about ourselves, not for the Nation or the common good,' he said.

(I should have taken these words to heart and come to my senses, that I was on a hiding to no satisfaction, as far as Sierra Leone was concerned, and did myself much mischief as I was to prove many months later.)

Monday 20/04/2009

9:20 a.m. Home. Called ACTB and left a message for Mark. I called Cluff Gold Ltd and left a message. I am going to make myself a coffee and head for the garden. The sun is shining.

11:30 a.m. I was speaking to John, freight forwarder and long-time supporter, who is now at RH Freight Services Ltd, Atlantic Terminal, Port of Liverpool.

Tuesday 21/04/2009

2:12 p.m. Home. I am going to put the shelving together. Arrange a meeting with supporter Peter who is an international development economist and has lived and worked in Sierra Leone for many years. Draft a letter for the Ministry of Education in Freetown. Called Cluff and spoke to Flavia, who is always helpful and supportive.

Wednesday 22/04/2009

8:35 a.m. Home. I have just called Nick, Jesuit priest and University Chaplain in Edinburgh, who tells me he is off to London to conduct a funeral. I am about to make a coffee, a piece of marmalade and toast, and head for the garden. The sun is shining. Blue sky above ma baldy heid.

12:15 p.m. Clouding over but still dry. I have been digging and hefting buckets of gravel up to the top pathway outside the shed which sits at the foot of the Creagh Mhor escarpment. Stopped for a break.

10:28 p.m. Late this afternoon I received an email from Jannah of ACTB Sierra Leone to confirm that she is coming up to Bonnie Scotland to view the educational resources in Glenrothes, possibly Friday of next week. Tomorrow: call Renwick and Gillian at Fife Council to determine whether the ACTB representative can be taken to see the resources.

Thursday 23/04/2009

6:44 a.m. I am aboard the MV *Argyle*. The vessel is rolling slightly towards Wemyss Bay. It is grey, soggy, and damp. I cycled in through the dreich, and tethered the bike. Today I am en route to Edinburgh to meet Peter, an African Hand and former economist with the World Bank in Sierra Leone. Hopefully he will clue me in a little more about that country and the best way in which to approach their government, its bureaucracy, and their representatives at their High Commission in London. I have been talking to Kenny, HGV driver, who drives one of MacKirdy's artics and who is always friendly and supportive. Gerry came up to me to offer some unwanted IT equipment. I did not wish to refuse. I value those individuals who offer something to me unconditionally. I am not feeling 100%. I gave him my card and told him to contact me.

11:45 a.m. I arrived at Cambridge Street, Edinburgh and went up the stairs to Peter's large flat. Peter served up fresh bread, cheese,

Thursday 23/04/2009

jam, and fresh coffee. I am grateful for his hospitality. He suggested I contact UNICEF United Nations Development Programme, the British Council, Department for Trade and Industrial Development (DFID) through to VSO, Scottish Government Aid people, and my MSP.

I later walked across town to the Morningside Library, where I dropped in to thank them for their recent donation of books, which are currently being stored down at Edinburgh Community Transport premises. I am now in conversation with Peter, who has made me a mug of coffee.

2:30 p.m. On the train for Glasgow Central from Edinburgh Haymarket. Toot toot, rumbling on.

I walked down the road from Peter, and now recall him cutting slices off a wholegrain loaf, which I had bought earlier that morning from Stromboli Bakers on Bruntsfield Road. Salami sausage, Lurpak butter, olives, and Peter's own aromatic filter coffee; he is a wise, sharp, friendly, and supportive human being, who knows the score from A to Z. I recommend his book, *An Economist's Tale. A consultant encounters hunger and the World Bank.* He is an Africa Hand who is the real deal. He gave me a few leads to follow up, and offered hospitality to me, should I ever be stuck in Auld Reekie.

'*This is Slateford.*' It's been a while since I have been on this route back tae the Big Green Place. I had got the **9:15 a.m.** bus for Edinburgh, from Glasgow Buchanan Street Bus Station, to St Andrews Bus Station where I paused for a pee. I bought a coffee and an egg sandwich from the counter and took a perch on a stool facing the bus rank, and was about to call Renwick in Glenrothes. I reached into my pocket, no spectacles, and as I shifted off my seat I spilled my coffee, '*Oh sh… one… t!*' I wiped up the mess and couldn't read the telephone number, ach weel, nothing for it but to move on.

I walked through the St James Centre and purchased a pair of specs from Boots. I can read with them; hopefully some thoughtful soul will return my lost pair, maybe I had never left home with them. I got a taxi up to the Morningside Library. I thanked Rhona and gave her one of the SESF calendars with correct dates. What a fiasco the first lot were. I seem prone to making messes; there is nothing else for it but to clean up my messes as much as possible and continue the journey on my private road.

The meeting with Peter was constructive, and very worthwhile. *(It was one of the highlights of many trips over the years 2005–2017 across the watta.)* His parting words to me were, '*I couldn't do what you are doing.*' I couldn't do your work either, Peter.

'*Next stop is Curry Hill.*' Rolling slowly through the beautiful, idyllic, West Lothian countryside of freshly ploughed fields. Some of them showing a hint of green shoots of grass and corn.

Chapter Eleven
I Meet the Secret Millionaire and Travel Far Further

Friday 01/05/2009

I am en route for Glasgow Airport. On the ferry, I met Iain from Irvine, who was driving a Bentley Sport and who has kindly given me a lift. He was curious to know who I am, and where I was going, when he met me standing opposite the Coffee Cabin; it must have been the suit I was wearing. He listened to my story and then, minutes later, went out of his way to give me a lift up to Glasgow Airport. He offered to assist me in my efforts, and his generous treatment of me, and kind offer, has unsettled me.

I hurriedly jot down the following words shortly after he arrives in the carpark on this bright, warm sunlight-filled morning. He switches off the engine and looks across at me and asks, '*Do you want your money back?*' For a moment I am lost for words. And I mumbled some words to the effect that I did not particularly care, but I was sure that those nearest and dearest to me would be more than happy that I did get their money back. And then Iain asked me again, '*Do you want your money back?*' This time I replied, '*Yes, if that were at all possible?*'

'*If that is the case, I want from you, an audited account of everything that you have spent so far on your charity,*' said Iain, looking straight at me. I think to myself that I had not got a clue of how much of our family's funds I had spent up to that point. And he tells me to let him know when I have this information. We shake hands before he drops me off and I part with high hopes, believing that finally, perhaps, just maybe, I have met someone who can help me to move up another notch. He has assured me that he can get me lots of publicity and that I need never have to bother selling my marmalade at the Port Bannatyne Gala Days again. At the very least, I have had the privilege of meeting a real toff and an unexpected upmarket hurl up the M8.

8:10 a.m. I am here in Glasgow Airport Arrivals to meet Jannah on Flight EFGBJ4K EasyJet from Luton.

8:20 a.m. Smarter types, in brains and dress, hauf ma years, who appear to be the real deal, flaunting their Blackberries, and who make this auld yin feel a bit of an impostor, are waiting to board the return flight south.

11:30 a.m. The Wee Diner, Shopping Centre, Glenrothes. The two of us are not long off the 9:30 a.m. bus from Buchanan Street Bus Station, Glasgow. On arrival in Glenrothes I called Renwick, the Fife Facilities and Asset Management Services Estates Surveyor, who has gone to get the key to Unit 3 and will soon meet us here. He arrives and takes us out to view the educational resources that were uplifted last December 2008, from the former Greyfriars Primary School in St Andrews. There is a lot of quality classroom furniture. Jannah snaps away with her camera and promises to send me the images. Renwick, another supporter, is always helpful and gives us a lift back to the shopping centre and we get the bus back to Glasgow.

I am having great difficulty in passing water; just as things are starting to go well, a possible turn up, and this happens to me. And to top it off, I am suffering another migraine. I bid Jannah goodbye and paid her fare up and back to Luton. A cheery soul from the USA. She is settled here in the United Kingdom. Her parents were missionaries in Africa.

(I was glad to make it home; that night, not long after arriving home,

Thursday 07/05/2009

I was in more pain and unable to pee. Marion and the bairns took me up to the hospital where I waited ages, puffing and groaning in agony, until the young doctor and nurse catheterised me and I was now on a bag. I had gone from the top of the hill back down into the muddy bog.)

Thursday 07/05/2009

3:29 p.m. Home. I have had another catheter inserted into my bladder since last Friday. I am far down in the dumps. Toothache etc. I have much to be thankful for, however.

I am going to call the Minister of Education in Grenada for about the umpteenth time. I spoke to Michelle, the secretary. This morning I received a letter from John, chairman of J&J Denholm Ltd with a cheque for £250 (BRILLIANT! Take a hug, you guys), which I deposited this afternoon into the SESF charity account, Royal Bank of Scotland, Rothesay.

That's Amy Elisabeth, bless her, who is going up to the health centre to collect a couple more pee bags and along to the chemist's to collect prescription pills, that I should have been taking ages ago, to shrink my prostate. I spoke to Michelle the Grenadian Government Ministry of Education secretary, who said she would try and move my request for assistance with the shipment of the three 40-foot containers of educational resources for their schools. I am going to apply to the Strathclyde Enterprise Challenge competition. I asked for application forms.

5:40 p.m. I have persevered and networked non-stop. Time will tell whether this effort will bring results. To do:
1. See that the educational resources currently stored in containers and in storage are inventoried.
2. Obtain suitable storage – a warehouse, an industrial unit, a facility somewhere in the central belt near to a transportation hub.

3. With teams from the Community Services Criminal Justice Department – give them real work and the opportunity to up-skill, to breathe new life into, refurbish, and bring up to a marketable standard IT kits that have been considered waste, junk, and surplus to requirements.
4. I need a showcase on the High Street and a warehouse for these educational resources.
5. Storage is a priority. I cannot take on any more donations of surplus educational resources until I have delivered what I have currently acquired.
6. I need marketing expertise.
7. Get business and accounting advice.
8. Get sponsors and sponsorship. I cannot continue to spend any more of the family's funds. Possible sources of financial support: ESA McIntosh; B&Q; IKEA; Thorpe Kilworth; ES Arnold and their ilk. I could approach educational manufacturers and their suppliers and distributors at the Scottish Learning Festival at the Scottish Exhibition Centre (SECC) in September.

Tuesday 12/05/2009

11:01 a.m. Home. The sun is shining brightly. I am out of doors. The district nurse came by to check my bladder. All clear and she has taken away all the paraphernalia of catheterisation. A good soul who trained in Edinburgh, she has been on the island 12 years now. I am going to call Howard. There is nothing else for it but to keep on trudging upward. Who says I can't? Why can't I?

1:10 p.m. I have sent emails to: Sian, personal assistant, thanks to Flavia the receptionist; Howard of Freight Container Services (Scotland) Ltd; and Renwick, Fife Council. I am now going to make a fried egg sandwich, warm the coffee, and sit outside in the sunshine.

Thursday 14/05/2009

2:35 p.m. Spoke with PA. '*We know all about you now,*' she said. (No assistance in that quarter was ever forthcoming.)

Wednesday 13/05/2009

1:25 p.m. Home. The sun is shining. Another beautiful day, there is not a cloud floating above my head. I have been putting up shelves under the deck.

I have just spoken to Gillian, estates surveyor and premier supporter, Fife Council, confirming that SESF will accept the surplus-to-requirements educational resources from the former Bell Baxter High School in Cupar. Risk and more risk; nothing ventured nothing gained. Archie and his teams from the Community Service Criminal Justice Department will uplift these resources and store them in Unit 3, Glenrothes, until such time as I can source a suitable longer term storage facility. Critically, friendly supportive partners, and ultimately worthy recipients in the developing world get the good of their pro bono help.

Thursday 14/05/2009

10:29 a.m. Home. I am on the phone to a reporter at the *Fife Herald* in Cupar about the prospective uplift of resources from the former Bell Baxter High School premises by a Community Service Team. Seeking publicity? I sent an email to Liz, journalist and supporter.

12:01 a.m. I am off into the metropolis to post letters and purchase something for Johanna, and my lunch.

2:30 p.m. I spoke with Leo at the Ministry of Education in Grenada. Sent an email. Heading back into town to arrange to have a banner made for my stall at the Port Bannatyne Gala Day. When I have prepared the relevant financial information, I can then go to W&B in Edinburgh, or their ilk, and ask them to prepare a statement for OSCR and the Companies House (dormant accounts) Limited Company account. I can get an external review rather than an audit. Will Iain pay the fee to have this done?

3:15 p.m. Home. I am off into the town again to post a letter. Iain had given me unnecessarily high hopes; I succumb to great expectations. Serves me right. Rely on no one else apart from your own dear self. Will I ever learn?

Thursday 28/05/2009

9:25 a.m. Home. I receive a call from Business Development at the local housing association. I received this call as I was trying to bring some order and organisation into the affairs of the Surplus Educational Supplies Foundation (SCO39331), a Scottish Registered Charity. I am gathering the relevant information to prepare SESF accounts for the Scottish Charities Regulator and Companies House.

10 a.m. I contact Murdo of M&K McLeod Construction Ltd, Lochgilphead. I had a very positive conversation with him. He appears to be in favour and supportive of my initiative. I am to call him in two weeks. I then sat own and wrote him a letter with information about SESF. But his words were a warning. '*We'll stand aside, it's up to you both,*' he said. Hmmm? What does he mean by that?

1:10 p.m. Amy is making lunch. Johanna is studying. This morning I was out at Ettrick Bay, which was cloudy and damp, but beautiful, with Marion and her Primary 1 and 2 class on a day-trip excursion from her school.

3:30 p.m. I am off to Rothesay to post a letter.

Friday 29/05/2009

8:18 a.m. Millennium Hotel, George Square, Glasgow. I am comfortably seated as though I am a regular in these surroundings, awaiting the arrival of Sanjay. I walked up from Central Station. It is a cool dry day and brightening morning. I am going to read *The Times*, dear boy.

10:54 a.m. The meeting with Sanjay was positive. He is receptive. Time will tell whether or not he can contribute anything that will move SESF ahead. Hopefully, together, we may be able to take SESF to another level.

I have just ordered a bottle of mineral water and two glasses from the young bartender. Here I am, sipping Strathmore aqua pura, *mon vieux. Salut*! The hotel chef came by handing out pancakes. The sunshine is cracking the sky above George's Square.

Priority:
1. SESF needs a recipient, 'customer', a deserving beneficiary – a committed, ethical dealing contact in the developing world, or an impoverished country in Eastern Europe, that genuinely needs surplus-to-requirements educational resources.
2. A beneficiary that is closer to Scotland than the Caribbean.
3. Marketing.
4. Funding. I am to contact Sanjay if and when I require help with face-to-face meetings with an accountant, and he wants me to send him details of the domain of my website?

'*We know very little but we are capable of a great deal.*' Peter Cochrane.

12:50 p.m. I am now on the train for Wemyss Bay. As I was walking along Platform 11 Central Station I met Harry and his wife from Rothesay, on their way to stay for three nights in a posh hotel, where they will be joined by their family from Denmark and other relatives to celebrate the latter's birthday.

There was sunshine on Glasgow city this afternoon; that was a positive meeting. Sanjay will contribute his IT, marketing and business liaison expertise, and assist in identifying the next beneficiary. I will see what happens next. He is keen, enthusiastic, and supportive. I am homeward bound. I found the Millennium Hotel staff welcoming, efficient, and pleasant.

Monday 01/06/2009

10:20 a.m. Home. It's a beautiful day full of sunshine. I got my face burned standing at the SESF table up at the Port Park yesterday. I am about to count the funds raised from the sale of 16 jars of my Caribbean Orange and Ginger Marmalade, bric-a-brac and books.

I made £102.75

Tuesday 02/06/2009

4:04 p.m. Home. I persist in being a nuisance. *'Ah know de whole story. She on annudah line. Ministah is outa de ilan,'* she said. I was calling the office of the Ministry of Education in Grenada. I had a brief conversation with Michelle, the Ministry of Education secretary.

Friday 05/06/2009

3 p.m. Home. I am feeling low. I cycled around the island this morning: there was sunshine on the back door. I have just called the Sierra Leone High Commission in London. I was trying to get hold of their Head of Chancery, Florence. *'She not on her seat!'* said the secretary. I called the Ministry of Education in Grenada. They are getting in touch with their High Commission in London. I then called Ellis Transport in Greenock regarding the possible use of one of their warehouses. I keep trying and getting nowhere at the moment. I have now more than nine 40-foot ocean freight containers than I know what do with.

Monday 08/06/2009

11:50 a.m. Home. It's a beautiful day of sunshine, but I have no energy. I am feeling low for no accountable reason. I am awaiting a call from Ellis Transport Ltd, Greenock. I am trying to locate storage, a warehouse for the large quantity of educational resources that SESF has accumulated to date. These resources cannot remain in the seven 40-foot ocean freight containers indefinitely. Where are they all?

MSKU6311690 contains library shelving, which was salvaged from what was once the Jubilee Gardens Library, Southall, West London, and is currently located courtesy of Freightliner Ltd, Eurocentral Freight Terminal Depot, Coatbridge.

MAEU6085656 is loaded with fit-for-purpose educational resources from the former Rothesay Academy. (see the article Friday, 7 March 2008, *The Buteman,* 'From Bute by Banana Boat') and is currently located at John G Russell Transport Ltd, Coatbridge depot.

OCLU1354487 is partially loaded with educational resources from the former St Andrews High School, Clydebank (see the article *Clydebank Post,* Wednesday, 22 July 2009, 'School Supplies are desk-lined for the sun' by Jamie Borthwick), and is currently stored at John G Russell Transport Ltd Coatbridge.

GATU4072944, which was loaded with surplus-to-requirements educational resources from Inveralmond Community High School, Livingston, is being stored at WH Malcolm Transport Ltd Muirhouse depot (see article, 'Kindness blows into Caribbean' by Scott McAngus, *Herald Post* Thursday, 9 July 2009).

TRIU5079422 is loaded with educational resources from the former Dunshalt Village Primary School and Fife schools (see article, 'Dunshalt furniture on its way to Grenada. School building put up for sale' by Liz Rougvie and Jane Howie, *Herald Citizen* Friday, 28 March 2008) and is located currently at Duncan Adams Transport Ltd yard, Grange Dock, Port of Grangemouth.

INBU4923875 is loaded, also with educational resources from Dunshalt Village Primary School, and is located at Duncan Adams Transport Ltd, Grange Dock (see article 'Old school equipment bound for Caribbean. Children living in one of the poorest parts of the world are eagerly awaiting the arrival of a very special gift from North East Fife' by Liz Rougvie, *Herald Citizen,* Friday, 25 December 2009).

SEAU4272551 is partially loaded with educational resources from the former Ladywood Primary School, Penicuick and is stored at Duncan Adams Transport Ltd Grange Dock.

Plus two pin-holed 40-foot containers over at Russell's, Deanside Road, Hillington.

What am I going to do with all these surplus-to-requirements educational resources? Who needs and wants these resources? Is there anybody willing to pay for them? Is there a more efficient way of doing what I am doing, now that I have all our family's remaining funds tied up in past-their-sell-by-date ocean freight containers? Are they are still seaworthy? I hope so. I have not been charged, billed, or invoiced for the parking of these containers. I can no longer presume on the goodwill of the aforementioned transport firms for haulage and storage at their depots. Sooner or later, I will be asked to remove them somewhere else if they have not been delivered to deserving consignees (see article 'Call for surplus school supplies to be donated. A retired teacher from Bute who has enlisted the support of 22 transport companies in diverting unwanted school resources from landfill to the developing world, is appealing to Scottish local authorities for formal recognition' by Simon Bain, *The Herald Business,* Monday, 13 July 2009).

I called the Bulgarian Embassy, who will return my call. They are going to contact two charities in Bulgaria that they support. I sent an email seeking help from Paul, one of our early supporters (he was with Ecosse World Express in 2005) to see if he can help me locate some storage in the central belt.

Tuesday 09/06/2009

10:50 a.m. Home. Sunshine. Pale blue sky above my head. I have just finished a fried egg and bacon sandwich which Amy, bless her, has just made. She's now off to work. I must call Ellis Transport before 1 p.m.

12:35 p.m. Calling the boss, who is not in the office until tomorrow. '*I'll get him to give you a call,*' he said.

2 p.m. Calling the Grenada High Commission in London. I spoke to Sam, who says that he will follow up the issue of whether or not the Government of Grenada want another three more 40-foot ocean freight deliveries of educational resources. There is another 40-foot ocean freight container shipment for the Grenada Boys' Secondary School ready to go and two shipments for schools in the islands of Carriacou and Petit Martinique.

Wednesday 10/06/2009

9:10 a.m. Home. I have just come indoors. I have been sitting on the deck, the perch mark three, enjoying a cup of coffee and a marmalade and toast piece. The sun is shining brightly and it is another beautiful day. There is a little rowing boat with an outboard motor chugging across the flat calm watta.

Roy, my neighbour, hauls pots and lives in the big house along the road. He and his sister, Jessica, a ceramicist, lived on the island of Inchmarnock. There is hardly any shipping up or down the Firth of Clyde. We are in recession times. I am going to call Murdo at M&K McLeod Construction Ltd. '*He's at a meeting call after 4 p.m,*' she said. I call Ellis in Greenock. '*He is in with someone at the moment. When he's finished, I'll get him to give you a wee phone,*' she said. I am waiting in the wings.

9:25 a.m. I am still waiting. A cool breeze is blowing up the corridor. I call Neil, the roofer

12 p.m. After all that hanging around Ellis can't offer me anything.

4:45 p.m. I call the Ministry of Education in Grenada to speak with the Permanent Secretary, Vida. '*Just hold on one second for me.*' She keeps me waiting. Supplicants must humble themselves and defer meekly. '*Yes, mam, three containers full, mam.*' Finally, she speaks and wants to know the cost of shipping containers to Grenada.

'*What we need are more people who specialise in the impossible.*' Theodore Roethke.

To do: acknowledge all the undeserved help I have received to date from the Scottish road haulage industry. One day, when I have the time, I will celebrate and acknowledge all their assistance in my record of the Surplus Educational Supplies Foundation. *(see* The Diary of a Shipping Clerk 2005–2017: Volumes, One, Two and Three*, to be published in 2022.)*

Thursday 11/06/2009

9:25 a.m. Home. I am back indoors as it has started to cloud over and now, as I look up, the sun is shining through once more. I am going to call Murdo. He said he will get back to me. You are a trusting soul. Call Matthew, the Tesco surveyor. Paul, formerly of Ecosse World Express, based at Glasgow Airport, whose firm airfreighted five boxes of new, basic, classroom educational resources to Grand Roy Government School Grenada in 2005, has replied to my email.

5:45 p.m. I received a reply from the Bulgarian Embassy to follow up leads.

Friday 12/06/2009

10:50 a.m. Home. I have been busy cleaning the house. Calling Popov mobile. Sent him an email. It is almost 11 a.m. I shall head into the town. The sun is shining brightly. Blue sky above ma heid.

12:30 p.m. Back home. I have done the messages. I am going to fix myself a bacon 'n' egg sandwich. The sun continues to shine. I am ahead of the curve, baby.

8:45 p.m. I received a call from Francis from Kenya, who is a teacher at Rothesay Joint Campus. He wants to send educational resources to his colleagues in Kenya. I have invited him and his family here for tea.

Monday 15/06/2009

7:05 a.m. Home. I am feeling somewhat frayed at the edges. There are light, squally showers, and grey clouds. I am going to make myself a bowl of porridge.
To do: send email to Roland, president of Seafreight Agencies Lines, Miami, Florida, asking him if his shipping company will take another three containers from Kingston, Jamaica to St George's, Grenada. I am reluctant to presume on their goodwill and previous generosity, but I will ask, needs must; see Lesley about VAT and HMRC forms.

9:33 a.m. Home. Call Gerry, site manager Interserve Projects Ltd, at Inveralmond Community High School to let me know when container GATU4072944 is fully loaded. I will contact the local press in Livingston, and would it be possible for us to visit Inveralmond Community High School at the end of the week? I make arrangements with Sanjay to accompany me on Friday 19 June to Livingston, if he wishes to do so.

Collect SESF banner from 'head quarters', the Caribbean Hurricane Relief Depot currently at the Boatyard, Port Bannatyne. Make arrangements with Carson Transport Ltd, Cumbernauld, to have the container collected as and when it is fully loaded.

10:39 a.m. I have sent emails to Roland, Vida, and Sanjay.

12:41 p.m. I have returned home from a delivery to the Rothesay Cowp, the dump and recycling centre, to find an email from Roland. Good news! Seafreight Agencies Lines, Miami, will take SESF containers pro bono down to Grenada from either the ports of Kingston or Manzanillo. *'How did ya manage that, then?'* asks John, the freight forwarder at India Docks, Port of Liverpool, who I have just called. He will try and work out the logistics and paperwork, from the United Kingdom to Kingston Jamaica. He will do it pro bono.

2:25 p.m. Home. Called Sam of Shanks Waste Management and left a message regarding a possible source of storage with their company.

2:42 p.m. Call Carson Transport Ltd, Cumbernauld. Can they pick up GATU4072944 and store it temporarily at their depot? *'You don't want to run out of favours, David,'* said Barry. Someone comes on the line. *'I can see big Ross floating about here. What is the weight of the box now?'* he asks. Couldn't tell him its weight. He will give me a call back.

The sun is shining brightly above my head and through the open door at the end of the corridor as I sit here awaiting return telephone calls. I contact the *West Lothian Courier*, 20–22 King

Street, Bathgate. I speak to Debbie. '*I was speaking to Duncan (Adams) a few minutes ago. I will l get John to give you a call.*' Small world as they all know one another in the Scottish road haulage industry.

For Tuesday 16 June: see Lesley regarding HMRC VAT forms; contact John in the Port of Liverpool, regarding freight costs to Jamaica and Panama; send fax regarding insurance query. We are all in a time of recession. The New Labour politicians, bankers and financiers have bankrupted the country, and my quixotic initiative has impoverished the family.

Tuesday 16/06/2009

9:24 a.m. Home. Speaking to John of Carson Transport and Lifting Solutions Ltd, Cumbernauld. His firm have generously offered to uplift the container from Inveralmond Community High School, Livingston, providing it can now be lifted. If not, Russell, who have a side ifter, will. If it can be lifted, Carson will store the container in their yard at Cumbernauld.

9:31 a.m. I called John, the freight forwarder, who did the paper work for our first shipment of salvaged resources to Grenada on Friday, 1 July 2005. John is based at the Port of Liverpool and worked for a subsidiary of J&J Denholm Ltd at the time. He is now with RH Freight Services Ltd. '*I know the managing director.*' He was referring to the Mediterranean Shipping Company, who have a feeder service from the Port of Grangemouth to Kingston, Jamaica.

9:40 a.m. I called Debbie, the journalist with the *West Lothian Courier*. She is cheery and helpful. '*If I need anything I will get back to you,*' she said. Grey skies overhead. I am going outside to work on what, one day, will be a fishpond.

9:53 a.m. Back at my desk. I called Gerry, site manager at Interserve Projects Ltd, whose company have the PFI/PPP contract to refurbish Inveralmond Community High School. I am to let him know that I am coming over on Friday. He told me that the 40-foot-high cube ocean freight container could be picked up over the weekend.

I call at Companies House in Edinburgh to seek advice and she tells me to click on '*Guidance booklet accounts and accountants reference. Then click on accounts prior to 6 April 2008, old version.*' I am none the wiser as I try to jot down what she is telling me to do. She continues to baffle me. '*Heading. Record the donations. Summarise, income from your sales at the Port Gala Days, sales of your containers; Heading: This is the receipt and payment of accounts for the year ended 31 March 2009; Total Income; Expenses that you paid for postage, telephone calls, travel, the Caribbean Hurricane Relief Depot banner, the 20-foot reefer etc. Total Expenses. Work out your surplus deficit. If your income is greater than your expenditure you have a surplus and that goes with the form. See Trustees Annual Report Templates at appendix on the OSCR website, print off and complete and send to us at Companies House by 6 December 2009,*' she said. I thanked her for the time she took to tell me what I should have been doing right from the start,

Before, I had taken on more than I could ever have handled on my own, which serves me right, Mr Big Heid.

'*Far better to dare mighty things, to win glorious triumphs, even though chequered by failure, than to rank with those poor spirits, who neither enjoy much, nor suffer much, because they live in the grey twilight that knows not victory, nor defeat,*' Theodore Roosevelt.

Wednesday 17/06/2009

8:49 a.m. Home. I call Carson Transport Ltd in Cumbernauld to ask them if they can pick up the container from ICHS on Friday afternoon. I decide to hold fire for a little while.

Wednesday 17/06/2009

8:56 a.m. Speaking to John, chief executive, Carson Transport Ltd. *'You were to let me know,'* he said. *Call him on Monday to confirm whether they can collect the container on Tuesday 23 June. Going to 'hot desk'*. I called the following: Jenny Simpson, W&B Accountants in Edinburgh, who is to call me back; contact OSCR.

9:40 a.m. Calling Ian, CEO of Recycle Scotland, Livingston. They can't help me with storage, their depot is chock a bloc; call Nick, at Edinburgh University regarding possible beneficiaries in Eastern Europe; call Zafar Iqbal, Education Aid, Pakistan; called Michael, surveyor at Jones Lang LaSalle – can they offer SESF any storage pro bono?; called Doreen, manager at CMA/CGM Shipping, in the Glasgow office, and Robert; called Lyn at MSC Shipping, and Adam at ESA McIntosh, Kirkcaldy.

11:14 a.m. I have contacted the media and communications officer at West Lothian Council regarding a possible 'puff' for West Lothian Council's 'donation'. (You mean salvage collection of surplus educational resources from Inveralmond Community High School that will save the council money from having to haul it to a landfill site.) I speak to Garry.

It has been raining all morning. I have taken the opportunity to sit here and 'Wheel and Deal' a *modus operandi* which, unfortunately, had annoyed my colleagues in a previous career. I am trying to locate suitable storage, transport, and sponsorship for three 40-foot ocean freight containers to the Port of Kingston, Jamaica and from there to be trans-shipped on to the Port of St George's, Grenada.

12:59 p.m. Zafar returns my call they do not want any SESF resources.

1:03 p.m. A letter confirming the SESF charity number

(SCO39331) transfer to HMRC. For the attention of Russell House, King Street, Ayr, for the attention of Jane.

2:30 p.m. Called Liz, journalist, *Fife Herald*, who suggested I contact Adam of the *Edinburgh Evening News*. He will call me back. I am appealing for help for the last leg of this journey of another shipment to Grenada, you mean.

2:52 p.m. I called Robin in Grenada, who tells me that he's under the cosh at the moment. What does he mean by that? He is always pleasant but does not deliver. I called the *Falkirk Herald* editor, James, and sent an email away – I await reply. I contacted them at the suggestion of journalist extra-special, Tanya.

4:53 p.m. I am now tired. I've tried to keep the Surplus Educational Supplies Foundation afloat. The problem is that I need to get out of the guddle regarding HMRC and Companies House soon. It was not necessary for me to have become a limited company or, for that matter, a registered Scottish Charity, given that my initiative was primarily self-funded. For Thursday, 18 June. Call Rachel, PR and Corporate Affairs, Hutchinson Ports (UK) Ltd, who was very supportive of my work and suggests I call Nick.

Thursday 18/06/2009

9:31 a.m. Home. Settling to work. Shaved and showered. I am conscious of physical comfort and many intangible blessings. I am calling the accountant, Jenny, in Edinburgh, who was not in the office. Called Norman at First Port. I called Stephen at ZIM Integrated Shipping Services Ltd, at the Port of Liverpool.

11:55 a.m. Sent email to Zafa; I received an email quote of the tariff to Kingston, Jamaica, West Indies from Birke at ZIM, who was very helpful.

Friday 19/06/2009

7:16 a.m. Home. I am reflecting on the events of yesterday, or rather, recording the events of yesterday.

I cycled into Rothesay. I left my bicycle at the pier. Took the ferry to Wemyss Bay and the train to Paisley and the bus to the Braehead Shopping Centre. I took Amy's cell phone to the Vodaphone shop and spent a good half hour with the young John being bamboozled by 21st century digital technology. I later sat in the M&S café waiting for the young Sanjay. He soon came, we went out to the car park and within minutes were in his car, onto the M8 and driving through to Livingston New Town, West Lothian. We eventually found Inveralmond Community High School, where we met the site manager, Gerry. Sanjay took some photographs of GATU4072944, which had been almost fully loaded with educational resources of excellent quality and by no means past their sell by date.

Apparently an inventory of the contents had not been taken as I had been assured it would be. I found it, after not having seen the big box for over six months, looking a little worse for wear. It was covered in rust bumps. We were taken on a tour of the Inveralmond Community High School to view the work of refurbishment that Interserve Projects Ltd had undertaken. There was virtually an entire new interior of the main building and new equipment. Much of the 'old' had been skipped, junked, thrown away, crushed, and trucked to landfill. Gerry was approachable, jaunty, keen and proud of what his team were doing, and he mentioned that this was their first Private Finance Initiative school contract, and they now had several more in the pipeline.

Sanjay later dropped me off at Livingston South Station. He still appears to be enthusiastic about my efforts. After a long wait I got the train to Edinburgh Haymarket Station, then back to Glasgow and home. Find out from Gerry about the firm AES in Hillington.

To do: Call Birke at ZIM and make arrangements to collect MAEU6085656 from Russells depot in Coatbridge and ship to Kingston, Jamaica. Seafreight Agencies Lines, Miami, will complete the final leg of the journey pro bono from there to St George's, Grenada. First confirm that the Grenada Boys' Secondary School do wish to receive another shipment of educational resources. Do they really want another load of fit-for-purpose educational resources?

What else can I do? I am now in a right pickle of my own making. I must make arrangements to collect containers INBU4923875 and TRIU5079422 from Duncan Adams Transport Ltd, Grange Dock. These shipments that are intended for the schools in Carriacou and Petit Martinique, but so far I have received no confirmation from the Government of Grenada that they are committed to accepting these two shipments and willing to defray my costs of shipping, and it is likely that I will be stuck with them. I sent an email to the acting principal of GBSS, Philip, and spoke to him over the telephone. I have no choice but to continue liaising with him for the time being.

Contact Dr Reginald Buckmire, regarding his interest in the St Andrew's Government School, Grenville.

Monday 22/06/2009

8:33 a.m. Home. Calling Carson Transport Ltd. '*I will tell him as soon as he comes in that you called,*' he said.

There were damp, thick clouds sitting heavily on my spirit as I drove Marion to the ferry this morning. Sunshine is beginning to break through.

9:26 a.m. Waiting, waiting. No reply from Carson Transport Ltd. I sent an email to the High Commissioner for Grenada in London.

10:31 a.m. I spoke to Birke at ZIM at the port in Liverpool, who tells me that I am to contact her as soon as I know the score with the Grenada Boys' Secondary School.

10:39 a.m. I was speaking to Norman at First Port in Edinburgh, who makes suggestions and more suggestions as to what I should do, but delivers nothing tangible. He says he has an appointment with a firm that has spare warehouse space in Inverclyde. He tells me to have photographs taken of the children's school before and after delivery of the SESF shipment of educational resources. Obvious. Gives me the name of Madge, who has a charity which supports an orphanage in the Republic of Georgia. However, I do appreciate the leads he gives me.

10:55 a.m. I am to call once I know when Carson Transport are able to lift the container at Inveralmond Community High School

2:38 p.m. I am calling Carson Transport Ltd.

Tuesday 23/06/2009

8:08 a.m. Home. I am making a start. *'May I speak to John, please?' 'He's on another line.' 'Hello, David. I've been very busy. I will try and get back to you, okay, for tomorrow. Ross will be in Bathgate and should be at Inveralmond Community High School by 9:30 a.m.,'* he said. I am beginning to feel a lot better after those words.

8:49 a.m. I called Gary at West Lothian Council Media and Communications, who tells me that they will have a photographer at the school. I then called Debbie, the journalist of the *West Lothian Courier*, who will also have a snapper at ICHS before 9:30 a.m. tomorrow.

I Meet the Secret Millionaire and Travel Far Further

Wednesday 24/06/2009

8:40 a.m. I am on a shoogling train bound for Edinburgh. I cycled into Rothesay and boarded the MV *Bute* 6:30 a.m. ferry for Wemyss Bay, caught the train to Glasgow Station and took a taxi up to Queen Street Station. I am en route on a slow train for ICHS, where I have arranged for Carson Transport Ltd to collect a SESF container that has been loaded with fit-for-purpose educational resources by Interserve Projects Ltd over the past six months.

I am aboard a slow train to Livingston South Station. Gary has arranged for a photographer to be there, also, David, the assistant head teacher, has indicated that he will have four teachers to hand over this donation of educational resources. I have also arranged for the *West Lothian Courier* newspaper to have one of their journalists there as well. Media overload! Carson Transport Ltd have kindly agreed to keep the container at their Cumbernauld depot until such time as I can empty it, store and inventory the contents, or deliver it as it is, assuming that the container will be seaworthy.

11:28 a.m. Sunshine is breaking through. I have just boarded another train from Edinburgh Haymarket.

Roll it back. The 9:28 a.m. train, earlier, took me through to Livingston South. I went into the Co-op and a very helpful lady called a taxi. I arrived at the school to meet Gerry, the site manager, who has offered me another container loaded with resources. '*Don't call me, I will call you,*' he said. There was the head teacher and Eddie, a lassie, the engineer who knows Graeme. The snapper from West Lothian Council took foties. I strung up the Surplus Educational Supplies Foundation banner at the back end of the container with help from John of Interserve Projects Ltd. Carson Transport Ltd had been and gone earlier, and had been unable to lift the container.

Wednesday 24/06/2009

'All things work together for good to those who love G-D and are called according to HIS purpose.' Romans 8:28
'This is Slateford, the next stop is Kings Knowe.'

11:36 a.m. It is a slow train and I am enjoying the ride back to Central Station. I am about to partake of a cheese and onion sandwich, and quaff a pumpkin milky coffee. Press on Gunga Din! *'The next stop is Currie Hill.'*

3:40 p.m. I am on the MV *Bute* once more. I have just had a cup of soup and met Keith and his missus from Yorkshire, who have come up on a Shearings bus. After his retirement from British Rail, he told me, he did a PhD in history. His subject was the economics of railway development. They now travel the world.

GATU4072944 is almost full to the door. Perhaps it is just as well that the Carson Transport Ltd lifter was unable to lift my 'box'. Eddie, the lassie engineer with Interserve Projects Ltd, wearing a white hard hat, mentioned St Kentigern's Primary School as another source of surplus educational resources. We'll have to wait and see about that one for at the moment. I am inundated with resources and I am unable to effectively handle any of it.

(In spite of the odds stacked against my folly, I was able to make the same logistic connections and the attendant word-of-mouth commitments successfully, thanks to the goodwill of the Scottish road haulage industry. And I did not, to my knowledge, let anyone down, only myself and my nearest and dearest.)

On the ferry coming back I met Malcolm, who was in my first P4/5 class at the Port School, who tells me that Andrew, his brother, is now one of the boatyard blacksmiths and is getting married – celebrations at the Kingarth Hotel and the Shinty Hut. Good on the couple. I kept my counsel. I bid adieu to Keith and his missus.

4:06 p.m. Home, home at last. I am now going to call John, managing director of John G. Russell Transport Ltd (Russell) based at Hillington Industrial Estate, regarding the loan of a sidelifter, apparently they have one, to collect my container, and the temporary storage of it. You are not asking much are you? They let me have two pin-holed fit-for-scrap 40-foot containers last year, which I covered with two of my tarpaulins, and which Kenny, one of their operatives, helped me to cover. I am also going to ask if they will repair the roofs and doors. '*I don't mean to cut you short, but I am going to another meeting.*' He is always civil to me. He used to live in the Port. He suggested I call his boss regarding the loan of the sidelifter, which I will do tomorrow.

5:12 p.m. It is time to switch off and stop work. My mission is to supply good quality, fit-for-purpose, surplus to requirements, educational resources salvaged from the Scottish Education system at point of need worldwide. That's my raison d'etre, but I do not have the means or finances to make the vision a reality.

Thursday 25/06/2009

7:29 a.m. Home. I am slow getting started. It's damp, humid, and overcast. To do: contact shippers to get quotes; call the chief executive of John G Russell Ltd to see if they will use their sidelifter to collect container GATU4072944 in Livingston and make arrangements to have MAEU6085656 moved over to the Freightliner Ltd Container Terminal if they are unable to move it from their yard direct to the Port of Tilbury. I cannot continue to expect any more favours. Contact John at WH Malcolm Ltd, at the Newhouse depot, to see whether they will store GATU4072944. This long-established haulage firm has always been helpful to SESF from the beginning of the initiative. We lived in the village of Kilbarchan, which is not far from Brookfield Village where this transport company had started up.

John said that they may be able to uplift the container from

Livingston and store it temporarily at the Newhouse depot, and allow me to empty the container and inventory the contents. I am so grateful to so many for making what I am attempting to accomplish possible. Contact West Lothian Council and the *West Lothian Courier* regarding media communications about obtaining copies of the articles and the digitals that were taken of the handover of the container that morning. Wait and see what was puffed.

9:06 a.m. I called John, CEO at Carson Transport Ltd, Cumbernauld, to thank them for bringing the lifter through to ICHS from Bathgate, and offer my sincere apologies that the container was too heavy, and that Ross had made a pointless journey. Embarrassing.

7:28 p.m. It has been a beautiful day. I went out to the boatyard this afternoon and emptied a box of tools, a donation from Robin's dad, the architect along the road who has a finial on their roof which is rusting away. I am going to knock off work. Enough for one day. And it just so happens that it is now.

(Home 5:05 p.m. Saturday, 2 July 2022 and I have been here at the keyboard since 1 p.m. editing this second volume of The Diary of a Shipping Clerk.*)*

Monday 29/06/2009

6:45 a.m. Home. Ablutions, and now I am ready to get back in the ring, bare knuckles, with the strains of Jimmy Cliff knocking out the beat. The family are away at The Grove in Kilbarchan.

'*Who are you going to call upon today?*' I ask myself aloud. I will call the supporters from early days; Rebecca, journalist supporter of *The Herald*, who wrote an excellent article about my efforts for the SESF a while back; Stephen, *The Herald* editor of the Society

Supplement; Leanna of the *Aberdeen Journal*. Publicity from their articles was much appreciated as it raised the profile of the Surplus Educational Supplies Foundation, as have the many articles Craig, editor of *The Buteman,* did so admirably from the beginning of my initiative way back in 2005. Is there a market for surplus and used educational resources? Find out. And if so, where? Supply and demand. What is in it for them? Feel good factor? I just want to do good, that is my basic motivation and rationale.

I must acknowledge the following companies and businesses that have assisted the Surplus Educational Supplies Foundation Registered Scottish Charity (SCO39331). There were so many individuals, at the other end of the telephone wire, many of whom I had never met or are ever likely to meet, who cut me a lot of slack. The public sector depends on their support, as does the continuing operation of my initiative the Surplus Educational Supplies Foundation.

- Jane Harris, the group commercial director at J&J Denholm Ltd, Glasgow;
- John Sas, freight forwarder at Denholm Bahr Ltd, Port of Liverpool;
- Martin and John Stirling of Stirling Yacht Services Ltd, Port Bannatyne;
- Freightliner Ltd, Coatbridge;
- J &J MacKirdy Haulier Ltd, Rothesay;
- EWL Lines, Port of Felixstowe;
- Andrew Wishart and Sons Ltd, Rosyth;
- Fife Warehousing Company Ltd, Kirkcaldy;
- Fleming Transport Ltd, Inverkeithen;
- Mr MacMillan, operations manager, Ben Mundell Transport Ltd, Tarbert;
- Duncan and Eric, Duncan Adams Transport Ltd, Grange Dock;
- Forth Ports Plc, Port of Grangemouth;
- John Murray, WH Malcolm Ltd, Newhouse and Linwood;

Monday 29/06/2009

- John Morrison, CEO, Carson Transport and Lifting Solutions Ltd, Cumbernauld;
- John G. Russell Ltd, Coatbridge and Hillington;
- ZIM Integrated Shipping Services Ltd, Port of Liverpool and Port of Tilbury;
- Pentalver Transport Ltd, Leeds and Port of Southampton;
- JA Steel & Son Ltd, Enfield;
- Cameron Geddes, general manager, and his team, Ecosse World Express Ltd, Unit11, Inchinnan, Glasgow Airport;
- Peter Timmsr, CEO, Flexi Tech Ltd, Rothesay;
- Philip Turley, Willmot Dixon Construction Ltd, Hitchin;
- Interserve Projects Ltd, Birmingham;
- James R. B. Ross, accountant, and his team, Ross and Company Ltd, Dunoon;
- Lesley Paul and her team, One 2 One Accountancy Services, Rothesay, Isle of Bute;
- The Bike Shed, 113 Montague Street, Isle of Bute;
- Euan Burns, storage adviser, Pickfords, Granton, Edinburgh;
- Sam Tweedlie, digital artisan, Rothesay Repair;
- Kevin, digital artisan, Isle of Bute;
- Gillian Parkinson, marketing operations, and team, at Lofthus Signs, Aberdeen and Edinburgh;
- Philip J. Kirkham, photographer, Picture Bute;
- John White, operations manager, James Walker, Devol, Greenock;
- Peter McGarry, transport manager, John G Russell (Transport) Ltd Container Base, Coatbridge;
- Colin Todd, surveyor, ICS Intermodal Container Surveyors W Ltd, Prestwick;
- Kenneth Brodie, regional manager, Advantage Worldwide, 159 Wright Street, Renfrew.

I am now going to contact *The Herald* business editor and see if, in some indirect way, I can have the foregoing companies mentioned through a brief article. A way of saying thank you; it's the least I can do. I call Ian McConnell, the business editorial. Mark Williamson, Tim Sharp, and Simon Bain.

9:56 a.m. I called Marie, section leader, Resources, Education and Cultural Services, West Dunbartonshire Council, who is unable to tell me who is in charge. '*They are all out of the office,*' she said.

11:39 a.m. I have sent an email to Dr Roselle Antoine MBE, who runs a company called TCS Tutorials Ltd for disaffected, failing students, and drop-out youth from Afro-Caribbean backgrounds in London, who, along with Julie Watson, Marion and I met at the Grenada Volunteer Hospital charity dinner at the Holiday Inn in London last year, and who recommended I get in contact. A question of identity. Who are you? Who am I? I am somebody. You are somebody.

It is now 12:09 p.m. and it is time I left this seat and had a bite to eat.

1:03 p.m. I am back on the phone, calling Sierra Leone High Commission in London, Head of Chancery. '*One moment please,*' she said. I am told to contact Julie Berseve in Freetown, Sierra Leone. Florence at SLHC has spoken to her and told me to contact the Director of Education, Mr Kuyateh.

It is now 1:31 p.m. I am calling Freetown. I called the *Falkirk Herald*. '*We'll try and get a local angle on that,*' he said.

1:38 p.m. I am beginning to inch forward, a little movement. I am making some progress. As Aristotle said, '*I need a lever long enough to shift the world,*' or words to that effect. I need a lever long enough to shift this increasingly massive stockpile of fit-for-purpose, surplus to requirements, educational resources, which I am diverting from destruction towards the right places worldwide. Your reach doesnae hauf exceed yur grasp auld yin; that's my problem to solve and the difficulty, the bed of nails, I have manufactured for myself. Now what do I do? Whatever I do, I cannot give up.

I am awaiting a return call from Garry of the West Lothian Council Media and Communications Department regarding the possibility of having some of their puff information – an assessment from the council's point of view of the donation handover of the reusable educational resources from Inveralmond Community High School on 24 June 2009. Mention to him that Adam of the *Edinburgh Evening News* was also interested in obtaining this information for an article.

'*Experience is not what happens to a man, it is what a man does with what happens to him,*' Aldous Huxley.

'*It is the cracked ones that let in the light,*' Old Chinese Proverb.

1:46 p.m. Back on the phone. I called Steve at the West Indies Freight Company Ltd, who is to call me back regarding the tariff to Kingston, Jamaica, West Indies.

3:23 p.m. It is a beautiful, sunshine-filled afternoon. I have taken a break and I have been power-washing the slabs at the back door and the granite setts at the front door. Now what next?

4 p.m. I called John Murray at WH Malcolm Transport Ltd Newhouse depot. He spoke to someone who will pass on my request for the loan and use of the sidelifter.

4:11 p.m. I called Gary Heron to thank him for the news release. He has to clear it first with the council supremo, and then he will pass it on to Adam, the journalist at the *Edinburgh Evening News*. Obtain copies of the puff.

4:30 p.m. Today? I made contact with Roselle Antoine MBE, Principal of TCS Tutorial College. I received a positive response from her, interested. West Lothian Council Media and Communications Department will put a brief article in their newsletter about the collection, 'The Donation of Educational Resources' from Inveralmond Community High School: it is no big deal to them, but it sure is to me, and the ultimate beneficiaries who receive them, and they will pass on their article to the *Edinburgh Evening News*, which gives some more coverage.

Wednesday 01/07/2009

9:37 a.m. Home. I got out of bed tired. Another sleepless night, but here I am with no other choice but to buckle under the pressure, or get on with the work in hand. I sent an email to Roselle, who has told me she had a meeting with the High Commissioner for Sierra Leone.

I am now about to call Simon Bain, business journalist at *The Herald*. We have a chat about 'the business', which SESF is definitely not. He has asked me to send that email again? *'I'll ask him to send you a copy of the final press release,'* he said. Fact check: there are about 2,720 council schools in Scotland – over the past decade 219 have been rebuilt and many refurbished. What happened to all of the fit-for-purpose educational resources?

11:38 a.m. I spoke with Charlotte at Scottish International Relief, who told me they don't take furniture and that Andrew Parker is based in Malawi.

Monday 06/07/2009

11:56 a.m. I have just returned home after having cycled round the island. It is a grey and muggy day with thick clouds sitting low on top of me. I managed to break through the barrier of my inertia and depression this morning. I am now calling Simon Bain at *The Herald*.

'It sounds like something we can make a good story of. Send me another email with a few broad details,' he said. His article, 'Call for School Supplies to be donated,' will be in *The Herald* on Monday, 13 July 2009.

12:36 p.m. I called the Bulgarian Embassy speaking to Aglika, the personal assistant to the ambassador. I then called Julian Popov, who is civil and interested. I am to call him after 13 July. He's returning to Bulgaria.

Tuesday 07/07/2009

1:35 p.m. Home. I received a call from Craig, Dunbartonshire Council Schools Estate Unit, Dunbarton. I have made an appointment to see him on Thursday 9 July.

Wednesday 08/07/2009

10:27 a.m. Home. 'You may know that several schools in Glasgow closed at the end of June and there may be some surplus stuff available? I explained to one of the principal officers what you did for others abroad and she said to contact her if you were still interested in items for abroad,' said Harry, who works for the council. I then called Linda at Glasgow District Council and she told me that there were six primary schools to be cleared next week. 'As the summer break started in Glasgow on Friday, 26 June, we have already cleared some buildings. If I can arrange access to the ones outstanding how soon can you be mobilised with labour and transport? I know one school with resources on the southside of Glasgow, but Friday is the deadline to be cleared,' she said.

I am frustrated and saddened to see all of these quality, fit-for-purpose educational resources being crushed and trucked to landfill sites. There is no way that I have the logistical capacity to take advantage of this offer and I had to decline.

Thursday 09/07/2007

9:50 a.m. Rigo's Café, 15 Castle Street, Dumbarton. I arrived in here a little while ago. I was grateful that I was able to use their facilities. *'Would you like any sauce?' 'No, thanks. Bacon roll and a cup of white coffee, please.'* I left the Isle of Bute on the MV *Bute* …

6:30 a.m. *'Where are yeh aff tae today?'* asks Calum, the steward fae Stornoway. It is a beautiful sun-filled day. I got the train and asked directions from the conductor on arrival at Central Station. Down to the next level, where I bought a ticket for the Dumbarton train from platform 17.

On arrival in Dumbarton I walked through the station and over to the Broad Meadow Industrial Estate. After walking around the block a few times, I eventually found the West Dunbartonshire Council Educational Services offices on Poplar Road, where I was met by a welcoming soul. I walk along the corridor. *'Good morning. I am early for my appointment, but is there any chance that I can meet Craig before 2 p.m.?'* The helpful soul phones him up. I am to see him at 11 a.m.

I walked back out and got a taxi to the Lennox Street newspaper offices of the *Clydebank Post*. The journalist I wished to speak to is in a meeting. I left my card and said I would return in 40 minutes. The pleasant receptionist has recommended the establishment where I write this note. My coffee has grown cold.

11:20 a.m. The meeting with Craig. He tells me that there will definitely be educational resources available at St Andrew's High School, North Douglas Street, off Dunbarton Road, Clydebank. They will contact me. (And they did sooner than I thought they would.) Get your skates on pal.

Later today I was in conversation with Roselle Antoine, do they want educational resources or not? Can her charity assist with the delivery of resources currently awaiting shipment to Grenada?

Tuesday 14/07/2009

Fine words, butter no parsnips. She says she has a meeting with the Sierra Leone High Commission Head of Chancery.

Friday 10/07/2009

7:50 a.m. Home. Beautiful sunlight-filled day. I am going to push myself to the limit on the bike. I can only wait and see what comes my way. I have done all I can for the time being. I can get some exercise. I cycled round the island and felt a lot better.

Tuesday 14/07/2009

7:59 a.m. Home. It is a wet and grey morning. I am getting on with it. Priority: sort through and record all my travelling expenses. Get the format of accounts required by OSCR and Companies House. I called Birke Owen at ZIM Integrated Shipping Ltd, Port of Liverpool, regarding their tariff for shipping the container to Jamaica from the Port of Tilbury.

A few moments ago I received a call from Stuart Laing, IT expert, who had seen the article in yesterday's *Herald* newspaper, 'Call For Surplus School Supplies To Be Donated,' by Simon Bain, and has kindly called me. He is offering computers from Stirling University and will store them for me at his brother's farm near Stirling. He told me that he had been out in Uganda and had visited some of their schools.

(That article was also seen by Ambassador Tom Kennedy, British Embassy, San José, Costa Rica. Allow me to quote from that letter:

'Dear David, This is just a short letter to show the Embassy's deep thanks and appreciation for all the effort that you have put into the first shipment of school materials for Bluefields in Nicaragua. It seems little short of miraculous to me that an article I read on the back of The Herald *while I was on holiday in the summer should have led to such a fruitful relationship being established between you and Bruce.*

And yet it has happened and we are delighted to know that the initial donation of books is on its way... Yours sincerely, Tom Kennedy'

Fast forward in The Diary of a Shipping Clerk, *later this year, when I was able to make a fact-finding trip to Bluefields, Costa Caribena, Nicaragua, Central America, in December.)*

Wednesday 15/07/2009

7:58 a.m. Home. What next? I am munching toast and marmalade and sipping coffee. I call Anne, South Lanarkshire Council, who called yesterday and left a message.

Thursday 16/07/2009

2:30 a.m. Home. Call from Kathy at West Dunbartonshire District Council about the uplift of educational resources from St Andrew's Secondary School, Clydebank, and Our Lady and St Patrick's in Dumbarton. I have got move quickly.

What was it Robert Hyslop, haulier, said to me once, bless him. *'You are the man for the job.'* He always had words of encouragement for me. He had asked me that morning, 25 April 2006, when he brought my first 40-foot ocean freight container purchase down from CT Engineering Services Ltd in Coatbridge to the boatyard in Port Bannatyne, *'Are you a born-again?'* Sometimes I feel like it; that morning, I certainly felt like it when I replied to his direct question in the affirmative, that I believed that I had been given a fresh start in life because of my faith and trust in THE LORD JESUS CHRIST. That is until later that day, when I saw the container was just a big box covered in rust bumps – but that disappointment was to change, at the end of the school day, when I went back over to the boatyard and saw Jim, the blacksmith, who kindly offered to help me out with a loan of a generator, grinder, goggles, gloves and a padlock, and brought the generator out to where it had been parked so I could get to work

Friday 17/07/2009

on it. I soon had '*Hanschell Freight*' scribbled in chalk all over it.

Enough of my reverie, this is where I am today. I make arrangements to have two containers, one at St Andrews Secondary in Clydebank and one at Our Lady and St Patrick's in Dumbarton. I make contact once more with Bishop's Move Ltd in Edinburgh, as they apparently have the contract with West Dunbartonshire District Council to do an uplift and inventory of the educational resources in the two schools. I contact David Bruce, managing director of that removal firm.

3:31 p.m. While I was out working in the garden, about an hour ago, I got a call from Jamie Borthwick, reporter at the *Clydebank Post* newspaper to tell me that that West Dunbartonshire Council had been in contact with his newspaper seeking publicity.

4:20 p.m. That's me. I have called Mark at Russell: he's on holiday. He gave me Peter McGarry's telephone number, who said he would speak to Graeme Russell. I then called John, their managing director, based at their Hillington Industrial Estate depot, regarding my two, scrap, pin-holed, 40-foot containers about the possibility of having them made watertight. Apparently, they don't have a welder on site! '*I'll see what I can do for you,*' he said. He tells me that he'd also seen the brief article in *The Herald*, where his firm, John G Russell Transport Ltd, had got an acknowledgement. '*We are mentioned right up there up among the big boys,*' he said.

Friday 17/07/2009

10:07 a.m. Home. I am going to do some darning and mending as I sit here and wait for a call from Peter at Russell in Coatbridge. Checking emails. I am going to call Madge in Edinburgh, who helps run a Georgia-based NGO trust charity orphanage where there is chronic poverty: alternatives for children in the Bulgarian

I Meet the Secret Millionaire and Travel Far Further

orphanage, an opportunity to export their music, Scottish links. In conversation with her, she is enthusiastic and positive. I told her that Norman Hill of First Port had suggested I contact her.

12:28 p.m. Called GHC in London. I spoke to Sam.

12:43 p.m. I am about to sew buttons on my trousers and darn socks. Going to call Peter McGarry, who said, '*We are pretty low on boxes. I'll leave it with you then.*'

2:13 p.m. Here I go again. I was speaking to Shirley at Duncan Adams Transport Ltd, Grange Dock depot, who is always pleasant. I spoke to Andy at Pentalver Transport Ltd, Leeds. That will be £575 plus VAT. Cheque is not possible to make it in time, so I will need to transfer funds from the bank. I am now about to make arrangements in a hurry to have the 40-foot container delivered to St Andrew's High School, North Douglas Street, Clydebank.

I am on my own and well and truly out on a shoogly branch. '*Well, David, if that's what you are going to do, be it on your own head.*' The words spoken to me as I stood at the door handing out hymn books at Sandyford Memorial Church, Kelvinhaugh Street, Glasgow one Sunday morning in June 1982 by Reverend George Philip, my Church of Scotland minister.

4 p.m. I have cycled into Rothesay and have had funds for the purchase of another container sent from Lloyds TSB, Montague Street. To do: confirm with Valerie at Duncan Adams Transport Ltd the estimated time of arrival of my SESF 40-foot container (OCLU1354487) to St Andrew's High School, Clydebank; let Jamie Borthwick, journalist, *Clydebank Post*, know when the container is due to arrive at the school; confirm with Andy that the payment has been received.

Monday 20/07/2009

11:26 a.m. Home. Valerie from DAT Ltd office called earlier to confirm arrival of the container for Wednesday, 22 July at 10 a.m. I had called Craig at West Dunbartonshire Council, but his mobile had been switched off.

11:30 a.m. I am now speaking to Jamie at the *Clydebank Post*, who tells me that the information I sent him last week was all he needed and that he might appear at St Andrew's High School on Wednesday to snap a few photographs. I called Andy at Pentalver Ltd in Leeds to confirm that SESF funds for container had gone into their account on Friday 17 July. Called Madge and left a message. I called Roselle Antoine, who tells me, '*The resources for Sierra Leone will definitely go ahead.*' We'll have to wait and see. Call the *Daily Record*. '*What's the fresh angle? We can't rehash the news,*' said Keith. I am trying to rustle up some more publicity tae shift this next shipment out of the doldrums of cynical indifference. For Tuesday 21 July: call Cathy at West Dunbartonshire Council to

The SESF collection of educational resources from Golden Hill Primary School, Clydebank, will go ahead.

confirm that the SESF collection of educational resources from Golden Hill Primary School, Clydebank, will go ahead.

Tuesday 21/07/2009

9:30 a.m. Home. Calling DAT Ltd, Grange Dock to confirm delivery of the SESF container to St Andrew's High School. Calling West Dunbartonshire Council Estates Unit to confirm for tomorrow.

9:37 a.m. I left a message for Cathy at West Dunbartonshire Council Estates unit. The container will be at the school DV tomorrow. I need to find a charitable accountant. Ha ha! A contradiction in terms. You got some hope.

2:19 p.m. I am listening to Georgian folk songs. A painful sound. I called Madge.

Wednesday 22/07/2009

11:35 a.m. St Andrew's High School, North Douglas Street, Clydebank, Glasgow. The team from Bishop's Move Ltd are currently loading SESF container OCLU1354487. I met Alastair, photographer, on the 6:30 a.m. boat and his chum Stephen, another snapper, met us with his car at Paisley Gilmour Street Station. He drove us through the Clyde Tunnel and down Dunbarton Road to Clydebank to the school, where we met the janny, John. I went out onto Dunbarton Road to a café and bought tea, coffee, and bacon rolls for the four of us. It was not long before the semi and trailer with the container, driven by Paul from Falkirk, arrived. He reversed the trailer round to the back premises of the school.

As I scribble this note I am at the same time attempting to keep count of the individual pupil tables and various quality solid kit being loaded into the container. It is a cloudy, overcast morning, but I am grateful just to be able to get on with it. Aircraft bound for Glasgow Airport are coming in to land low over North Douglas Street. Earlier, I met David, general manager of Bishop's Move Ltd, who is over from Edinburgh to supervise the removal. I also met a representative of the West Dunbartonshire District Council Estates Unit who was here to say what could and could not be taken. I am concentrating on tables and chairs.

It is now almost midday. The team of young lads from Bishop's Move have just gone for their lunch break. The container is partially loaded with desks and chairs, which have all been carefully stacked. It's a rusty box but I'll have it painted one day. I have been on the cliff-edge of a migraine headache all morning. I am keeping going. Paul, the Duncan Adams Transport Ltd artic driver, is chilling out in the cab. I have just had a chat with John the janitor here at St Andrew's High School, who tells me his son is a teacher.

'*The council moves us around from school to school. You are doing good work,*' he said. That will do me for a compliment. It is starting to cloud over, with spots of rain.

School resources to be exported.

1:40 p.m. I am, once more, helping with the loading of the container. Approximately 30 big tables; 60 small, single, pupil tables; 50 chairs; 6 book cases; 2 filing cabinets; and 2 table tennis tables.

The container is now only just half full, and the removers have quit at 3 p.m.! Alastair, the photographer, and I accompany the container to Russell's depot, Gartsherrie Road, Coatbridge, where we meet Peter, who gives me a 'lecture'. I take it on the chin.

(See *Clydebank Post*, Wednesday, 22 July 2009, '*School supplies are desk-lined for the sun. Retired teacher gives chairs and tables to hurricane ravaged schools in Caribbean,*' by Jamie Borthwick.)

Thursday 23/07/2009

11:05 a.m. Home. I have had a frontal headache all morning. I am going slow at the moment.

3:56 p.m. Call from Sanjay. Bless him.

Friday 24/07/2009

10:11 a.m. Home. I have received a message from a teacher, Randall Patton, at Saint Dominic's High School in Belfast saying that they are disposing of school furniture. I called the *Clydebank Post*. They ran the article and will send me a copy of the newspaper in which it was printed.

I received some very bad news. They tell me that while the Surplus Educational Supplies Foundation (SCO39331) ocean freight container was being loaded several hundred laptops were stolen. Why is it that, with things that I have worked so hard to bring about, there is always something that occurs to spoil or taint the achievement?

I am heading into the little town to see if Michael can repair my watch strap.

Tuesday 28/07/2009

1:38 p.m. Calling Randall in Belfast. '*I'll get him to return your call,*' he said.

2:27 p.m. A beautiful sun-filled afternoon. I have returned from a cycle to Kerrcroy with Marion.

2:36 p.m. I have spoken to the High Commissioner for Grenada, who is personable. She told me that she will continue to see whether or not the Government of Grenada wants any more shipments of educational resources for their schools.

Later I spoke to John, the freight forwarder at India buildings, Port of Liverpool, who said he would send me templates of the documentation necessary to ship goods. 'Bill of lading (also referred to as BOL) is a document issued by the carrier acknowledging that the carrier has received the specified goods on board as cargo for transportation to a named place for delivery to the consignee who is usually identified.'

Monday 27/07/2009

9:08 a.m. Home. I have just had a call from Randall of St Dominic's High School in Belfast to ask me if SESF still wanted their school furniture, which he had to consign to the skip. I can't win them all. My reach has always exceeded my grasp.

Tuesday 28/07/2009

8 a.m. I am on the boat where I meet Tony, who is multi-skilled: a paramedic, writer, bicycle repair mechanic, and shop owner, who has given me the addresses of Abel Miller of Skilled Scotland, Brown McFarlane, Carntyne and that of Jackie Agnew in Bathgate who ships furniture out to St Vincent de Paul charity shops in the USA.

12:40 p.m. I am sitting in the carriage of the train for Wemyss Bay, Platform 11 Central Station, Glasgow, my adopted city. '*Please have your tickets ready for inspection,*' she said. I have not long walked down from Borders Books, where I had a meeting in Starbucks café with Graeme and Karen of Circola Communications. They appeared interested in SESF. They told me that they need to go away and think about whether or not they can assist SESF to move up a notch or two.

Wednesday 29/07/2009

7:12 p.m. Home. Marion and Johanna have just gone out on a kayak club message.

Earlier today I set off on the 6:30 a.m. ferry boat. I took the train to Central Station, a taxi up to Queen Street Station, a train to Edinburgh Haymarket and a taxi to Gilmour Street where I met Madge, who gave me scrambled egg and salmon, and a mug of tea. I met her fellow chorister of Gregorian Chants who has come to Scotland from the Republic of Georgia. I gave them what information and contacts I had in the transportation industry and offered my support for their work in the orphanage in Georgia. I told my hosts that I am thinking about the possibility of delivering educational resources to anglophone Costa Caribena, Moskito Schools, Nicaragua, Central America. Time will tell where this leads.

I made my way home. There is slight migraine numbness and tingling in my left hand. There is so much I want done and resolved, vis-à-vis the containers that are loaded with educational resources at five different depots across Scotland and what is currently available from the closure of schools in the Scottish Education system with falling rolls. I'll just have to do what I can and remain awake to seize the opportunities as they arise. Is this somewhere that could do with one of these boxes? Nicaragua. Cayos Miskitos, Porto Cabezas. I contact the mayor of Puerto

Cabezas, Guillermo Espinoza, City of Bluefields, Costa Caribena. Formerly a British protectorate. Once a bolthole for escaped slaves from the European Caribbean Colonies. (See Stephen Gibb's BBC article, *'Travels to Nicaragua's Mosquito Coast to find out why the Miskito People are pushing for independence.'* Hector Williams, Leader Wihta Tara, Great Judge of the Miskitos. *'They have taken everything from us, and given nothing back,'* said Oscar Hodgson, lawyer.)

Monday 03/08/2009

4:29 p.m. I have sat down in the carriage of the next train to Wemyss Bay.

Earlier today I picked up the telephone and called Abel Miller, businessman, engineer, and political refugee from Zimbabwe. He had worked on the railway. He was doing good work, by his account, in a refugee camp and had fallen foul of Mugabe's thugs who wanted him out of the way; miraculously he survived and was rescued before assassins threw his half-dead body to the lions. He was picked up, barely alive, by a game warden's helicopter. After a long time recovering from his injuries he got blackwater fever. His family paid for his treatment in the United Kingdom and he arrived in Glasgow, where he received life-saving treatment. Tony Edwards told me about him at our chance meeting last week and had given me his telephone number. Abel has the use of the former Brown & McFarlane (Steel stockholders) premises in Carntyne. I decided to give him a call and made an appointment to see him. I caught the 11 a.m. boat and train later from Wemyss Bay. On arrival at Central Station I got a taxi, otherwise it would have taken me the rest of the day to find his office and unit in Carntyne.

'Are ya a businessman?' asks the taxi driver. *'I guess so. I am sort of one. Let's say I'm a learner businessman-cum-entrepreneurial charity worker, who has gone into great self-imposed debt so he can deliver*

good stuff and make good things happen for other people,' I said.

I try always to be smartly dressed and can at least look the part of something at any rate. Handsome is as handsome does. First impressions last. Abel seems to be the sort of person who is facing many unnecessary difficulties and obstructions from those who could quite easily make it easier for his enterprise to flourish. They said that they would have to charge me/SESF to keep my containers in their large yard and educational resources in their warehouse. They said they were running on a shoestring. Abel however has a vision and strikes me as a genuine social entrepreneur. His favoured expertise is the provision of clean water.

He gave me a lift back down the road to the bus stop in Parkhead, where I got a bus to Bellgrove Station in Dennistoun, and where I lived in a sublet flat on Garthland Drive 1980–1982. I got the train to Queen Street Station lower level and then hoofed it down Buchanan Street to Central Station, and here I am, where I managed to get my mobile phone, my 66th birthday present from Marion, tae wuk and called Amy Elisabeth. Contact, ya beezer. Heading hame.

9:20 p.m. Home. Before heading for bed yesterday evening I received an email from Regina Da Silva from Brazil, who is doing a Public Health course at Edinburgh University, to tell me she has now received 13 boxes of children's toys, games, and books, which she has collected for SESF from the manager, Luanda, while working at the Cancer Research UK shop at 87 Morningside Road. We had met at an Edinburgh Chamber of Commerce Social Enterprise conference at the Grosvenor Hotel earlier this year. I emailed her back with Jimmy of Edinburgh Community Transport's telephone number.

On my return home this evening there was an email from Regina to say that Jimmy and his team had come round to her home to collect these boxes. This news made my day; goodwill and no-strings-attached kindness that makes the wheels of charitable initiatives birl. Regina has started her own business. '*My congratulations, you are doing a lovely work with your company,*' she said. Luanda is an encouraging, cheery, and lovely soul.

Tuesday 04/08/2009

5:31 p.m. Home. It took me a while to get going. I finally managed to get on the bike and cycled round the island. On my return I met up with Amy Elisabeth walking back from the town. She is making supper. Bless her. I am calling Grenada Chamber of Industry and Commerce (GCIC). I am reluctant to move, it's another break-point; I must crash through my inertia barrier or suffer the consequences of self-destruction. Why should I bother anymore? Make the move and overcome the difficulty. I am the only person who can and will: accept and take responsibility, you're your actions. I spoke to Hazel Ann, CEO of the GCIC. Will her members assist to defray costs of shipping SESF educational resources to Grenada Governments schools?

Wednesday 05/08/2009

11:34 a.m. Home. The sun is shining through the overhead skylight out of a pale, clear blue sky. I went into Rothesay to Print Point to have more puff sheets photocopied. I purchased envelopes and bought a book by Richard Branson, *Business Stripped Bare*. He is not a role model for me, but I might learn something. I stopped by The Bike Shed and chatted to David Kilpatrick, a supporter from early days who is always welcoming, and he put some air in my tyres gratis, which makes a big difference to my progress.

11:54 a.m. I am writing a letter to John. S. Denholm, chairman of J&J Denholm Ltd.

I MEET THE SECRET MILLIONAIRE AND TRAVEL FAR FURTHER

Friday 07/08/2009

11:02 a.m. Home. I called Jimmy at Edinburgh Community Transport, the Lothian and Borders Community Justice Authority, and Regina Da Silva to express my appreciation for the recent uplift of 13 boxes of resources (children's books, toys and games) which were collected from the Cancer Charity shop on Morningside Road.

11:14 a.m. Jimmy has called and has confirmed that Edinburgh Community Transport will collect resources from anywhere in the capital city! And what's more, they will store them temporarily at their Elizafield Industrial Estate unit off the Newhaven Road. Great news!

2:40 p.m. I spoke with the High Commissioner for Grenada, who said she was trying to elicit support from the alumni of Grenada Boys' Secondary School: apparently, everyone in the Grenadian community in London and back on the Isle of Spices is focused on enjoying their carnival. Such is life under tropical skies. I continue to keep knocking on that door. Why? I am now going to cycle into the town to get some messages for Marion and purchase a new watch strap. The sun is shining brightly.

4:20 p.m. While in the town I met the Gatongi family, who are from Kenya. Francis told me that his former head teacher is coming to Scotland. We chatted and I told him that I would give him Abel Miller's telephone number. I have just called Abel to let him know that I had spoken to Francis.

Monday 10/08/2009

10:23 a.m. Home. I called Mick, Port resident, who some time ago had offered me a printer that works. He had called me weeks ago

Monday 10/08/2009

and I should have called him before now. I said that I would be at the Caribbean Hurricane Relief Depot later today. I apologised to him for the delay.

Contact Peter Kilfoyle MP, who has links with the Mosquito Coast through the Peace and Hope Trust, regarding the Surplus Educational Supplies Foundation Charity's offer to donate a pallet-load of library books, gifted by Morningside Library months ago, and perhaps basic classroom educational resources at a later date, should the initial shipment prove successful. I sent him an email outlining my proposal. I called his Liverpool constituency office. *'He's a very hands on, Member of Parliament. He is on holiday in Italy at the moment. Surgery hours are the first Friday of the month and are held at Anfield CP School, 6–7 p.m. And the third Friday of every month, Northcote PS, Cavendish Drive 5–6 p.m. opposite Sainsbury,'* she said. When he's not on holiday, methinks.

12:30 p.m. I have received a call from David Alexander, merchant seaman, who has arrived in Hamburg, where I wandered in the Raperbahn and recall passing a nightclub where the Beatles were performing their music. I was homeless, rootless, and aimless on the waterfront streets of that city in the late winter of 1965 after a failed attempt to become a Grolier Encyclopaedia salesman. I was attempting to sell encyclopaedias to American military personnel – I was reluctant to have them sign on the dotted line of the book contract, since if they defaulted they would be court martialled.

'I will call again tomorrow. I am on watch and have to go up to the bridge,' he said. Bless him. I called Roselle Antoine MBE earlier today. She said that she would get in touch later in the week, that she had arranged meetings with the Sierra Leone High Commission, and tells me that she liaises directly with their Head of Chancery and has contacts in the Grenada Government's Ministry of Education. Roselle is a well-connected individual. She had told me that she would get back to me some time ago, so I took the initiative and called her. See Google! Called my link to

ACTB the Sierra Leone charity. Check them out. Mark Green left a message and now he does not return my calls? No word either from Terry. What's up with these people?

4:25 p.m. I called Philip, construction manager with Willmot Dixon Construction Ltd, regarding the Hackney School refurbishment. He had told me last year that there would be educational resources available.

Tuesday 11/08/2009

1:21 p.m. Home. I am working, with Marion's indispensable assistance, on updating the IT slide presentation of the SESF charity and social enterprise business.

3:30 p.m. I am heading up into the town to post my donation to Reforesting Scotland's Highland Gathering next month: I don't know whether I will make it.

Wednesday 12/08/2009

12:56 p.m. Home. This morning I had an appointment with the MP for Argyll and Bute, Alan Reid, held at his Rothesay Pavilion surgery. I gave him an updated dossier of SESF's activities since we last met. He has been supportive and we'll see what further efforts he can make on my foundation's behalf.

While at the Isle of Bute Agricultural Society cattle show this morning, I met Dan, retired Glasgow CID inspector, who asked me in a very direct manner if I would man the car park for the Bute Highland Games next Saturday. I said, '*Yes!*' taken somewhat off guard. My willing disposition gets the better of me. He told me that he would call me to confirm. I presume he has to clear this on-the-spot appointment with his Rotary Club committee. Dreich showery wi' smirry rain up there at The Meadows. I was

Wednesday 12/08/2009

chatting to Neil the roofer, who tells me that he has a lot on his slate. I offered him solidarity by listening.

I wandered around the showground to see the livestock and bought myself a hamburger with a splashing of mustard and a coffee. It was time for me to head back up the road. Marion's chum Wilma, from Langbank, came over and she and Amy have not long left here to have lunch at the Kingarth Hotel.

1:07 p.m. I am not feeling too good. Inertia and inert, not catatonic, but in that state of being in limbo. *'What do I do now?'* or as Eric said to me way back in 2006, *'What's next?'*

I can try and develop the recent contact with the British Embassy in Costa Rica and their ambassador Tom Kennedy, who, while visiting family in Glasgow, read Simon Bain's article on Monday, 13 July, 'Call For Surplus School Supplies To Be Donated.' The British Ambassador had expressed a wish to have educational resources, in this case library books, shipped to some schools on Nicaragua's Costa Caribena, many of whom are English speakers. An idea? A breakthrough of sorts! We could start with a pallet-load of books, delivered to the community of English speakers in the town of Bluefields, Puerto Cabezas, Mosquito Coast, Nicaragua, Meso-America, and see how that goes. I am going to call John at RH Freight Services Ltd. How do I get a pallet-load of library books to Bluefields, Mosquito Coast, Nicaragua?

After speaking to him, he calls me back with two leads. He is always chatty, cheerful, and encourages me in his distinctive Scouse accent. *'I'm off to Spain on holiday,'* he tells me. KLM and Luftwaffe Air Freight have a good service to South America, and also Managua Sea Freight. I will follow up these firms. Also Fallow International Freight Ltd. I can ask the question, *'Will they give SESF a charity rate?'*

Kestrel Liner Agencies, agents for Tropical Global Logistics: I speak with Andy, who is personable. He tells me that Otis Roberts is Jason Roberts' uncle (who plays for Blackburn Rovers) and has a charity that sends stuff to Grenada. He suggested I contact the footballer's uncle.

Friday 14/08/2009

11 a.m. Home. It is grey and wet. I am reading The Scramble for Africa by Thomas Pakenham. The white race and its people, in my view, have much to answer for for the sorry state that the African continent and its own people are in today. The phone rings: '*You have just won an all-inclusive tour to the Caribbean.*' I put the phone down. I am going to try and contact Sam at the Grenada High Commission once more. He said he would get Otis Roberts' number for me. '*I kan't find his numba. Ah'll kall you in de aftanoon,*' he said.

I speak with David at Kestrel Liner Agencies, who tells me that they will ship a pallet-load of books to Managua, no bother, for approximately £155, providing I can deliver the pallet to Manchester. I send an email to Bruce Callow, c/o British Embassy, San José, Costa Rica. They must now move towards my efforts and initiative in response to their ambassador's request.

4 p.m. I've received a call from Francis Gatongi asking if it would be convenient for him to bring around his friend Joe from Kenya, who is a doctor in Fife. I give them hospitality and lots of leads to follow up contacts. It's now up to them.

Tuesday 18/08/2009

9:46 a.m. Home. Grey and wet. I am not feeling 100% – there is a tingling numbness in my right hand, and now it has gone. Worrying. What's wrong with my nervous system? I shall press on regardless. Durward, neurologist at the Royal Infirmary, who my GP in Ruchazie had referred me to, told me way back when (in the seventies), to stay clear of doctors, which was good advice.

Wednesday 19/08/2009

I am going to call the Scottish Book Trust and see if I can drum up some support for the shipment of the Argyll and Bute Council Libraries, Morningside Library, and Stirling Library books to the Mosquito Coast prisons and schools.

10:45 a.m. I called Matthew, Tesco surveyor. He tells me that they may have warehouse space for me in Paisley. He's always positive and encouraging. I am typing up my notes at the moment. The washing machine technician man has come and gone.

11:03 a.m. I give IKEA HQ customer services a call and I sent an email to their PR department. No joy there.

12:36 p.m. I am going to stop typing and have some lunch.

2:32 p.m. I call Sierra Leone High Commission and the Head of Chancery, who gives me the name of Persima, who is in charge of educational resources at their Ministry of Education in Freetown. I am to call SLHC tomorrow and they will give me his telephone number. Why do I continue to call these people? Eventually, I speak to Vanessa at DFID, Freetown, Sierra Leone, who tells me something interesting. '*The government of Sierra Leone has developed a 10-year education plan, which DFID stands ready to support with other donors. This has been endorsed by the Education For All Fast Track Initiative,*' she said. Sounds good. I call Crawford, McLaren House, Falkirk Council, regarding surplus resources and technical equipment which they are disposing into landfill. No joy there either.

Wednesday 19/08/2009

---

4 p.m. Home. I am about to call the SLHC for the second time. '*She's in a meetin,*' she said. There is no joy the second time round. I called Crawford and left a message. He is in a meeting. I received an email from Patrick Kilfoyle to tell me that the Warrant Group Ltd international are the freight forwarders. He and his team were constructive to deal with. He's in the freight delivery business. I will deal with him. I was given this contact by Bruce Callow, who works in the British Embassy in San José, Costa Rica.

Thursday 20/08/2009

11:46 a.m. Home. I have just received a call from M&K McLeod Construction Ltd, Lochgilphead. I confirmed with the caller that I was still interested in acquiring the resources that remained in the former secondary school buildings. Irene will contact me regarding the uplift of the resources. My hopes are raised once more. Why didn't I say, *'No, thank you. I am no longer collecting surplus educational resources.'* Instead, my pride is my downfall and I press on ahead, recklessly.

1:18 p.m. Calling SLHC yet again. I am speaking to Florence, who is on a first name basis. *'I have been in talks with the mining companies. I will do something,'* she said.

Friday 21/08/2009

10:39 a.m. The sun is shining through cloud cover and patches of blue sky. I don't feel like cycling around the Isle of Bute, but I am going to, once again, and make an effort of will.

Tuesday 25/08/2009

9:45 a.m. Home. I have just come in from outside, where the sun is shining brightly out of a pale cloudy sky, to receive a message from Jamie Borthwick, journalist at the *Clydebank Post* asking me to call him, which I do. He asked me if I knew anything about the theft of 60 laptops from St Andrew's High School, Clydebank.

Wednesday 26/08/2009

Thieves, claiming that they were charity workers in order to gain entry to the school on the day that the SESF was there making a collection, took the opportunity, while we were busy, to carry out this despicable crime. The opposition strikes just went I am gathering up a few threads to make some progress. He told me that David at Bishop's Move Ltd had been in touch with him.

10:59 a.m. I got a call from Ailsa and had to think for a minute. *'Who is this?'* I ask myself. *'Would you mind raising your voice?'* – my wee ploy to give me a few seconds to remember who I was speaking to. I must remember to wear my hearing aid.

She told me that the former pupils of the high school were going to have a fundraiser party before the building was demolished. I told her that M&K McLeod Construction Ltd had been in touch with me offering SESF the opportunity to salvage the resources that remained in the former school building prior to its demolition. I suggested she get in touch with them. She asked me about the next Argyll and Bute Social Enterprise Network (ABSEN) meeting; frankly I have ignored all their posts, but did not tell her that.

11:49 a.m. Call from Billy the janitor at St Andrew's Primary School to inform me that he had left a set of encyclopaedias, a bag of handbags from a local charity shop, a computer (which he assured me still works) and an unwanted video camera that had belonged to the head teacher. *'Martin had told me to put them in the "wheel house,"'* he said. Thank you, Billy, for all your trouble.

Wednesday 26/08/2009

9:01 a.m. Home. I am calling Daniel, information officer at the Social Enterprise Academy, Edinburgh, who sent me an email yesterday offering me a place on their graduate coaching scheme? I am going for it. All donations gratefully received: there are four

90-minute sessions with an executive coach. We'll see what comes from this.

Thursday 27/08/2009

11:39 a.m. Home. Typing notes. The sun is shining, beginning to beam through once more. I am going to cycle round the island. Austin calls to tell me that there is little left at the high school that is worth taking. I thought as much a while ago.

2:36 p.m. I have spoken to Matt, who tells me that the Paisley site is not suitable, but there may be premises available in Stirling. He will get back to me. He is keen that I find suitable storage. '*Let's make it happen,*' he said.

Friday 28/08/2009

11:41 a.m. Home. I received a call earlier from of M&K Construction Ltd to say that they there was indeed equipment and educational resources at the former Lochgilphead High School premises worth salvaging. He thought I had meant IT equipment. He told me to call Tony to arrange another appointment. I then called Ailsa to tell her of this development. She then told me that the housing association board meeting yesterday had agreed to donate £400 to the Surplus Educational Supplies Foundation to cover costs for the removal of educational resources, and that she would continue with her efforts to have a fundraiser.

My hopes are raised once more. I am a sucker for punishment. I have spent the morning writing letters to Tom Fordyce, supporter and Prayer Partner, and Matthew, surveyor and asset disposal manager with Tesco headquarters. It has been a wet, wet, dreich day so far, and I am going to cycle in to Rothesay to post correspondence and get some messages.

Sunday 30/08/2009

4:30 p.m. Home. I received a call from David, the doctor from Kenya who has been shown the educational resources in Unit 3 Glenrothes by Renwick Cowan, to tell me that some of it is broken. Okay. You don't need to take it. He is making arrangements with the Kenyan government. He tells me he wants IT equipment. I suggested he contact schools in Kirkcaldy directly.

Thursday 03/09/2009

2:39 p.m. Home. I have just cycled back from having lunch with Gordon, who was showing me his digital snaps of his recent trip to Madeira and Alt Berlin, where he was posted with the British Army on the Rhine, and is a lad o' many pairts from Greenock City. He told me that his secondary school geography teacher would send his class down to the port as an assignment to research the ships and cargoes that had docked at Ocean Terminal. I told Gordon that was a teacher after my own heart.

Checking emails. *'I am in the middle of a meeting right now. I'll call you back when I am free,'* said Peter, transport manager. He is brusque. I eat humble pie. For the meek shall inherit the earth, for their faces are already in it.

3:06 p.m. I sit here and wait. It was worth waiting.

3:51 p.m. I spoke with Peter once more, who said Russell would pick up, gratis, the boxes of library books from the Edinburgh Community Transport depot at the Elizafield Industrial Estate on Monday and would pallet them. I am so grateful; these acts of kindness encourage me to keep on keeping on with this initiative. I have just called Jimmy, the team leader, to let him know and asked him if he could get some digitals of his team loading Russell's vehicle. I then called Patrick at Warrant Freight

Ltd in Liverpool to let him know that the Surplus Educational Supplies Foundation donation of library books for the Bluefields Community on Nicaragua's Mosquito Coast was underway.

Friday 04/09/2009

10:27 a.m. Home. I called Adam, the journalist at the Edinburgh News, and asked if they could highlight the important work done by Edinburgh Community Transport service teams, in particular the work that their teams had carried out in the collection and storage of boxes of library books for over two years now. I left a message. He has not replied. Stale news. I call the Morningside Library; I speak with Rhona. Their surplus shelving may become available later in the year when the library is due to be refurbished.

2:34 p.m. That's Marion and Johanna left to go kayaking. I am going to go for a cycle round the island. The sun is shining through the windows at the end of the corridor. I am using my will.

5:45 p.m. I return to an empty home.

Monday 07/09/2009

2:42 p.m. Home. With Marion. Overhead the sun is shining out of a clear blue sky, after a very wet last few days; it is a blessing for me to see the sun shining through once more. Marion is making plum jam with oor ain plums. '*We plan for tomorrow and live for today,*' sang Mr Jimmy Cliff.

Earlier today I called Jimmy at Edinburgh Community Transport to learn that Russell, Coatbridge, had sent a vehicle through to pick up the 40-plus boxes from their storage unit at the Elizafield Industrial unit, Newhaven Road; that's another leg of the journey out to Bluefields, Mosquito Coast, completed. Now Russell will pallet approximately one cubic metre (1,000 kg) of books, which will be delivered down to the Warrant Group Vanguard Freight Ltd. I will pay the tariff to Nicaragua.

Tuesday 08/09/2009

4:40 p.m. Home. I have been speaking to Jimmy, the team leader of Edinburgh Community Transport. I hope to meet up with him tomorrow after my 'coaching session' at the Social Enterprise Academy. I am calling George McGuire, St George's University, Grenada. I spoke to him. *'We'll see what we can do, we keep our standards high,'* he said. So do I! I then called Philip, who is now principal of the Grenada Boys' Secondary.

'You have to fail to learn,' said Peter Cochrane. In that case, Peter, I have sure done an awful lot of learning.

Wednesday 09/09/2009

8:36 a.m. It is a beautiful sun-lit morning as the bus bumps its way up Cathedral Street. It has stopped at the lights opposite Allan Glen Road. The sun is shining into my face and now through some trees planted at the edge of the car park across from the Royal Infirmary.

The bus is moving a lot faster now that we are on the M8 motorway. The sun is shining out of cloudless sky. On my arrival earlier at Central Station I had walked up Buchanan Street to the bus station, having resisted the temptation to take a taxi. I noticed the massive wrought-iron gates at the entrance to the railway station and reflected on the amount of collaborative skills that had gone into making them many years ago, and the almost endless litany of glorious names that had laid down their lives for freedom 1914–1918.

We will see what I can learn today. A long traffic jam stretches its way into the city as we head east into more sunshine.

3:40 p.m. I am on the train back tae Glesga Queen Street looking back the way: I usually face the direction in which I am travelling. Okay, after the British breakfast at the British Home Stores café on Rose Street, I walked back up the street to number 5 and up tae the third floor, where I was welcomed by Daniel and ushered through the open-plan office to meet Barry from Ulster, the coach who is casually smart. He says he tells it like it is and he would let me know at the end of the session whether or not he would see me for another; he wanted my personal history and assured me that everything I said would be confidential. Ha ha!

He wanted to know whether I was financially challenged. He gave me a short personality profile and thinking style test. I'm in the right-brained quadrant, along with the other 65% of the population. I could have told him it fits the entrepreneurial profile, blah, blah. He told me that I would have trouble with the other 35%, the left-brained, logical thinking geeks, bureaucrats, number-crunching, nit-picking, and risk averse population. He said we can meet again on 22 September at 1:30 p.m., when he wishes for us to discuss my 'business plan and executive summary'. I told him that I needed assistance from those who fit the 35% profile in order for my social enterprise initiative to succeed financially. I have said that as much already, if he had bothered to read my brief profile, which I had submitted in the application for this Social Academy coaching course.

Okay, where do we go from here? For Coach Barry, the problem for me is: 'How do we package what you have to offer?' At least that's something to focus on. The hour and a half session went quickly. Coach Barry kept to the time allotted as he had another appointment. I showed him my folder, which he glanced at and said, '*I don't want to be dismissive.*' I left there and got a taxi out to the Elizafield Industrial Estate, Newhaven Road.

I had phoned Jimmy. I am learning how to use my 66th birthday present mobile phone. Many thanks Marion, my luv. Jimmy had arranged to meet me. I met their current team, who were sorting through piles of library books. I was made a cup of tea. I can work with them and it is a privilege to meet these youngsters engaged in constructive and useful projects: there will be an ongoing supply of books, and there were more resources to collect. They will call me at the end of the month when they have several pallets. Contact Russell in Coatbridge to make the collection. We'll see when the time comes. Presume on none. The team at Edinburgh Community Transport, Elizafield Industrial Estate, are positive: they want me to write a brief article for their monthly magazine. The sun has continued to shine all afternoon.

I got a bus back to Princes Street, eventually, from a bus stop on Newhaven Road. I then walked back to Haymarket Station. Impulsively I stopped off at Danzig Accountants, where I met one of their partners, Donald, who heard me out. No pro bono expertise from that quarter.

6:30 p.m. Aboard the MV *Argyle* as usual. I am on deck and the sun is shining on Rothesay Bay.

Thursday 10/09/2009

10:25 p.m. Home. I am back in the doldrums, stuck in the Sargasso Sea, where I feel that I am going nowhere. The typeface on the word processor has changed: frustration and annoyance. Leave it be for the time being. I am going to head out and cycle once more round the Isle of Bute. This time, for me, is the worst – anticipating the struggle of cycling up those wee, long, hills with no energy to speak of. There are thick banks of damp grey cloud above of me.

Friday 11/09/2009

6:29 p.m. Home. The sun shone brightly this morning and it is still a beautiful day. I try to take the weather as it comes. One day at a time. I had toothache and migraine but I managed to keep going. I walked into Rothesay via Canada Hill and doon the Minister's Brae, and stopped off at Cowal builders' merchants to purchase a wire brush for the grinder; I get a welcome from Ronny and Christo. I helped myself to a cup of free soup from the machine and stepped outside to enjoy it in the sunshine. I walked on past the library and met my former colleague at the Port, who comes from St Catherine's, Ontario, and shot the breeze for a few minutes. On and down Bishop's Street and into Print Point to buy ink for the printer, and round the block into Bute Naturally to collect SESF brochures, which Phil proprietor of Bute Naturally, had printed off for me.

6:36 p.m. 'Dad!' That's Johanna calling me for supper.

Monday 14/09/2009

11:06 a.m. Home. I have arrived back from the Toon. I had been to see Harry, the dentist. He gave me a reprieve from having the offending tooth pulled and prescribed another course of penicillin, then I walked along to the Victoria Hotel for a white coffee and a look the oot windae. A light, cool breeze blew off the Kyle of Bute and Rothesay Bay. I had a quick read of *The Scotsman*. Earlier I had been to RBS, where helpful Caroline sorted my cheque books. On the way out of town I stopped to speak to Margaret, who sits at the entrance to her café and tells me that Paula is counting the days till a certain person comes home. I then stepped a few yards along the pavement and stopped in at Bute Naturally to chat briefly with Anne (Phil is off the island), and then on to the Co-op and got some messages. I met Michael coming out. '*Hi, Mike,*' I said. You are a gregarious soul: so be it, I am a social being and in these days of Global Village pandemic, total cultural reset, analogue social interaction cannot be a thing of the past, because I don't do social media and we need each other, for better or worse.

When I got home I called Patrick regarding the shipment of books to the Mosquito Coast. He will contact his dad, Peter Kilfoyle MP, who has returned from Nicaragua. Patrick told me that the Ministry of Education in Managua would waive the charges to Bluefields. We'll have to wait and see. The Warrant Group deals with Vanguard.

Tuesday 15/09/2009

11:06 a.m. Home. I have returned from the health centre where I saw Andrew, who prescribed another medicine for migraine pain. Co-codamol? I whizzed back down Castle Street and stopped off at Print Point for more publicity stuff, copies of articles about the work of SESF that have appeared in the press, and then along to Bute Naturally for more of the same, which was not ready. Then back up the main drag to the Victoria Hotel for a coffee, where I was chatting to Emilio who comes from Bratislava in Slovakia. He is unhappy with his lot here on the island as he wishes to return to Wyoming, USA, where he had been living until immigration authorities told him to leave the country. He tells me that he has a friend in Nicaragua. And here I am back on our hearth. What do I do now? Finish folding another stack of SESF brochures.

Wednesday 16/09/2009

7:46 a.m. Home. Marion has just called to tell me that there is a message from Grenada, which had come yesterday afternoon when I had gone out for a walk after tea.

10:10 a.m. The printer has packed up. I am going to push pedal myself once more around the island.

1:01 p.m. I have arrived back at the cottage; there is sunshine on the door step. I am going to make myself a sardine sandwich and sit outside.

It was not for long. I am now calling the Grenada Boys' Secondary School. *'What's your package, David?'* asked Social Enterprise Academy Coach Barry. My reply to him was: *'Matching the fit-for-purpose educational resources that SESF currently has stored in warehouses and in ocean freight containers to what the partner schools in the underdeveloped nations of the world require.'*

I was speaking to Stuart, trying to elicit more publicity. My news is stale. Calling Andy at Pentalver Transport Ltd, Leeds, who has cut me so much slack in the past but who tells me, *'Ah got nowt, David!'* I call Howard, he can sell me a 40-foot ocean freight container for £980, but he cannot assure me that it is seaworthy. He takes no prisoners. I then call Carson Transport Ltd, Cumbernauld – £1,667.50 for a 40-foot high cube. They don't take any prisoners either. There is no sentiment in business. What do I expect from these people? A free handout? I will continue to pay my way, and the going rate for ocean freight containers for as long as I am able to do so.

3:45 p.m. Calling GBSS. I wrote a thank-you letter to Fraser, the operations manager at Freightliner Ltd, Coatbridge.

Thursday 17/09/2009

9:45 a.m. Home. I received a call from Peter, the transport manager with Russell, Coatbridge, to say they do not have any 'boxes' for sale. I took the opportunity and I thanked him for giving me the time of day, and for all the pro bono assistance I have received from John G Russell Transport Ltd. Being civil, appreciative, cheerful, helpful and, above all, gracious online, and face-to-face goes a long way in my book. Peter told me that Russell would waive their charges for collecting the boxes of library books for Nicaragua, Bluefields Schools, from the Edinburgh Community

Transport storage unit, paletting them for uplift by Vanguard Transport Ltd and the delivery to Manchester.

What more can I ask? But in return I will continue to acknowledge and celebrate their assistance and many others in the pages of my diary.

10:57 a.m. It's high time I stopped tapping out these scribbles. The sun is shining and I am going to sit outside for a while and harvest a few sunbeams. I do not sit still for long as I will not get anywhere fast otherwise. I am going to make another call to Stuart at Pentalver Transport Ltd in the Port of Southampton. I was speaking to Mandy in the office, who is helpful and tells me to call back later. No joy!

12:42 p.m. I am going to cycle into the town to post another cheque to Active 24, the Norway-based outfit that hosts www.haitirelief.org.uk.

Friday 18/09/2009

11:50 a.m. Home. I am back from Greenock City where I had an appointment with James Ross, Chartered Accountant, Brougham Street at 9:30 a.m. After a hard pedal against the wind and drizzle I barely managed to make the 6:30 a.m. ferry. *'You don't need to pay,'* she said. Ticket office. I forgot and am not accustomed to this travelling across the watta for free. On the way over I was chatting to the Mellish family, who were among the supportive parents, who tell me that they are keen to send educational supplies to Tanzania. They had a tree planter/forester from that country talking to the pupils. They know someone in that country who teaches 60 pupils in the morning and another 60 pupils in the afternoon. They ask, *'You think you had it hard at the Port?'*

While on the boat I met a friendly couple with their little dogs, who they were taking to the vet, and they kindly gave me a lift as far as Tesco. I walked round the block, and past Clyde Port Marine Terminal storage yards with boxes stacked to the skies. I left an SESF brochure with the guard at the gate security on the port's Patrick Street entrance and walked back up the road to Tesco's café for a roll 'n' egg and pot of tea, scanned *The Herald*, and on the way out bought a copy of *The Big Issue*. Back up the Gourock Road to meet James Ross Junior at 9:30 a.m.

I trust him completely, and let him and his Dunoon-based firm get on with it. He wears a Rotary badge pinned to the lapel of his jacket. He tells me that a group from the town got resources from Dunoon Academy before I did and sent a container load to Africa. Brilliant work! He told me that he does a lot of work for charities. I left my two folders of records and container purchase invoices with him. Jim has a sense of humour and my gut instinct is to leave all this information with him. He has a firm handshake and is certainly shrewd. More importantly, he and his firm have offered more than I had ever the right to expect – to audit the Surplus Educational Supplies Foundation, Scottish Registered Charity (SCO39331), and Company Registered in Scotland, No. 337348, accounts on a no-fee basis., which is absolutely wonderful of him!

12:03 p.m. I am going to chill out for a wee while. It is dry and cool autumn weather.

12:51 p.m. I am still not chilling. I called Yvonne, the sales person at Eldapoint Containers Ltd, Grangemouth, about boxes. She is always helpful and is going to call me back. I send an email to Steve, DFID, East Kilbride. I received an email from Patrick at Warrant Freight Ltd, who tells me that the pallet-load of library books left the Port of Felixstowe: they were loaded aboard the Maersk Danbury bound for Managua, Nicaragua. I spoke with Rachel at Warrant reception who said, '*You sound really happy.*' '*Yes, Rachel, I am very happy,*' I said for my heart was bursting with

Friday 18/09/2009

Dinamarca school staff sorting the shipment.

thanksgiving, in spite of all the trachles it took for me to get that modest shipment of books to where they would do some good, instead of being pulped and tipped into landfill. That was my reward.

Monday 21/09/2009

1 p.m. Home. That was David Alexander who just called. He arrived back home in Scotland last night and stayed with Gran, Marion, and Johanna in Kilbarchan. They went up to Glasgow this morning to do some shopping. I have been waiting for him to return safely. Bless his heart. He has been at sea for the last six months. It is a blanket grey sky with continuous smirry rain. I'll continue to hold the fort here for the present.

2:15 p.m. Johanna has come home from school not feeling well, she was asked, '*Is there any one at home?*' You bet there is, her dad!

Obtain VAT information from Lesley and her team at One 2 One Accountancy Services, Rothesay.

Tuesday 22/09/2009

8:47 a.m. I am on the Citylink bus bound for Edinburgh. The sun is shining down on Cathedral Street. I noticed earlier that the trees that had been planted beside Buchanan Street Station have grown. The streets are thronged with students. Cheery bus driver. I have made an early start.

I have an appointment with social enterprise coach Barry, which is not until 1:30 p.m. I will visit the National Portrait Gallery.

1:22 p.m. 5 Rose Street. The Melting Pot, 4th Floor. I have just arrived.

Earlier I had walked through Princes Street Gardens. Sunshine breaking through. I stopped off at the National Galleries of

Tuesday 22/09/2009

Scotland. Lots of children from private schools dutifully pausing to absorb a visual feast, and a little group of tinies from a nursery school seated in front of a painting of a monkey eating fruit. The great portraitists are in abundance: Constable, Raeburn, Raphael. Too much for me to take in all at once. Into the café for a cheese 'n' tomato sandwich and a pot of tea. I looked out the big window, east towards the George IV bridge with double-decker buses crossing to and fro, and, out of sight, Arthur's Seat.

I walked on and stopped at the big baroque fountain and looked up to Castlerock and the castle. On I strolled to St Cuthbert's churchyard and met Anna, the gardener, and we got into conversation. She knows Jean Rennie, who was my Moray House College of Education, Post Graduate Certificate in Education, practice teacher at Silverknowes Primary School, Pilton, North Edinburgh in the autumn of 1974. She said that she would tell her that we had met.

(And as I type these words this evening of Tuesday, 25 January 2022 I recall that Marion told me earlier Jean passed away to a better place last Thursday, 20 January 2022. Rest in Peace, my dear friend.)

Anna the gardener said she also knew Iain Lusk, my mathematics lecturer at what was Moray House College of Education, down the Royal Mile. I have come full circle. I am not finished yet. No way, José!

Here I record hurriedly taken notes from that second 'coaching session' with Coach Barry, who tells me he has an MBA. I record some of what he said: *'Did you have a plan for your visit to Grenada? You must get tactical and operational. You must get problem solving on the ground. You need to look at the strategy.'*

Now there's a word, strategy, I had not thought of before. *'You need to be strategic. You must get the overall picture and put it in context, you need to describe the big picture,'* he said.

I am not sure at this point what this will involve as I hurriedly try to jot down these pearls of business administration wisdom.

He continues, '*When you return from your fact-finding mission, this is what you will say: Here are the schools and this what they need. Deliver your story about these schools. You need: a board; to build a business plan that looks like this; your supporters; and you need some funding. All sorts of questions that the directors, the funders, wait to ask you. It will be a Dragon's Den interrogation.*

'*Here's the overarching need. Look, you must be on a businesslike footing, or it will fail. It will not last, it must be run in a businesslike way. What do you do about partners? You need an advisory board. Here's an inventory of need from the British Embassy in Central America, they are desperate for stuff. You have to solve problems, David, I repeat, your project will not last. There must be a rational way of getting through this. You have not got a clear idea of what is required and what the need is, and you need to quantify it. You have to get this initiative of yours into a rational form. Listen, and have the big picture story. Show proof obtained from the British Embassy in Central America. Enlist and get their support. Keep Ambassador Tom Kennedy on side and nurture him back to focus.*'

All of what he said had me baffled, and I was overwhelmed. This session had me feeling that I had not achieved very much for all my hard work, at no little personal cost, over the past four years. This session had brought home to me how disorganised I was and as someone had said, 'you move from one crisis to the next.'

(*I did not know it at the time, but several months later I did indeed make a short fact-finding trip to Bluefields, Nicaragua, Central America at the behest of the British Embassy in San José, Costa Rica [see diary notes 14/12/2009–18/12/2009] where I saw for myself what was required by a number of schools. And I would, over the next eight years, attempt to put into practice the advice given to me that afternoon by Coach Barry. I was later that year to send an email to Bruce Callow, British Embassy official.* 'Bruce, I need to have a clear sense, an indication of what the anglophone schools in Bluefields and El Bluff require. Please help me.' *I never got from him or the ambassador what the educational needs of the hurricane devastated schools in Bluefields and the outlying communities of the Costa Caribena were. I must record here that I was never to receive this crucial information.*)

Thursday 24/09/2009

6:37 a.m. I am onboard a humming and shuddering MV *Argyle* heading for Wemyss Bay. The MacKirdy driver, who took the containers to Russell Transport depot in Coatbridge last year, has bought me a coffee. His act of kindness sets me up for the rest of the day. Here I am, perched, going to Stirling to meet with surveyor Iain, who will show me a possible unit for the storage of educational resources and parking space for ocean freight containers. I told him that I would be at 31 Kerse Road, a former Pickford's Removal warehouse.

I just made the ferry before it shoved off. It is a damp and humid morning. I stepped, or should I shipped, out another journey across the watta, trusting and trying, which is all I can do. And whatever the end result of this initiative for the Surplus Educational Supplies Foundation, Scottish Registered Charity (SCO39331) and Scottish Registered Company No. 337348, I will be confident that I did all that I was capable of doing and I had left, as the saying goes, 'no stone unturned.'

Yesterday, I attended the Scottish Learning and Teaching Festival at the Scottish Exhibition Centre in Glasgow. I managed to distribute my flyers to a good few Scottish local authorities, a number of trade stands and individual teachers and visitors. And I can only await the results of that marketing and publicity seeking effort. I also pitched my spiel to the principal of Newbattle College.

The day before I was in Edinburgh for a coaching session with Barry, tutor at the Social Enterprise Academy, whose advice was to stay small so that I don't lose control and get to the stage where I am unable to manage. Remain focused on Grenada, West Indies and find out whether there is still a need for fit-for-purpose educational resources in their government schools since the devastation wrought by Hurricane Ivan on 7 September 2004. I have already, to some extent, been following that advice.

11:25 a.m. Corn Exchange Pub, Stirling, where I have consumed their full Scottish breakfast. I'll need to walk some distance in order to burn that off. The sun is shining on the road outside. I arrived in this town by bus from Glasgow Buchanan Street Station. A slow journey through the towns of Kilsyth, Denny, and Bankrock. On arrival I walked up to the taxi rank opposite the railway station and asked the taxi driver to take me to 31 Kerse Road in the Stirling Enterprise Park.

I am in familiar surroundings as I had walked past this industrial estate last year, when I was doing the 'prepare a business plan' course, courtesy of the Edinburgh Social Enterprise Academy. If this is the warehouse, it will have to do for the time being. I did not need to hang around, took the taxi back into the town centre and was dropped off at the Stirling Library, up the street from where I am, writing up my diary and trying to keep track of my safari. What's next? I will walk around the town until 2 p.m. and then make my way back across to the Kerse Road warehouse.

2:55 p.m. I am sitting on a low brick wall at the entrance to the Stirling Enterprise Park. The sun is shining on the page as I write these words, and nearby is what was once a Pickford's Removal depot. I must sit and wait for the arrival of Iain the surveyor.

Roll it back a few hours. I had walked down from the full Scottish cooked breakfast hostelry and stopped in at Jessops Digital Photographers, and purchased a small camera and a pair of binoculars for Marion from a very helpful and switched-on sales assistant, the young Andrew, who was on my wavelength regarding climate change and the impending collapse of the Blue Planet ecosystem. He complimented me on my efforts to do something about it. I walked under the shopping centre, and around and under the roundabout, and up past Kentucky Fried Chicken. Here I had had supper one evening last year.

The sun continues to shine brightly.

3:09 p.m. I have just got on the wrong train! This one is going to Edinburgh! Ach weel, the helpful conductor told me to get off at Larbert Station and in 15 minutes I'd get the train for Glasgow.

3:31 p.m. Sun shining. No panic. Keep calm and carry on. Haud yer piece and don't lose yur peace, and possess your soul in patience. Well, what of the appointment with the surveyor?

Iain turned up on time, as he said he would, and prior to that I had a long read of David Alexander's gift to me of Pirates. Somali Thugs. The premises are suitable. The dead seagull on the warehouse floor unsettled me from the start – apart from that, no complaints, beggars can't be choosers. Iain is now going to clear the lease with his superiors at Tesco and his boss Matthew. He was approachable and open about the background of the property, and has two other properties adjacent to Number 31, but they did not have parking space for containers. Well, nothing is ever definite, but there is the likelihood that I may be a little closer to finding a base of operation in the central belt for the Surplus Educational Supplies Foundation social enterprise.

Friday 25/09/2009

8:30 a.m. Home. I call Eldapoint in Grangemouth and speak to Yvonne in sales. I call the Grenada High Commission in London and speak with officials to determine to what extent, does there still exist, a need for educational resources in Grenada's schools post Hurricane Ivan? I pose the question. The ball is in my court to find out. Research. Is it worth my while to get back out there

The Galt Transport team.

and find out for myself? If so, I will need some funding for this.

Call Tom Walker regarding ISO inspection of the container at Eldapoint depot. Send emails to the business people who handed me their business cards at SEEC on Wednesday.

11:11 a.m. Amy is safely back in Scotland.
'*Hi, David, its Gerry from Interserve, can you give me a wee call please on … I need to know what kind of stuff you are looking for. I think I have more stuff that would interest you. Want to give me a call please?*' This turns out to be a ploy for me to get in touch with him. I call him. The site manager of Interserve Projects Ltd, he informs me that the SESF container GATU4072944 happens to still be in the Inveralmond Community High School, Livingston, car park and must be shifted soon. It was not moved by WH

Malcolm Transport Ltd to their depot at Newhouse, as had been arranged weeks ago.

I am calling Philip, who is now the principal of Grenada Boys' Secondary School, St George's, Grenada. He tells me that he is in a meeting. Do I persist with my solo attempts to send another 40-foot container shipment of educational resources to this school? I certainly have to persevere with the Surplus Educational Supplies Foundation for the forseeable future.

(I was not to know then that I was to make two further shipments to Grenada government schools in 2011 and 2016. However it appeared to me then that I would have to draw a line under sending any more educational resources to that part of the Blue Planet. As it turned out, I shipped another 40-foot container of educational resources (MAEU6085656) on 16 October 2010 to the Grenada Boys' Secondary School. Thanks for this shipment must go to: Peter, transport manager, John G Russell (Transport) Ltd, Coatbridge; Fraser Russell, operations manager, Freightliner Ltd, Coatbridge; Roland Malins-Smith, president, Seafreight Agencies Lines Inc., Miami.)

4:53 p.m. I have just spoken to the First Secretary of the Grenada High Commission in London and all I get from them is a lot of sweet talk.

5:05 p.m. Calling Patrick at Warrant Freight Ltd, Port of Liverpool, regarding the shipment of 40 boxes of library books to Bluefields, Nicaragua. I tell him that I would like to speak to his dad, the Member of Parliament, if it were possible and if he could he give me Bruce Callow's (the British Embassy official in San José, Costa Rica) telephone number. I hope to find out from him what educational resources are most needed by schools and colleges in Bluefields.

8:15 p.m. Philip, principal of GBSS has just called while Amy was showing us the digital images of her stay in Blantyre, Malawi, and her voluntary work in an orphanage there for the charity Open Arms. She has done a lot of good work in six weeks. Philip wanted to contribute to the cost of shipping the container to Grenada Boys' Secondary School.

I told him that was not necessary. Somehow or other I will see if firms in Grenada will give me, the SESF, a charity tariff rate just to Kingston, Jamaica; from there Seafreight Agencies Lines Inc will do the rest, pro bono, to deliver the container to St George's, Grenada.

Saturday 26/09/2009

2:01 p.m. Home. For next week. To do:
1. Research current situation post Hurricane Ivan.
2. I will need to bring my container at ICHS Livingston to 'my depot' in Stirling. I await news from Iain, the surveyor for Tesco, owner of the property, as he awaits instructions from Matthew.
3. Make arrangements to ship container MAEU8065656 full of educational resources to GBBS, since by Philip's account they want the resources (tables, chairs etc.) that I and the team uplifted last year from the former Rothesay Academy, or was it the year before in 2007? The container is at Russell, Coatbridge. I must try and get some clearance from the Grenada Government representatives at their High Commission in London.
4. Contact John, the freight forwarder, who is now no longer with Denholm Bahr Ltd.
5. Contact Birke Owen at ZIM, also in Port of Liverpool, and Louise of Knight Swanson Ltd Freight Forwarders, Port of Grangemouth for quotes.
6. Contact Yvonne, sales at Eldapoint container dealers, regarding my recent purchase of a 40-foot container. I sent them a cheque last week.

Monday 28/09/2009

7. Contact Tom Walker, container surveyor, regarding a possible ISO inspection of the container.
8. Find out from Archie, Graeme, and team leaders, Community Services Criminal Justice Department, Glenrothes, if they can supply SESF with a team to load the container.
9. Collect VAT data from Lesley and her team at One 2 One Accountancy Services.

Monday 28/09/2009

8:20 a.m. Home. I am making arrangements to ship MAEU8065656. Obtaining quotes from Scotland to Kingston, Jamaica, West Indies. I am trying to maintain the focus. Get the facts. Funding – not much of that at the moment. I am to see Coach Barry at Edinburgh Social Enterprise Academy for the final session, and possibly Sanjay afterwards. I spoke with John Sas, the freight forwarder, regarding quotes to Kingston, Jamaica. '*Leave it with me, I will call you back,*' he said. John keeps his word. We met over the phone on Friday, 1 July 2005, when he helped me ship my first container to Grenada.

I call Birke Owen at ZIM, Port of Liverpool, for a quote. I spoke to Donya, who tells me, '*Birke is on holiday. I'll see what I can do for you.*' Then I called Patrick at Warrant Freight Ltd in Liverpool, who will give me a quote. '*I suggest you ship your container from Grangemouth, as it is always best from Scotland.*' The tariff he gives me is £1,055. He is informative, cheerful, and helpful, but he will not give me Bruce's Callow's telephone number. Why not?

I called the Grenada High Commission and sent a message to Leonie. I sent another email to Denholm Bahr Ltd, Port of Liverpool. Ray Perkins, who was very helpful to me, has retired. To call: Yvonne at Eldapoint Ltd depot in Port of Grangemouth

10:40 a.m. I have just received a quote from Donya at ZIM:

£2,616 including haulage. Called Sanjay, and sent him an SESF flyer. Called Alan at A&M Parcels. He is going across to the mainland later this week and says he may be able to deliver the boxes at the Caribbean Hurricane Relief Depot, Port Bannatyne, to my container at Russell, Coatbridge. Contact Peter, transport manager, Russell, to let him know that I hope to ship MAEU6085656 to the Grenada Boys' Secondary School, Grenada and will need to paint over the Maersk decals and I will need his permission to come into the yard. I spoke to Paul? As it turned out the decals remained.

Send an email to Donya at ZIM with details regarding shipment to Grenada. Contact Gary, freight forwarder at Knight Watson Ltd, Grangemouth for their quote.

4:33 p.m. I am awaiting a return call from Paul? at Russell, Coatbridge. I am to call again tomorrow. Will Russell waive haulage? Call Fraser, Russell accounts manager, Freightliner Ltd Container Base, Coatbridge, next week, regarding rail freight of container to the Port of Tilbury. Will they waive the haulage? I can only ask. Another 'free haul' of which I have had not a few. I know that there is no such thing as a 'free lunch' or a 'free lift'.

Tuesday 29/09/2009

9:15 a.m. Home. I called Eldapoint Ltd regarding the recent container purchase. I left a message for Paul at Russell, Coatbridge. Posed the question – will they waive the cost of haulage of SESF container MAEU6085656 to the Port of Tilbury?

As it turned out, Freightliner Ltd, Coatbridge waived 'haulage' for the rail freight all the way. Brilliant! Goodwill! Pro Bono! I am so grateful and encouraged, notwithstanding the personal cost and the toll it has taken on every member of the Family Hanschell since this initiative began. A leg up is all I need.

Wednesday 30/09/2009

9:22 a.m. I called Yvonne, Eldapoint Ltd, regarding GATU4033193, who tells me that it can stay onsite for the time being. I then called Renwick, estates surveyor, Fife Council, who reassured me that there is no need to uplift the educational resources that are stored in Unit 3 just yet. GREAT! Good on him and Gillian!

Then I called One 2 One Accountancy Services Ltd, Rothesay, who tell me I can collect VAT returns to send on to Ross & Co Accountants, Dunoon. Both of these firms have given me, the Surplus Educational Supplies Foundation, their services free of charge and by doing so have made it possible for the foundation to function as a viable and credible entity – whether or not the prime mover, CEO, is such is another matter for you reader to decide. My besetting sin is, when given intuitive and instinctive gut feeling warnings, I press on. I will not please everyone and and will antagonise many.

11 a.m. I cycled into the town to collect VAT Returns from Lesley and then over to hand them to Jim Ross at their Rothesay office who said they would be in contact with me.

1:20 p.m. Home alone and not alone. David Alexander has gone up to the gym at Rothesay Baths.

'Happiness is more valuable than all the riches in the world, and doing the right thing the most important of all,' Peter Cochran.

Wednesday 30/09/2009

10:41 a.m. Home. David is scraping the wallpaper off the walls of his bedroom. He is no slacker. Bless him.

I am about to call Steve at the Department for International Development (DFID) Abercrombie House, East Kilbride. I sent him an email on 18 September and I have had no reply since. Called Tim Byam in Grenada, who is an associate of Robin Swaisland and is currently engaged in building a marina. *'He's a lay preacher.*' I called on 27 September. No answer, called again at 10:45 p.m. Left message. '*He's in a meetin' right now.*'

I'm off to the post office. Call Active 24 in Norway: I am customer. I am unable to access www.grenadarelief.org.uk, the site that was built for me by Kevin Sayers pro bono. (Now www.haiti-relief.org.uk thanks to Sam Tweedlie.)

Monday 05/10/2009

1:01 p.m. Home. I am in the midst of making contact with many individuals and companies via the telephone. I call Jim, container control at John G. Russell (Transport) Ltd, Coatbridge. He has told me that it will be okay for John MacKirdy Transport Ltd, Rothesay, to drop off the pallet of boxes that they collected this morning from the Caribbean Hurricane Relief Depot, Port Bannatyne. I am so grateful. Jim tells me that container MAEU6085656 has been shifted over to Freightliner Ltd, who will deliver it, rail freight, to the Port of Tilbury. As always I am most grateful for his unstinting assistance and advice.

Then I spoke with John MacKirdy Junior to see if it was okay for them to take the pallet of boxes up this evening and drop it off at Russell Coatbridge. He told me that they could do it for me. Check invoices.

1:45 p.m. BE STILL! David Alexander has gone to the gym up at the Rothesay Baths and I am going to do the dishes. Here I outline, briefly, the process of delivering a container of educational resources from Scotland to a secondary school in Grenada, West Indies.

1. MacKirdy Transport Ltd, the local haulier since 1870, collect boxes from the Caribbean Hurricane Relief Depot at Stirling Yacht Services Ltd, Boat Yard, Port Bannatyne, which they pallet and shrink-wrap at their warehouse, and which they deliver to Russell, Coatbridge, later that day 5 October 2009.

2. The boxes were loaded into my SESF container by myself, with help from Raymond on 6 October 2009.
3. The container was transferred across to Freightliner Ltd, rail-freighted to the Port of Tilbury and shipped by ZIM Lines to Kingston, Jamaica.
4. The container was shipped by Seafreight Agencies Lines, Miami, from Kingston to St George's, Grenada on 22 October 2009.
5. Container MAEU6085656 arrives St George's, Grenada, 19 November 2009.
6. The contents of the container were received by GBSS on 25 November 2009.

'We all need to make a positive contribution to as many activities as possible, to the best of our ability,' Peter Cochran.

I move forward with the process of solving the problems involved in shipping another container. I must obtain the invoice from Eldapoint Ltd for the SESF purchase of GATU4033193. They tell me that their head office in Liverpool will send it to me. I am going to ask accountant Jim in the Dunoon office to send me a letter. He wants to know who the SESF cheques were for. He continues to be a tower of support, and his firm have not billed me for the services that SESF has received from them.

4:21 p.m. I have just had a call from Matthew, the Tesco stores surveyor down south somewhere, to say that providing I pay 20% of the rates, they are happy to let me have the use of what was formerly Pickfords Removals warehouse in Stirling. I may be able to persuade Stirling Council to reduce, or better still waive, the rates altogether. Time will tell.

I Meet the Secret Millionaire and Travel Far Further

Tuesday 06/10/2009

7:15 a.m. I am on a creaking, moving train leaving Wemyss Bay Station en route for Glasgow and Coatbridge (Sunnyside), and along to John G Russell (Transport) Ltd. I hope to squeeze another 19 boxes of educational resources, which I have collected over many months, from inside my Grey Adams 20-foot reefer at the Caribbean Hurricane Relief Depot into the bigger box, the 40-foot ocean freight container MAEU6085656. My second SESF shipment of fit-for-purpose, surplus to requirements, educational resources for the Grenada Government's Ministry of Education Grenada Boys' Secondary School.

Here begins another working day for me. Some time ago now a near neighbour described my charitable social enterprise initiative as an expensive hobby. Well a hobby it definitely is not and I would rather on this day be doing some physical and practical work, gardening out the back of Delhi Cottage below the Craigmore Cliff.

10 a.m. Drizzling, dreich morning where I am in this huge container and road transport depot. There are 40-foot ocean freight containers stacked all around me – up to 10 of them. Cries of gulls. It must be rough out on the high seas for them to be so far inland. Jim O'Donnell, the container transport manager, has brought me from his office to my SESF container. I am glad that it belongs to me. Ownership of property is a great feeling.

He has asked a forklift driver from his team to bring the shrink-wrapped pallet-load of boxes over from a massive warehouse not far from where we were standing. Initially, Jim had thought that the pallet had not been delivered. I experienced worry, anxiety, and disappoint all at once, but I kept my cool, I stayed calm (HIS PEACE) and called John MacKirdy the haulier in Rothesay. John assured me that the pallet had, in fact, been delivered and so here I am, about to climb into my boiler suit, don my high-viz yellow

Wednesday 07/10/2009

fluorescent jacket, get stuck in and complete this donation of another top-quality shipment of educational resources to the Isle of Spices. I scribble this aide memoir as I sit on a very comfortable upholstered IT swivel chair, which I salvaged almost a year and a half ago. I must never, never, give up.

Expect a big turn up sooner or later. In all labour there is profit. I am here this morning in front of one of my big boxes thanks to Peter and Trish Timms of Flexi Tech Ltd, Rothesay, who suggested some time ago that I contact John G. Russell. (See their note, which they had left at the front door of Delhi Cottage, that I contact John G Russell.) Okay, stop looking at the piece of work in front of you and get tae wuk and load up.

11:46 a.m. Sunnyside Railway Station platform Coatbridge, Lanarkshire. It is grey, overcast, muggy, and damp. I have not long walked from Gartsherrie Road. Raymond, bless him, made me breakfast of fried egg an' spam, mushrooms, bread, and a mug of tea. He and Michael, who works in the office, are still on deck.

I met Eddie before I left the depot. He said that he had some football strips for the Surplus Educational Supplies Foundation; that's part of the job done, accomplished, only through the goodwill, pro bono assistance, of the people mentioned in the entry for today. I am heading home. 'The next stop is Easterhouse.'

3:17 p.m. Home. David has just made me a mug of coffee. Message from Fraser Russell at Freightliner Ltd, who is to call me tomorrow.

Wednesday 07/10/2009

8:05 a.m. Home. I am up shaved and showered. I am in a limbo-like state of feeling that I am going nowhere. I am down in the dumps. Is it time to draw the line under this seat-of-the-pants shoestring charitable initiative?

No way! I cannot quit at this juncture. I will have to persevere until there are no loose ends such as warehouses and ocean freight containers at sites across the length and breadth of Scotland, where educational resources remain to be shipped worldwide to deserving beneficiaries.

Johanna is getting ready for school and David Alexander is upstairs asleep. I await a call from Fraser Russell, accounts manager at Freightliner Ltd, Coatbridge, and from Matthew, surveyor at Tesco stores property department, to confirm the handover loan of their warehouse property at 31 Kerse Road, Stirling.

I got a reply from my email to Tim Byam in Grenada.

5:36 p.m. I arrived back home to find David Alexander working away redecorating his bedroom. He is no slouch. Bless him.

I had set off this morning for Greenock for my appointment with the optician in the Oak Mall Shopping Centre, which was for 2 p.m. I wanted to get over there well before time. I met Robert, solicitor, on the boat on his way to the Greenock Sheriff Court. He is an encourager and supporter, and kindly gave me a lift to Cardwell Bay. I went into the garden centre and bought some bulbs, sheltered from the rain and then walked along the Cloch Road to Gourock and the rest of the way to within the Greenock City limits. A long walk! Then I got the bus to the bus rank across from the Oak Mall and later got the bus back to Wemyss Bay, otherwise I would still be walking.

For tomorrow: call Ross & Co Accountants regarding the format and VAT break down. What does it mean? The numbers? I won't have the RBS statement for the Surplus Educational Supplies Foundation account until next week; call Nathan at Warrant Freight Ltd, Port of Liverpool, to make sure he has Roland Malins-Smith's (CEO at Seafreight Agencies Lines, Miami, Florida) telephone number and email.

I have just called Tim Byam in Grenada. You don't half use the telephone and burn up transatlantic copper wires. He tells me that he is going to speak with the Minister of Education, senator Alexis Franka Bernadine. '*It shouldn't be too much of a problem for me to speak with her,*' he said. He tells me he grew up with her and with Roland Malins-Smith. Call Stirling Council. Will they waive the rates on 31 Kerse Road?

Thursday 08/10/2009

10:15 a.m. Home. I have just returned from the town of Rothesay by the Clyde. While pedalling up Castle Street I stopped to speak to Mrs Shepherd, an Ardbeg Baptist Church stalwart who along with her husband always gave me a friendly welcome. '*My husband is up in the Annex Thomson Home. It is awfully sad,*' she said, and went on to tell me that her son, a consultant in the Glasgow Royal Infirmary, has gone on a cruise. '*You should have gone with them,*' I said. Her son is in the Brethren Assembly in Hamilton where my friends Bill and Margaret Jones were members.

I had gone in to collect dust bags for the sander from Cowal Builders. David Alexander has got stuck in. We'll do 15 minutes each. Then I cycled round to The Electric Bakery for two meat bridies and a chicken pie. I cycled in in the rain and back out in sunshine.

I called Ross & Co Accountants in Dunoon for a breakdown of how VAT was calculated. Go and see Lesley, Paul, Vanessa, and Donna, the team at One 2 One Accountancy Services here on the island tomorrow, who are BRILLIANT!

Friday 09/10/2009

7:20 a.m. Home. I am up and waiting for Sam Tweedlie Senior to appear, who is helping David refurbish his bedroom.

He arrived shortly after 8:30 a.m. I gave David a shout and later held the fort while he and Amy went to the gym at the Rothesay Baths. I cycled in at 12:40 p.m. to get the one o'clock boat bus to Greenock with Raymond, who lives further along the road, to Mount Stuart. He was on his way up to Gartnavel Hospital (or is it now the Western or Victoria Infirmaries?) for his thrice-weekly session of dialysis. He deserves many medals for his fortitude. Bless him.

I went to Millers store in the Oak Mall Shopping Centre and dithered over purchasing a pair of walking boots. I needed another fluorescent jacket, but neither were in my size. Into M&S and I found a pair of cords to suit, but there was a long queue to wait in and the staff seemed not too bothered about shifting, so I walked out and over to the opticians to collect another pair of spectacles on a new prescription. I walked back under the underpass and got a slow Largs bus via Gourock. I enjoyed the ride. Ferry home. Sam reappeared to help David paper his room.

Saturday 10/10/2009

7:10 a.m. Amy Elisabeth, the Surplus Educational Supplies Foundation company secretary and fellow director of Scottish Registered Company No. 337348 have just had a business meeting. See the minutes book for what we discussed and decided upon. I called Philip, principal of the Grenada Boys' Secondary School, who tells me that they have had another fire and this time in their administration office. Suspected arson, as what had caused the fire the last time. I told him that the 40-foot container of educational resources for the school should be on its way to them next week. I asked him if he could give me a fax number to which I could send an inventory of container contents. I also gave him Tim Byam's telephone number and suggested that this person might prove to be a useful ally and supporter of the school's attempt to get back on its feet, so to speak. I then also gave the latter a call and left a message for him.

This morning, Graham of Edinburgh Community Transport, Northwest Community Services, Muirhouse, called me to say that a pallet of boxes of library books would be ready to be uplifted on Monday 12 October. I called Peter, transport manager at Russell, Coatbridge to see if they would collect the pallet and transfer it to SESF container OCLU1354487, which I, along with a team from Bishop's Move Removals Ltd from Edinburgh, had only partially loaded with educational resources (mainly quality classroom furniture) from the former Saint Andrews High School, Clydebank, on 22 July, as they had quit at 3 p.m. The container which Alastair Middleton, the photographer, and I had delivered to Russell at Coatbridge later that afternoon.

Monday 12/10/2009

9:23 a.m. Home. David is putting another coat of clear varnish on the floor of his room. He has done a superb job of redecorating, with a little help from Sam, the man of many trades. It is a beautiful day with light cloud floating under a blue sky and the sun shining across the blue Clyde watta.

I called RBS regarding the bank statement of the SESF charity account, Scottish Registered Charity (SCO39331), for the first part of 2009, which I now collect and send on to the accountants. I called One 2 One Accountancy Services Ltd to obtain a breakdown of the input VAT reclaimed from £1,278.38 for the period 1 July 2008 to 31 December 2008. They told me they would have it by Wednesday. I replied to an email from Gillian, surveyor, Fife Council.

Tuesday 13/10/2009

9:25 a.m. Home. Grey and overcast and I feel like that as well.

10:15 a.m. Vanessa at One 2 One Accountancy Services Ltd has just called to say that they had received the numbers for their VAT rebate for my SESF charity, which I will collect later today.

7:15 p.m. This afternoon I cycled into Rothesay twice. Once to post information on my VAT account to Ross & Co Accountants, Dunoon, which I had collected earlier from Vanessa. I then returned to the town to pay MacKirdy Hauliers Ltd for taking the pallet of boxes to Coatbridge; it is not all free lifts in that quarter, just to set the record straight.

Next week the Grenadian Minister for Education and Human Development visits London. Prepare an inventory of the educational resources in container MAEU6085656 for George McGuire, St George University, Grenada and send him a copy, and also to GHC in London. I have already spoken to Sam Sandy to let him know I was faxing an inventory of the container contents. Find out who Vanguard Logistics Services Ltd are.

Wednesday 14/10/2009

3:10 p.m. I am on the train bound for Wemyss Bay. Platform 11 Glasgow Central Station. Roll it back.

I left the house in the dark. It was a damp morning. Overcast. Lights flashing on the Clyde watta. I just got to the boat in time. As usual, Frank the steward asked me how I was. I told him I was great, but not travelling as fast as I would like. I gave him an anecdote from 16 December 2006 of an afternoon uplift given to me from Duncan Adams Transport Ltd depot at Grange Dock to Falkirk High Station in Eric's Porsche Carrera. That was at some speed, and when he dropped me off he turned to me, and said, *'You find the shipping lines and we will take your containers to any port in the United Kingdom.'* What more encouragement than that to get airborne?

Arrive at Central Station. I walked briskly up to Buchanan Street Bus Station where I got the 9 o'clock bus to Edinburgh Bus Station and walked out into Saint Andrew's Square. The day was beginning to brighten up. The leaves were turning into many golden colours. While crossing the square I called Jean Rennie,

Wednesday 14/10/2009

who was my first teacher and mentor on my first teaching practice session on my PGCE course at Moray House College of Education in September 1974 at Silverknowes Primary School in Pilton, North Edinburgh. No answer.

I called Norman Hill at First Port and spoke to Naomi for a few minutes, and then got through to Norman when I became aware, self-conscious, that I was calling attention to myself. My voice probably too loud and speaking too freely. I could feel the vibe. '*Who on earth does he think he is? Mr Big Head?*' At that moment my mobile ran out of juice. Serves me right, so I decided to make my way over the First Port office in the New Town.

I continued on down George Street to Charlotte Square, through the vennel beside West Register House, on past Saint Margaret's Cathedral and, finally, found the address I was looking for: up the stairs of this Georgian mansion of many offices, tucked away behind unvarnished doors. I chatted with Norman, who was as usual full of suggestions as to what I should be doing. I wanted to bring him up to date on what the Surplus Educational Supplies Foundation had achieved since we last spoke.

I, as usual, am always on the scrounge for any positive words of encouragement, for which I am aye grateful, and, of course, practical assistance. I walked back up to George Street and stopped off at the Undercroft Café below the Kirk. I ordered a toasted teacake and coffee. I was given a friendly reception; an uncomplicated ambience. I felt comfortable and secure in that setting, among a clientele of a certain age who have done it and seen it all.

It's time to get to my meeting at 1 p.m. with Barry, executive coach at the Edinburgh Scottish Social Enterprise Academy. Fresh bottle of iced water on the boardroom table. Pot of flowers on the windowsill. Welcome. He is smartly but casually dressed. Purple velvet sports jacket, bespoke faded blue jeans, black brogues, checked shirt. His first words to me were, '*You have nice handwriting, you have a fantastic project.*' Do I really? He has bowled me over and within a split second I have dropped my guard. I am disarmed.

I received what I think is more of his advice. He tells me, '*In order for your Surplus Educational Supplies Foundation initiative to last you must leave a legacy. You must need to become less of a blizzard and start making a snowman. In other words, you are all over the place, David. You need to become businesslike. Quantify. Let's have less of your wee stories and more analysis.*' I am not sure what this entails, but I get his drift. Okay, I take on board what he says. Where do I go from here?

I agreed with him that I would try and create an advisory board. Who? How? Well, already I have Sanjay – see his suggestions if I can find them. I reconnect with Ambassador Tom Kennedy at the British Embassy and his assistant Bruce at their offices in the British Embassy, San José, Costa Rica. Here's another anecdote. A wee story. Sorry, Coach. See *The Herald* article by journalist Simon Bain.

Research. Find out precisely what are the needs of the schools on the Costa Caribena Mosquito Coast. Can they give us the facts and the numbers? This is what it means to be businesslike I guess. Is it necessary for me to visit Bluefields? I am beginning to feel threatened by Coach Barry's criticism. He does not give me the opportunity to rebut, take issue with his negative criticism. One positive note. He was pleased, impressed, with the email that I had received from Ambassador Tom. At least here was tangible evidence that I was not a complete plonker. After all, up to this point, and in the previous meetings with the executive life coach, I had a track record. I had done positive stuff, made things happen like, for instance, I had shipped half a dozen ocean freight containers of educational resources to an island in the West Indies that had been devastated by a hurricane in 2004, and received significant pro bono logistics support from the Scottish road haulage industry and several shipping companies. As for the numbers, I had spent a small fortune of my and our, the Hanschell

Wednesday 14/10/2009

family, funds. He suggested I follow this contact with the British Embassy as soon as possible, something I was going to do anyway.

I mentioned the stonewalling difficulty of dealing with the Nicaraguan Government. He suggested I should network. With whom? I had been a member of the Edinburgh Chamber of Commerce and I had met some good people, like Peter Griffiths, marketing and development economist, Gillian Anderson, business development at Lofthus Signs Ltd, and Bahram Ajodani, successful entrepreneur and businessman, to name a few. He did not give me any names or introductions, connections or contacts, and ignored what I had achieved. He suggested I see if the Embassy in Costa Rica can link me with the Foreign Office representative for Grenada. *'You can't go off half-cocked.'* And he told me I needed to know and have a clear idea of the situation regarding the need, the requirements, for educational resources in both Grenada and Nicaragua. Only then can you return to those who have already helped for further assistance, and funding from potential donors. He said that they will soon stop granting me favours. This I know well enough. I told him that there might be the possibility of me going to either the Isle of Spices or the Costa Caribena, Nicaragua, prior to our next 'coaching session'. His parting words to me were, *'You like to fix things. You are a fixer. But I guarantee that in two or three years' time you will be getting nowhere.'*

That's what you think, but you have been paid handsomely for these coaching sessions and not once have you offered me one concrete bit of constructive assistance. There are no lucky break connections coming from you, Coach. I keep these thoughts to myself. Unlike the slack I was cut by the many individuals and firms mentioned previously in the pages of the Diary of the Shipping Clerk, typified by the words of Eric of Duncan Adams Transport Ltd, *'We will do it for you.'* (see diary for 8 December 2006). I accept the challenge from executive coach Barry that I will try to become more 'businesslike', 'rational', and 'strategic', not ad hoc, without having to pay another a fortune for advice from someone with an MBA.

I had told him that I was reading, Second Bounce of The Ball. How to turn Risk into Opportunity, by Ronald Cohen. So what? I don't need to ingratiate myself to anyone ever again. Some will help you spontaneously, most of those you meet will not. No matter how likely they appear to be able to do so.

He was full of sweet talk. We shook hands and I hoofed it back along Rose Street, all the way on my own to Haymarket Street Station where I bought myself a ploughman's cheese and pickle cutter, an Americano brew and savoured the purvey on the journey back tae Glesga. I met approachable youngsters Connor and Yvonne, studying art at the Glasgow School of Art. I engaged them in conversation and then proceeded to impose with enthusiasm of my own all-consuming work of art. You ebullient fool, buttonholer, doorstepper. I have benefited from another session. I just hope and pray it all sinks in and all he has said, which I know does ring true up to a point, I will be able to put into practice and move what I began on 7 September 2004 up a few notches. The train moves on and has just left Port Glasgow.

8:22 p.m. Home. Returned after a day in Edinburgh, where I saw Norman Hill at First Port and later, from 1 p.m. to 2 p.m., attended an 'Executive Coaching' session with Barry. Both meetings went well. The sun shone through the clouds as I walked down George Street to Charlotte Square on my way to Manor Place. While I was waiting to board MV *Bute* I met Harry, the dentist, Kevin, who is working at the Kingarth Hotel, and later Janet from the new houses adjacent to the Craigmore Pier, who told me that her husband, Godfrey, is in the Inverclyde Royal Infirmary and very unwell. I assured her of my support.

David Alexander had our tea ready. Pizza, homemade chips, and a can of Coke. To do: fax inventory of container MAEU6085656 contents to Grenada Boys' Secondary School and to the Ministry of Education; develop contact with Ambassador Tom Kennedy and Bruce Callow, Political and Communications Officer, British Embassy, Foreign and Commonwealth Office, San José, Costa Rica. Can they assist me with contacts with DFID headquarters in Barbados to improve Grenada links; establish an advisory board for SESF and follow up Coach Barry's challenge and advice of today.

I will jot down some more of what Coach Barry had said to me, *'Do you want this to be your legacy?'* And I said that I hoped it would be my legacy. *'After a while the first few famous people will get tired of you.'* His parting words were, *'Be careful you don't become part of the problem.'*

Thursday 15/10/2009

8:37 p.m. Home. Marion, Amy, David, and Johanna are here. I woke this morning not feeling too good. There was tingling numbness in my hands and a sharp pain behind my right eye: there was nothing else for it but to take to my bed until the afternoon. It was a beautiful day out of doors. My eyes could not take the bright sunlight.

Later this afternoon Bill, the local IT wizard, came by as he had said he would when I had met him walking his dog on my way home yesterday. We had a long chat over coffee at the kitchen table. He sure knows a thing or two. He is accomplished in many areas of technical expertise, joinery, construction, drafting, music, and photography. He was crucial in enabling me to scan and attach the packing list inventory of the recent SESF donation of library books, which had come from the Morningside Library in Edinburgh, to the anglophone community of Bluefields, Costa Caribena, Central America, which has now arrived in Miami, Florida. Nathan and Patrick of Warrant Freight Ltd, Port of Liverpool, had emailed me a request for the packing list. The fact that Bill was here had made it possible for me to send it with my signature.

I received a call from Norman of First Port to tell me that he had been in touch with Inverclyde Regeneration Ltd and said he enquired after warehouse space. To do: develop, if possible, a link with the British Embassy in Costa Rica for my contribution to schools, or a school, in Bluefields, Mosquito Coast; see how far I and the Surplus Educational Supplies Foundation can take this initiative; call Bruce at the British Embassy, San José, Costa Rica; await result of the email I sent to the High Commissioner of Grenada, High Commission in London, which had been forwarded to the Ministry of Education and Human Development, Grenada.

Friday 16/10/2009

10:54 a.m. Home. It is a beautiful day of full-on sunshine. I have just called Matthew, surveyor with Tesco stores, who is always pleasant. 'I'll call Iain Rhodes and get this sorted out. Are you planning to take up our offer of the warehouse in Stirling?'

I called Patrick at Warrant Freight Ltd, who has received the packing list. All in order. He said he would call Bruce at the British Embassy in Costa Rica. Patrick said he would mention to him about the possibility of my fact-finding trip to Bluefields to determine what the educational requirements were of the schools on the Mosquito Coast. Called Alyson accountant at Ross & Co; they have the numerical data so they can show that the Surplus Educational Supplies Foundation is discharging its statutory responsibilities and will keep my files for a little while longer. I realised too late that I need not have become a registered company; I am exceedingly grateful to her and all at Ross & Co, Dunoon, and for Lesley Paul and her team at One 2 One Accountancy Services for carrying out this work pro bono, which shows to all and sundry where the funds are coming from.

Monday 19/10/2009

10:56 a.m. Home. Marion has the vacuum going. David Alexander and Johanna are asleep. It is a grey and damp morning. I received an encouraging email from Coach Barry.

5:07 p.m. '*If I put some tatties in the basin will you go and peel them for me?*' asked Marion '*Yes, I can manage that nae bother,*' I replied.

Tuesday 27/10/2009

9:53 a.m. Home. Raindrops bouncing off the skylight window above my head. I called First Port, where I had met someone on my previous visit who seemed supportive, and left a message for Norman regarding his mention of a warehouse in Inverclyde that might become available. I called Matthew, the Tesco surveyor, and left a message.

  '*The most important job we ever have is to be good parents,*' Peter Cochran.

Wednesday 28/10/2009

11:17 a.m. Home. The sun is shining. I look up through the skylight window and there are no clouds. I don't feel like doing very much, so I will get on my bicycle and cycle round the Isle of Bute. I have been having a go at my Spanish.

2:15 p.m. Arrived back and I am feeling a lot better than I did, with my self-respect restored. It stayed dry. I saw seven swans land in a harvested field not far from the Isle of Bute landing strip. I could have hugged them!

2:22 p.m. Returning a call to the Sierra Leone High Commission in London, to their Head of Chancery and Foreign Affairs,

Florence, who had called while I was away and wished to speak with me. At least after having made many attempts to speak with her, she tells me that, '*The government of Sierra Leone has developed a 10-year education plan which DFID stands ready to support with other donors, which has been endorsed by the Education For All Fast Track Initiative.*' What does this mean for SESF?

Thursday 29/10/2009

9:55 a.m. Home. I had my piece of toast with marmalade and marmite, and mug of coffee.

11:01 a.m. Sporadic development. I am engaged in a work of intermittent and provisional progress. I was speaking to Sanjay earlier, who tells me to keep bringing the pieces of the jigsaw together and that I must harness support; that's all very well but whose support am I to harness?

10:47 a.m. '*It's all systems go,*' said Matthew. Is it?

11:31 a.m. I am calling the Sierra High Commission. Make arrangements to see Jim, business adviser at the Stirling Enterprise Park, the next time I am in Stirling.

4:45 a.m. Her Excellency Florence Bangali of SLHC has passed me on to speak with Zainab Hainab Bangura, Minister of Foreign Affairs in President Koroma's cabinet: the ball is in their court. I send her an email and get no reply. She has told me that she is working at the United Nations in New York and she will call me again from Freetown. '*When I return to my village der are hundreds of children and I want to give dem books,*' said Minister Bangura. I had waited all day to speak with her, and finally as I was in the midst of making our tea the phone went. Florence Bangali to say that the Minister of Foreign Affairs for Sierra Leone was there in her London office waiting to speak with me. I sent an email to her, for which I still await a reply.

Friday 30/10/2009

9:30 a.m. Home. I am going nowhere at the moment. I am just hanging on with the long and winding road, on which I have to travel, ahead of me. I expect to hear from Iain the surveyor who is responsible for 31 Kerse Road, the former Pickfords Removal warehouse. Why the delay? (Good question as I was soon to discover.) I am going to have a go at some Spanish.

1:45 p.m. Called Matthew, who is always helpful. Positive. He said that he would chase up their surveyor in Scotland – 'I'll give him a poke.'

2 p.m.–5 p.m. Bill, IT savant, has been helping me to build a new website www.educationalsurplus.co.uk New domain name integrity fee £40.

7 p.m. Received a call from Madge to tell me that she has bought a house in Tbilisi. As frenetic as ever. She is making plans to bring a severely disabled Georgian lad to Edinburgh for medical treatment and wants to acquire good quality furniture and suitable school resources for the physically disabled. She asked me if I planned on going to the Social Enterprise Academy ceilidh? No thanks. The family are here this evening. Gran is staying with us for the weekend. It has been raining all day. I am counting my blessings.

Monday 02/11/2009

2:10 p.m. Home. Grey, overcast, and damp. I am going to call Iain the surveyor once more. Left a message; if nothing else, I am a persistent nuisance. To do: contact Ross & Co in Dunoon and let them know that Companies House are looking for my accounts. The pressure and price that goes with the territory of being a social entrepreneur do-gooder. The deadline for them to be handed on time is 6 December 2009. Were it not for the pro bono cooperation and willing assistance from this firm I would be sunk.

Tuesday 03/11/2009

11:50 a.m. Home. I am feeling rotten. Another sleepless night. I woke with pains behind my eyes. I am lying low. That was Peter, the pharmacist primero uno at the Rothesay Health Centre, who has just called. I phoned yesterday to make arrangements to receive any vaccinations that would be necessary should I make a trip to Bluefields, Mosquito Coast, Costa Caribena, next month. He said he would call me this afternoon. He is always a great help. So I press on in weakness and crushing feelings of inadequacy for the task. We'll see.

4:30 p.m. Peter called, as he said he would, and I made an appointment with him for jags on 9 November 2009 at 2 p.m. for a cocktail of prophylactics.

Thursday 05/11/2009

11:22 a.m. Home. I have not long returned from the Caribbean Hurricane Relief Depot at the boatyard where I had dropped off two boxes of Bibles and hymn books that I had collected from the Russell Street Hall in the town. Thanks due to Ivor Gibb, antiquarian, who I had met that day way back in May 1990 at the Bute Museum prior to walking up the High Street for a job interview. He was knapping a piece of flint and is a Museum trustee and supporter of my initiative. There has been no word from Iain

Friday 06/11/2009.

the surveyor. I've just called Matt at Tesco, who hasn't poked him hard enough, and left a message.

I received a call from Gerry, Interserve Projects Ltd, at Inveralmond Community High School in Livingston, who wants me to shift container GATU4072944. I have nowhere to park it at present.

2:15 p.m. I made another call to Matthew and left a message. He returned my call.

Friday 06/11/2009.

9:45 a.m. Home. Amy has just left with David to drive him down to the house he's working on with Sam Senior in Kilchattan Bay. Johanna left earlier for school. I spoke earlier with Elisa of Barrhead Travel in Glasgow, enquiring after flights to Nicaragua. She is to call me back. '*I will bring you back a coconut,*' I said.

It is raining heavily. I am pressing forward. I called Howard Clack of Freight Container Services (Scotland) Ltd who gave me these contacts: Container Lift Ltd and Tom at Dunlop's.

10:25 a.m. Call Ross & Co about SESF accounts.

10:57 a.m. I received a call from Jim, transport manager at John G. Russell Transport Ltd, Coatbridge, to tell me that the pallet had been collected from Edinburgh Community Council's warehouse, which was in the Elizafield Industrial Estate Muirhouse. He told me that I could come and shift my container at any time. He also told me that Craighead Primary School in Lanarkshire was due to close on 18 December: he said that he and his wife would give me the name of someone to contact if I wished to salvage the educational resources from that school. I asked him to give my regards to his colleagues Peter, Raymond, and Michael.

12:15 p.m. £1,022 cost of the flight 14–19 December to Nicaragua. Elisa at Barrhead Travel is on the ball.

1:15 p.m. That was Tom down south, who said that his firm will provide a sidelifter to pick up container from ICHS Livingston and would deliver it to 13/31 Kerse Road, Stirling.

I will now call Gerry at Interserve Projects Ltd and let him know that as soon as I get the space I will make arrangements to have the container uplifted.

1:34 p.m. I was speaking to Elisa of Barrhead Travel Ltd, regarding the flight from Heathrow to Managua, Nicaragua via Miami. I have just looked at the flight details and there has been an error. I have been booked to fly on 14 November and it should be 14 December. There is many a slip betwixt the cup and the lip. I am now trying to get Elisa and Allanah to sort the error. I will need to spend two nights in Miami in order to get the return flight. Problem. I don't look forward to spending two days hanging around Miami International Airport, so I contact Art Gold of the charity Food For The Poor and Roland Malins-Smith at Seafreight Agencies Lines in Miami, hopefully either might be able to suggest somewhere to stay, and I scan my passport and email to Elisa.

4:19 p.m. It has been a busy day with emails criss-crossing to Barrhead Travel in Glasgow, to Bruce Callow at the British Embassy in San José, Costa, Rica, to Coach Barry in Edinburgh and to Roland Malins-Smith in Miami Florida. It is now time to take a break; a day's work of logistics. '*That's just a big word, David,*' said Eric.

Monday 09/11/2009

8:47 a.m. Home. Call Ross & Co. Post letters, collect vaccine and get jag from Rothesay Health Centre.

10:35 a.m. It has now turned grey and cold.

3:29 p.m. I received a call from Stephen Edgerson to tell me that they might consider sponsoring the shipment of one of my containers and they can put their logo of a forklift truck on it. I tell him that, in all, the Surplus Educational Supplies Foundation has 10 40-foot ocean freight containers at five transport depots all over Scotland. I can give his firm some publicity in return for corporate social responsibility sponsorship. (This promising lead did not materialise.)

3:50 p.m. I have had my hepatitis and anti-tetanus injections from Peter. I stopped off at Lloyds Pharmacy to purchase some chloroquine tablets.

Tuesday 10/11/2009

10 a.m. Home. I have just had a call from David, purporting to be from the Tax Office, wanting details. I told him I knew nothing about it. He said I had put in a claim.

I have finally received an email from Iain the surveyor to let me know that Semple Fraser Solicitors in Glasgow will prepare a 'Licence to Occupy' document, which will enable me to occupy the Tesco premises at 31 Kerse Road, Stirling, providing I pay the cost of their fee of £750. I said. '*Go ahead.*' I must be off my head!

Don't forget to take my Seaman's Book when I travel; I may be able to stay at the Seaman's Hostel in Miami. Confirm visa to the USA. Call Barrhead Travel.

11:30 a.m. Ray, prawn fisherman from Port Bannatyne, arrived at the door to pay me for the generator he purchased from me for £80 some time ago. We had coffee and a long chat together. It improves the cash flow somewhat.

Wednesday 11/11/2009

9:09 a.m. Home. 'You've got mail.' Junk mail you mean.

3:21 p.m. Lyndsey Barr of Semple Fraser Glasgow, who is drafting the licence to occupy document, has called me back with the terms of the lease; it seems to me that it is all in Tesco's favour. Elisa, Barrhead Travel, called with revised details of my flight to Nicaragua on 14 December.

7:02 p.m. I was speaking to Salim of Spice Isle Retreaders Ltd in Grenada. He wants me to send him a fax of the container MAEU6085656 purchase invoice. The container has arrived in Kingston, Jamaica.

Thursday 12/11/2009

8:43 a.m. Home. I have a pain behind my right eye and slight numbness in my right hand, which began in my little finger. I called Lyndsey, the solicitor at Fraser Semple, who said she would have to show 'the document' to Tesco first: and contact me eventually. What a lot of paperwork, expense, and an inordinate amount of toeing and froing to acquire some storage space. A process that I have brought on myself.

12:44 p.m. I am calling Jim, the accountant, who tells me, '*The investment element of my funds are a return on sustainable philanthropy.*' What does that mean? I am calling the Grenada Boys' Secondary School regarding the port charges. I spoke with their school administrator to find out if the shipment had received authorisation from the Ministry of Education. I received a reply from Salim of Spice Isle Automotive Sales Ltd, Frequente Industrial Park, querying these arrangements. He is offering to pay me US$1,200 for the container, which should be free of duties providing the Port Authority waive charges. He wants to know the estimated time of arrival of the container. I am call Warrant Freight Ltd, Liverpool, and spoke to Anthony who did not know the ETA of the container.

'Don't be encumbered by history, go off and do something wonderful,' Robert Noyce.

Friday 13/11/2009

10:17 a.m. Home. It is a beautiful sunlight-filled day, but cold, and I am dithering here at this desk as to what I should do next. Amy has made me a cup of tea, bless her.

Saturday 14/11/2009

8:29 p.m. Home. I have not long sat down. Showered, clean clothes. Thank you, Marion. I have done the dishes, washed the kitchen floor, cleaned the toilets and shower, and emptied the compost bucket.

While I was walking home this afternoon, I crossed the road to speak to Tom Shaw, who asks me, *'Do ye keep a diary, David?'* I tell him that I keep a scribbly diary of sorts. My mind is preoccupied with this move from the Caribbean Hurricane Relief Depot at the Stirling Yacht Services Ltd boatyard at Port Bannatyne into the warehouse at 31 Kerse Road, Stirling, and with the impending visit to Bluefields, Mosquito Coast, Nicaragua. I can only continue trying to make something out of the Surplus Educational Supplies Foundation. My priority remains Marion, Amy, David, and Johanna. Gran Morrison is spending the weekend with us.

I Meet the Secret Millionaire and Travel Far Further

Monday 16/11/2009

7:53 a.m. I call Barrhead Travel Ltd. They will send tickets, travel insurance, and invoice. I call Stephen Phillips, solicitor at Burness in Glasgow. We became acquainted a while back.

Tuesday 17/11/2009

10:20 a.m. I am now sitting in front of a cup of coffee and a toasted teacake in the Undercroft Café under the Kirk on George Street, just along from St Andrew's Square, Edinburgh. I came into the city on the express from Buchanan Street Bus Station, Glasgow.

It was a slow journey. Traffic was piling up on both sides of the motorway. I'll sit here and chill among the clientele, and I had better drink up my coffee before it turns cold. Beautiful, clear, sunshine morning. A wind is blowing in off the Firth of Forth. I have an appointment with executive coach Barry at midday.

11:50 a.m. I have arrived at Thorn House, Rose Street, ready to go. These are some of the notes I jotted during the meeting with the executive coach.

He tells me to do so much, but he does not give me much time to take proper notes, so I scribble away. I note that it is too nice a day to be indoors. He tells me that I have got to be hard-headed. Here are some of the points I am finding out about this one-man band. I am my own worst enemy and critic. Look, Coach, just give me the advice. Let's have your MBA analysis insight, that's what the Social Enterprise Academy are paying you for. He thinks that I am all over the place, which is true; that's what it is like when you have to do everything yourself. I know full well the amount of work, sustained effort and money that I have ploughed into this venture, and the goodwill and pro bono support that has come without payment from many good folk. You don't need to tell me what I already know. I'm too deferential to tell him that.

Tuesday 17/11/2009

Verbatim: '*Take strategic decisions. Deciding what you don't do. You need to be more focused. You are operating like an anarchist renegade. You should not be paying for this project yourself. Everything is dependent on cash flow. You need dosh ... David, you do not know what you are talking about. You are out of your depth. Keep your trap shut for a change and start listening to people.*' Okay, point taken.

I let his comments go past me. I know these statements are true. I know that. But it is not everything about me, thank goodness. I agree, and so will Marion, with a lot of what he has to say. I tell him that I accept what he says. I am not here to argy bargy with him. I need his support. I have 10 40-foot ocean freight containers and have salvaged quality educational resources by the truck full. He has already told me that I have a track record and in his words, '*A fantastic project.*' So? True. I know I am a rebel with a chip on his shoulder. I have been an outsider for as long as I can remember. I am certainly not one of the boys like yourself, casually dressed in a purple velvet jacket, designer jeans, and checked shirt. What I have achieved these past 49 years has been grafted for every step of the way. '*I dug for it, sir.*' Fun, Family, Finance, and Future. So where do I go from here?

Coach Barry goes into a long description of how companies grow and why they eventually die. He mentions the management guru Yitchak Adizes. Yes, we are all part of a life cycle. '*Why do companies grow and die?*' Yes, that makes sense, but where do I go from here? He tells me that the Surplus Educational Supplies Foundation is at the baby stage of development. A long way from maturity. I know that much: that I have been at an arrested stage of development on many levels for as long as I can remember, but I have done my best with what I had to work with at the time. He goes into another description of the way International Aid is distributed and how it is dependent on geopolitics. He tells me that US Aid money is now dispersed under the control of the US State Department, and likewise the UK Government DFID etc. '*True, Coach, but I do not move in those circles,*' I am thinking to myself as

Coach Barry patters on with his insider knowledge. *'How are you going to help me?'* I am thinking to myself. *'Can you help me, in the here and now, to move forward? Can you show me how to access funding if you think I have such a great project? You know my situation.'* I am now skint after shipping six ocean freight container-loads of educational resources to four Grenada government schools that were devastated by Hurricane Ivan in 2004. I'm a retiree OAP for goodness sake. What is at issue here, this afternoon: can you and your contacts assist me in helping these children in Bluefields and the Mosquito Coast?

I have a new focus for my life, apart from my family. It was once my teaching vocation, then Grenada, and now Costa Caribena anglophone Nicaragua, which came through my own efforts. I need not be ashamed of my struggles to achieve something worthwhile with my life. What would you do, Bruce, Roland, whoever, if you were me?

He tells me that I have to appear as a serious player, and look and be corporate. I am not sure what he means by that. More smoke and mirrors you mean. He relates an anecdote about his time in New York, where he made his fortune apparently; he has already mentioned more than once how successful he was in setting up his own company and selling it later on, before returning to the United Kingdom, and how the fountain pen he used sent a message of corporate success and confidence, to such an extent that the people he was working with all went out and bought the same model of fountain pen. He then shifts from being critical of my work so far and turns to being more helpful, and here I attempt to record what he has to say almost verbatim.

'You need to put together a proper business plan. You must be businesslike. You need to use concrete words like: focus, inventories, strategy, market, business mode. You have to get into a business mode. Use their vocabulary. What you are attempting to accomplish must be put on a business footing or it will not last. Your project must be run in a businesslike way.'

Tuesday 17/11/2009

I tell him that I have had a go at that already, thanks to the Social Enterprise Academy courses. I tell him about my attempt at an executive summary of such a plan, but he is not interested in discussing it with me.

'You have to solve the problem. I repeat it will not last. There must be a rational way through this. Plan your visit to Bluefields, be operational. You must get tactical problem solving on the ground. You need to look at the strategy. You need to be strategic to get the overall picture when you get there. You have not got a clear idea of what is required and what the need is, and you must be able to quantify it. You need a clear sense, an indication from Bruce at the British Embassy in Costa Rica, or whoever you deal with, of what the schools, in this case Bluefields, require. Please give me a list. You must be aware of what they need. What are the precise needs? Please send me an inventory. Can you help here please? Be careful that you don't become part of the problem. After the first few benefactors, famous people, they will become tired of you. You are going to run out of people. One the first few challenges you will face. You want to be sure you are doing this project properly.

'*You need an advisory board. It's called governance. A chairman. Two or three people. One to do the money and another to do the public relations, publicity, and funding.*'

You have told me all of that before, Coach. I need people to help me that's for sure, but who?

'*You need to be able to tell a short story. Here are these schools. This is what they need. You relate what you do now to help children in the area where you grew up. You have always had a connection with the Caribbean, the West Indies, and there has always between a connection between Scotland and the Caribbean. You need to be able to tell the story for a journalist, PR person, an audience, in order to raise the profile. What is it that the community, the children, parents, and teachers in Bluefields really need? It may NOT be educational furniture, unwanted, salvaged, classroom furniture, but new up-to-date IT equipment,*' he said.

A fair bit of the storytelling, the publicity aspect of the Surplus Educational Supplies Foundation's work has been done already. See newspaper articles, the SESF flyer, PowerPoint presentation and talks, and the website.

'You need to tell the people in Bluefields, Mosquito Coast, Costa Caribena, Nicaragua Meso-America, and at the F & Co British Embassy, Costa Rica, San José Office/DFID what I require from them is a plan. You mention the connection between Scotland, the Mosquito Coast, and the Darien Peninsula Scheme, of settlers from Scotland in the 16th and 17th centuries that promised so much, that went bottoms up: the fortunes that bankrupted Scotland, the lives that were lost etc. There are links that go back a long way. Find out if there is anyone of Scottish descent living in Bluefields and the Mosquito Coast. Tell Bruce Callow and Ambassador Tom Kennedy at the British Embassy, Costa Rica, if they don't already know, what it is, exactly, that the Bluefields community need.

'*Prepare a well-prepared pitch book of your story, the SESF initiative project, so that on your return from the trip you will have something to show, pitch to funders,*' he said.

Notes for my story continued. (After another session with Coach Barry I spent four days in Bluefields.)

He continues his talk and does not give me the chance to engage with him in a constructive dialogue. 'You plan how you are going to operate. You are going to TRANSFORM a random blizzard, snowstorm, into a snowman. You clarify the need. Your story must be utterly clear. You, David Miles-Hanschell, are the product. The way you come across with the project must be FOCUSED. So that on your return you have something to pitch to funders … for the ring binder. Don't talk so much, learn to listen more. When you are talking to Bruce, keep it tight. Don't go off on your tangents. You must become more self-aware, especially with those with whom you are conducting business. Build a business plan that looks like this "XY gave me this," [see the two

Wednesday 18/11/2009

audited financial statements prepared by Ross & Co Accountants for OSCR and Companies House, and the budget forecast for 2011–2013]. Your supporters will want answers to all sorts of questions; here's the overarching need. Get straight to the financial side. You have no money, but you do have lots of enthusiasm, energy, experience, and a proven track record. Identify the consumer need and organise your business, the Surplus Educational Supplies Foundation, to meet that need and, if possible, make a profit. How do you convince the British Embassy DFID etc. that you are a serious player? Be crisp, don't waffle. Tell it straight. How do you become a cash cow, and not a dead duck? [2005–2017. Nothing was ever easy there were hurdles to overcome at every bend in the road.] What do you need to focus on? Your attention to detail. Your USP, you do things differently than others. CREATIVITY. Attention to detail. SERVICE.

'What is the contribution you are making? See track record. What is the LEGACY you are going to leave behind when you are gone. Do you want SESF to be your legacy?' He asks me that question for the second time. *'Yes. I do.'* I replied. Thanks for the advice coach.

Wednesday 18/11/2009

2:20 p.m. Back home. It has been raining all day. This morning I drove to Dunoon for an appointment with accountant Jim at 11 a.m. He had already prepared a draft of the Surplus Educational Supplies Foundation accounts, which we discussed together with his colleague Alyson. I walked around the town afterwards and went into a draper's shop on the High Street. The salesman's son works for Duncan Adams Transport Ltd. It's a small world! I can't get an internet connection. Annoying. I am at sixes and sevens at the moment. I will just have to get on with it and tough it out. I sent them an email describing the shipment of MAEU6085656 to Grenada Boys' Secondary School. The container should be in

St George's, Grenada, today. Scan a picture of the container. Amy will help me.

Thursday 19/11/2009

5:32 p.m. Home. I have just called Leslie, the editor of the *Grenada Voice* who said that he had received my email and would open it prior to leaving his office. He is positive and recognises my contribution. I asked him to send me a copy of the newspaper, should a story about the donated shipment of educational resources be published.

Earlier I cycled through the wind and rain to the town and deposited approximately £400 into the RBS account. Purchased *The Times* and *The Herald* and went along to Print Point, the stationers, to fax the container purchase invoice to Spice Isle Retreaders Ltd. I then cycled back in the rain. I then called Salim Rahaman, the chief executive, to check that he had received the fax, which he had not. I called Warrant Freight Ltd, Port of Liverpool: a sociable soul gave me their managing director's number, who was happy to put their logo on my boxes.

I was really low earlier today. I kept going, folding SESF flyers while listening to Pete Seeger plinking away.

Friday 20/11/2009

7:23 a.m. Home. I call Gray Adams Ltd in Dunfermline, the reefer manufacturer. I told them that my 20-footer was for sale. Mike said he would speak to their managing director and will keep a record of my interest in selling it. I called Elisa, the travel agent, at Barrhead Travel Ltd, who told me that the travel arrangements paperwork was in the post. I said I would bring her back a coconut from the Mosquito Coast.

Monday 23/11/2009

12:49 p.m. Home. It has been raining heavily all morning. It's beginning to lighten up overhead from what I can see through the big skylight window. I am weighed down with the cost of operating my charitable foundation, the 'Social Enterprise.' I am typing up the notes that I gave to Jim the accountant: what I paid for each of the containers and the cost to ship each one, which came out of my, you mean our family's, pockets. '*It is our money!*' Will we ever get it back? I am weighing up what it has cost in breaking my relationship with my best friend, partner, helpmeet, and wife, Marion. It is a fractured relationship at the moment.

Apart, from that I am not feeling physically 100%. Words from Barry, high flying coach at the Edinburgh Social Academy, come to mind, or words similar, '*It's the families of do-gooders, the agents of virtue, who pay the price.*' The sun is shining through and I am going to cycle in and post a letter for Amy Elisabeth.

3:30 p.m. I called Semple Fraser Solicitors, they are giving me no quarter. I then I called Stephen at Burness – the former has been on to him. Why? To check that I pay my bill.

Tuesday 24/11/2009

6:35 a.m. Home. Johanna is asleep, Marion and David have left for work and college. I've shaved, showered, dressed, and am going to make myself a bowl of porridge. Do I take this empty and vacant-for-some-time warehouse in Stirling, or not? I call Stephen at Burness to see if Semple Fraser have taken on board his comments on the wording of their drafting of their licence to occupy document.

I will need to try and get the container at Inveralmond High School, Livingston moved. But where to? How? Who?

Clean the oven.

10:03 a.m. I have not long spoken to Lyndsey at Semple Fraser LLP and Stephen at Burness solicitors. I am swithering, undecided about taking up the Junson Properties Ltd 'offer' (Tesco Stores Ltd) of 13/31 Kerse Road, Springbank Road, Stirling. I have sought advice from Stephen, the solicitor, who has been faultless in the prompt reply to my request for advice. '*All in all SESF now has a much more satisfactory position, but there are still elements that are not ideal and, or which, involve some risk for SESF. Against that, this is being offered on a rent-free basis. Please do phone me if there any issues on which you are not clear. Best regards. Stephen.*' Stephen Phillips, Partner.

I was speaking to Sanjay. He wants a meeting soon to draft a plan for the next steps? Going for it. I have been making supper for the family. The tea: haggis, mashed potatoes, clapshot, turnip, carrots. Set the table. Cleaned the oven. Brought the bin in. I emptied the compost bucket. Not in that order. In the words of Jimmy Cliff, '*I am a struggling, man, and I got to move on.*'

Call John at WH Malcolm Transport Ltd, Muirhouse depot. Call Archie, team leader, Community Services Criminal Justice Department, Glenrothes regarding Unit3 uplift of resources before the end of the year. Call Tom Walker, container surveyor, regarding where I might be able to hire a sidelifter. A message was left on the answerphone by Jim O'Donnell at Russell to call Linda Kerr, Hamilton Council. '*I am always pushing the boat out,*' I said in conversation with Jim. He replied, '*David, that's the name of the game.*'

Wednesday 25/11/2009

9:06 a.m. Home. I set off before 6 a.m. in the darkness and arrived at the pier to learn that the ferry would not sail until 8 a.m. I swithered. Do I wait or head back home, which I did. Contact Gerry regarding uplift of the container at ICHS. I met Marion at her car and we drove with a passenger to Rhubodach and just missed the

Wednesday 25/11/2009

ferry. A wait in the queue. I decided not to chance being stranded on the mainland and so began walking back to Rothesay against a strong wind and a light rain. I soon got a lift from the engineer at the Ardmaleish boatyard who lives in Portavadie. I walked on from there into Port Bannatyne and on into the town to arrange the collection and delivery of container GATU4072944 from Inveralmond High School, Livingston, where it has been parked for over a year, to Stirling.

I call Alan Galt Transport Ltd, Dumbarton. They will call me back. I have received an email from Ashley at Semple Fraser solicitors in Glasgow to say I can sign the licence to occupy documentation. Ominous. I have misgivings. Warning. Calling Gerry at Interserve Projects Ltd to let him know that I have made arrangements to have the container collected. *'This person's phone is switched off.'* I then made a call to the Ardmaleish Boat Building & Dry Dock Co. Ltd to thank Alan the engineer from Portavadie for his lift to a stranger, and for recommending Alan Galt Transport Ltd to me so I could hire a high hab sidelifter. My steps and stops are overruled. Called First Port and spoke to Elaine from Tighnabruaich, and with Norman, who always makes suggestions but never delivers anything concrete. I then called SCVO to let them know that I could not make their conference being held at the Glasgow City Chambers. Left a message for Helen. I need to get a refund of £35.

12:08 p.m. I have been sitting here since 9 a.m. and it is time I took a break. I have achieved, at long last, arrangements to collect the container, a place to park it and somewhere to store the contents. I have arranged to sign the licence to occupy document tomorrow morning.

1:39 p.m. Left messages for Peter Griffiths, Archie Melville, and Iain Rhodes.

2:53 p.m. Called Jim Fraser, Business Gateway Stirling Enterprise Park seeking advice about persuading tenants to no longer park their cars in the warehouse car park at 13/31 Kerse Road.

3:57 p.m. Speaking to Carol, the receptionist at Mcfarlane Gray Guest House, regarding the possibility of a donation from the motorists in the Castlecraig Business Park. This can be a problem. An issue. I was speaking to Valerie and Brian in the office at Duncan Adams Ltd, Grange Dock, who are always friendly and helpful. Called Eldapoint Ltd and spoke to Louise, who I am to contact when I am ready, to move GATU4033193. '*We can move it whenever and to where you want it for £270.*'

The ferry is likely to be off again tomorrow. I now need to consider the issue of insurance relating to my intended occupation of 31 Kerse Street/Springbank Road. How am I covered as a charity? My indemnity insurance – is it covered? I am taking on the liability of cars in the car park and possible damage to the warehouse car park caused by the weight of the containers. The issue has to be resolved.

Apart from anything, the solicitors are charging me a fortune just to sign a piece of paper that can make me responsible for any problems that may arise from Surplus Education Supplies Foundation occupancy of these premises. I am now having second thoughts. This anticipated move has been, and continues to be, complicated. More so than it need be. I am in great potential difficulty here and well out of my depth. I am unclear as to my responsibility regarding the issues of indemnity and liability for anything to happen to the property. Apparently, the warehouse car park has been used for a long time by car owners. I was not told this fact.

I call Elaine at Semple Fraser regarding my misgivings. If anything goes wrong in the car park, and for that matter the warehouse in Stirling, I am carrying the can. With regret, I am unable to occupy the premises. Bill McCord, the IT specialist, was here and after much discussion with him about the implications of the consequences of moving to that site, I acted on his advice, which saved me from what could have been another pickle of my own construction. Thank you, Bill, you saved me from being embroiled in another pickle of my own making.

So I picked up the phone and called Alan Galt and cancelled arrangements with his firm to have the container uplifted from ICHS Livingston to Stirling. I am now no further ahead. I am greatly disappointed after what has been a long process to move to somewhere where good quality, fit-for-purpose educational resources could have been salvaged from landfill and safely stored, refurbished, and inventoried prior to shipment.

So far everything has been a struggle, and an expensive one at times. But what else can I do? The educational resources that I have salvaged from THE WASTE STREAM must, somehow, be redistributed to schools and institutions where they can still be fit for purpose. Only then can I draw a line under the Surplus Educational Supplies Foundation project. I must now renew the task of locating a suitable storage facility.

Monday 30/11/2009

10:33 a.m. Home. Beautiful day. Sunshine at last, and it's a fresh and clear winter's morning. I can see no clouds above my head. I have just cycled back from the town. Into the bank and along to the post office. Send another email to SCVO and call Nancy regarding the refund of my £35 conference fee. Some questions: what are my liabilities and does insurance cover them, or do I have to take out insurance?.

Tuesday 01/12/2009

11:13 a.m. Tom Walker, the container inspector, called me back earlier. He was glad that I had been able to locate a sidelifter/high hab and found temporary storage for GATU4072944.

2:37 p.m. It is blowing a wet gale up the Firth of Clyde. I have set the table and put the sweet potatoes and mince on to boil.

Wednesday 02/12/2009

10:30 a.m. Home. An icy wind and rain. I am struggling onwards in the face of it. Get out the violins. I called Clyde Port Ocean Terminal to ask them whether or not I could come over to the container base and inventory the contents of my container.

11:38 a.m. I called Patrick at Warrant Freight Ltd in Liverpool to make arrangements for them to collect the container from the Port of Greenock. I then called Alan Galt Transport Ltd, Dumbarton, and left a message for Alan, who is on holiday.

3:52 p.m. I spoke to Jim, the accountant, who will let Jeremy Sandle at Nightingale Estates Ltd have my Companies House certificate of incorporation.

Thursday 03/12/2009

12:41 p.m. Home. I received a call from Hugh, operations manager at Clydeport Ocean Terminal container base, Port of Greenock, who told me, '*We are happy to store your containers free of charge.*' And Clydeport Ocean Terminal, Peel Ports Ltd, will take a couple more ocean freight containers into storage for me; that news has made me feel a lot better. WONDERFUL NEWS!

Friday 04/12/2009

1:32 p.m. Home. I am not feeling up to scratch. I go up and down. I called Bentley Cars Ltd in Bellshill. Do they know Iain Murray? '*Whit dae yeh want tae know him fur?*' he might have asked. He apparently does live in Irvine. Iain had told me to get in touch with him once I had had my accounts audited, as he would support my initiative. Which I was able to do thanks to the pro bono generosity of Ross & Co of Dunoon. I sent a copy of the Surplus Educational Supplies Foundation accounts to Iain, c/o the Bentley dealership in Bellshill, who had said they would forward my letter on to him, but I have had no reply since.

I called Lloyds Pharmacy regarding my prescription.

Saturday 05/12/2009

11:22 a.m. Home. I have not long arrived at Haymarket Station and got a taxi to take me up to Companies House. We talked about Auld Reekie being guy dreichie this morning. On to Mo's Moroccan Bakery.

I put the Surplus Educational Supplies Foundation, Company No. 337348, accounts through the letter box and walked up to Lothian Road. When I saw Edinburgh Castle, I got my bearings. I crossed the busy main road, went down past the Edinburgh Playhouse, along and across Lothian Road once more, and up the steps into the Sheraton Hotel. I needed to answer a call of nature pretty quickly: plush carpets, civilised gentility, couthiness. *'May I have a pot of tea please?'* I made myself comfortable. I paid the bill. Tipped the young lad and disappeared for a wee moment. I called Marion to let her know where I was. I will chill here for a bit and then give Peter, the marketing economist who lives on Cambridge Street a couple of blocks away, a call. He welcomes me and makes coffee. He has been an encouraging supporter of my efforts to salvage fit-for-purpose, surplus to requirements, educational resources and deliver them to where they can be put to good use; we have a discussion.

I record here briefly what Peter, development and marketing economist, said to me. *'What would it cost DFID, OXFAM, Tear Fund etc. to equip a classroom in a primary and a secondary school in Bluefields? Their costs, your costs. The DFID Nicaragua programme will be managed from the DFID Caribbean office in Barbados, and will be delivered through partnership with the World Bank [Peter once worked for them see his book An Economists Tale] and their development partners. The British Embassy supports small projects in Nicaragua with a particular focus on the Caribbean Coast region, where it has been undertaking a prison reform campaign to improve conditions for juvenile and women prisoners in the Bluefields jail,*' he said.

I contact the British Embassy consular official Sheila Pacheco and Dr José Taboada, Honorary Consul, Managua. Peter mentions the name of Andrew Mitchell MP, who he said is conscientious and approachable and is now the titular head of DFID, also: The Nicaraguan British Association, Michael Jackson, British Association, Managua; Greg Pope MP, House of Commons, Westminster; Peter Goldring, Member of Parliament for Edmonton East and Opposition, Foreign Affairs; Bruce La Rochelle. I call these people and email them and get absolutely nowhere.

Monday 07/12/2009

9:49 a.m. Home. The house is quiet. I have brushed my teeth. It's raining. What's ahead? I am going to contact John at WH Malcolm Transport Ltd and see if they will give me some space to park my 'boxes' and/or warehouse space for educational resources. 'He's upstairs I'll get him to phone you,' he said helpfully.

I have just had a call from Norman Hill at First Port. Norman tells me about Ian Strachan at REUSE in Motherwell, to whom he has given my email. Networking. I called him. Perhaps he can store my container? I left a message for Archie, team leader, Community Services, Glenrothes. He is to call me back. Called Renwick, surveyor Fife Council, Glenrothes, to keep him posted. I was speaking to John at WH Malcolm Transport Ltd, who tells me that they will pick up the SESF container from Eldapoint Ltd, and take it across to their Fould Dubs depot in Grangemouth.

I am overwhelmed by this KINDNESS, GOODNESS, and

Monday 07/12/2009

GOODWILL. The pro bono corporate assistance that has enabled me to stay afloat for so long. So far, I have not run out of favours. I have never expected or presumed on such help, but it has been the underlying theme of this initiative from the start and what drives me to see this project through to completion.

12:47 p.m. I call Fife Council and try to speak to Ken Greer, chief executive. *'Mr Greer has gone out to lunch,'* she said.

1:24 p.m. I am awaiting replies to messages. I am to call John Murray next week.

1:43 p.m. I call Maersk AP Moller Group. I wish to be directed to the person in charge of corporate and social responsibility, and speak with Helene. Her response does not offer much hope. I am to write a begging bowl letter to Kate, AP Moller Group, Maersk House, Braham Street, London. *'May I charter for free, all crewed, just one of your six container ships currently tied up in Loch Striven. I have some shipments to make?'*

You have some nerve. Who do you think you are? Just me, that's all. No, that was not what I said, it was just another crazy thought that crossed my mind.

I called Archie Melville again and spoke to Craig, of Community Services Criminal Justice Dept., to make arrangements with them to supply one of their teams to assist me in the loading of container GATU4033193 with the educational resources currently stored in one of their industrial units. Call Renwick, Fife Council surveyor, for the address of the unit. (Call him on Tuesday 8 December.) Call John Murray once transport is arranged. I call Archie again at the Community Services Criminal Justice Department and spoke with Craig regarding the collection of educational resources, the loading of the container and the need to take an inventory of the resources that are loaded. I set in place the collection and uplift for Friday 11 December.

MY WORD and YOUR WORD IS OUR BOND. Once the above is all in place, call Renwick for address of Unit 3, Southfield Industrial Estate. The resources have been there a while (see earlier diary notes) and perhaps moved.

4:57 p.m. Home. I call John Murray at WH Malcolm Transport Ltd, who said he would speak to John Boal to see whether I could use their depot at Fould Dubs in Grangemouth to temporarily store my 'boxes.' My ambition, and the gap between that and my actuality: my reach exceeds my grasp.

I am to call Bill on Tuesday, 26 January 2010 regarding the website. All delays on the website that he is building can't be finalised until the salvaged educational resources are located in a new storage base. Fould Dubs, Faulds Point Park, Gourock, Inverclyde. You can't put the cart before the horse. I need to have the salvaged educational resources in situ and they must be properly inventoried, and costed/priced before resale.

Tuesday 08/12/2009

9:54 a.m. Home. Here I am, hot-desking. I continue to make numerous telephone calls. I am wheelin' an dealin', if that's what you want to call it. The collection of the container GATU4033193 from Eldapoint Ltd and delivery to Glenrothes has been arranged in collaboration with many good-hearted individuals.

10:12 a.m. All systems go. Ready for Friday 11 December 2009. Liz, journalist, *Fife Herald*, will have a reporter on site. I will be there on the spot, all being well. I have not managed this project by remote control. I have borne the responsibility of it and carried my share of the burdens involved in all of the organisation of shipments so far.

11:07 a.m. I have just received a return call from Archie,

Thursday 10/11/2009

Community Services project officer, to confirm for Friday morning 11 December. BRILLIANT! I have lined up all the players and I am speechless with gratitude. TOGETHER WE MADE IT HAPPEN. It certainly has not been all my own work. SESF has been a joint work and achievement from the start.

3:29 p.m. I have returned from Rothesay, cycling against the wind. I had gone in to DC Murray Decorators paint shop and picture framers to collect some framed Manning and Hanschell old family photographs and paid the bill. As I was about to stop off at the post office, I saw Iain standing outside the Taverna pub at the corner of Guildford Square. I stopped to speak to him. He asked me how the trip to Bluefields went. I told him that I did not leave until Sunday. He invited me into the Taverna for coffee and introduced me to his friend Ken, who is a ship's engineer who works on a North Sea oil rig. He tells me that he has been all over the world – he knows the Pacific Coast of the south and the Caribbean coast of Central America like the back of his hand. In the course of the conversation I mentioned that my son was a deck officer cadet, his reply to this was, '*Has he been lobotomised yet?*' I let the remark pass me by.

On the way out of the pub I met Donald the taxi driver sitting at the bar. He asked me if I could get him a CD-ROM for a laptop, and I told him I would ask Bill McCord for one. I went along the street to Print Point and asked Martin if he'd make a couple of small laminated posters for the container, for a price of course. All stationery publicity costs have been borne by me.

Email from Stephen Phillips, Burness solicitors, Glasgow, with a lease document attached for the warehouse at Faulds Park, Platform 2, which has cost me more than I needed, or could, afford.

Thursday 10/11/2009

11:25 a.m. Home. I am slow to move. I am finding it difficult to get into, for want of a better word, the flow. But there is nothing else for it, I just have to get on with it. I am going to call all those individuals who are about to be engaged in the process of removing educational resources tomorrow morning from Unit 3, The Food Centre warehouse, Glenrothes, just to make sure that all parts of this system of removal and storage are ready to go, that the LOGISTICS of it is in place. '*That's just a big word,*' said Eric, as he whisked me up the road to Falkirk High Street railway station in his very top-of-the-range motor that afternoon, way back on Saturday 16 December 2006.

To do: call the following – John Murray at WH Malcolm Transport Ltd; Craig Pearson, Community Services; Renwick, the surveyor with Fife Council, who will be there with a key to open the unit; Liz of the fourth estate to make sure we all get a bit of publicity for the collection.

11:35 a.m. Everything okay with WH Malcolm Transport Ltd. They will have the SESF container at the Glenrothes Food Centre complex at 10 a.m.

1:00 a.m. '*Call me when you are at the Glenrothes Bus Station and I will be here to open the unit for you,*' said Renwick.

11:43 a.m. '*Liz will know all about it,*' said the helpful journalist at the *Fife Free Press*, Cupar office. I am fighting my way at the moment through the inertia barrier.

12:59 p.m. Back home. The sun is still shining. I met Iain on his way to the pub and walked with him to the Co-op car park, and went across the road and into Print Point where I met Caroline and chatted for a bit. Then Liz was telling me about her son Duncan's recent trans-Saharan journey via Mauretania and Mali in an old banger, which had to be rerouted because of the threat of being kidnapped. I gave her a donation for his trip. I then cycled back up the road.

Friday 11/12/2009

3:02 p.m. The financial statement accounts for SESF have finally arrived. It is a good thing I pressed for a faxed copy last Friday, which I was able to deliver the following day 'par la main' into Companies House letter box, and which I hope they find all in order. I called Ross & Co to thank them and asked if they could send a copy to OSCR the Scottish Charities Regulator. Bless them once again, that is Jim, Allison, and the team in Dunoon.

Friday 11/12/2009

8:30 a.m. '*Is this the Glenrothes bus?*' I have not long boarded the Saint Andrews' bus, which is now moving out of Buchanan Street Bus Station. Thick, cold mist is lying heavily over the city. I walked up from Glasgow Central railway station. I had taken the train up from Wemyss Bay. Ferry over from Rothesay. I cycled in under a starry sky and a bright crescent moon. On my journey once more.

2:10 p.m. I have just boarded the train at Polmont Station. Thanks to the taxi driver who picked me up from the rank on Bowen Road in Grangemouth. When I asked if he would take me up to Falkirk High railway station he questioned it because of the delay caused by a burst water main, and so it was to Polmont Station. He tells me that he knows Eric. '*Elisabeth hires and fires,*' he said. He went on to tell me about his return from working in Saudi Arabia and told me that Eric ran the family's hotel, where he had his 25th wedding anniversary. '*He couldn't do enough for me,*' he said. Nice recommendation, which I seconded. That's Eric, who he said plays bowls with his brother. Well roll it back as this train rolls along.

I arrived at Glenrothes town centre at 10:15 a.m. I got a taxi, and the driver could not find the Viewfield Industrial Estate Food Centre, which was overshadowed by thick fog, so I went into the HRW Freight Forwarders office in the Fife Food and Business Centre, Southfield Industrial Estate. Thanks to Linda their office manager, who phoned Gillian and who in turn called Renwick and Craig. The container had arrived and the Community Services Teams had already begun to load it. I wandered around to the other side of this vast warehouse unit to find the SESF container on a trailer attached to a WH Malcolm Transport artic/rig and got stuck in with the team of brilliant young folk. I met Colin their supervisor and team leader, and young Justine who was busy taking an inventory of the educational resources that her team were busily loading into the container. The young team stacked the school furniture to the ceiling of the 40-foot ocean freight container. Justine's list: The following educational resources were loaded into container GATU4033193. 268 wooden chairs; 125 metal-legged, plastic-seated chairs; 25 large Formica-topped tables; 17 small desks; 10 office desks; 6 small filing cabinets; 10 bookshelves; 24 metal stools; 2 office chairs; 2 wooden boxes; 2 nursery play-equipment structures; 17 trolley pigeon tray holders; 72 small tables; 1 bed.'

Please thank Justine who took this inventory. Stephen, the driver, took our photograph and gave me a lift back to Grange Dock, Port of Grangemouth. The container will be parked at their Fould Dubs rail and road depot. I thought for a moment that I would drop in at the Duncan Adams Transport Ltd Grange Dock depot down the road, but stayed focused and headed for home.

5:03 p.m. Home. When I got into Central Station, with just a few minutes to spare, I managed to get the Wemyss Bay train from Platform 9 at 2:50 p.m. On the ferry I met Janet from the new houses along the road, who was going home to an empty house. She recently lost Geoffrey, who sat at their front window overlooking the Kyle of Bute and would give me a wave as I cycled past on my home from school. We chatted over a hot chocolate.

Chapter Twelve

The Trip To Bluefields, Costa Caribena, Nicaragua, Meso-America

Monday 14/12/2009

5:25 p.m. Terminal E2, Miami International Airport, Florida, United States of America. I am sitting here in a lounge looking into the west, where a big orange sun has gone down behind the tail fins of two American Airlines planes parked on the other side of a huge plate-glass window. I've just met Brendan from New York State, who is also on his way to Managua. He has got a brace around his neck. He tells me that he fell off a dump truck and hurt his neck. He told me that he is fortunate to be walking.

Well, here I am en route for Bluefields, Costa Caribena, Nicaragua, Central America. The flight leaves in an hour's time. I arrived from Heathrow at 2:30 p.m. (7:30 p.m. UK time). I am glad to be off that flight. I travelled with a Jamaican Brit and her dear children who are going 'home' for Christmas. She is studying accounting and business at London Metropolitan University. I have made a long-distance call to Marion, thanks to Laura, who is a resident of the Turks and Caicos Islands. I was struggling to put the right number of coins into the payphone and she was sitting nearby and came to my rescue. Later I called Roland Malins-Smith to let him know I'll make my own way to the Seafreight Agencies Lines in Miami Doral when I return on Friday, so he need not have the trouble of coming to meet me.

I am now in at the deep end and will just have to try and cool down. Yes, and LISTEN! As I walked up a long, sloping upwards corridor from the currency exchange counter, I reached into my pocket to find that I had dropped my passport folder with passport and airline tickets. OUCH! I had not walked many yards back to the airport lounge wondering to myself, '*What on earth do I do now?*' and was about to retrace my steps, when a smart young Ivy League couple appeared from behind me and handed it to me. I thanked them effusively and felt a complete idiot – definitely not off to a good start – you prat!

I started falteringly on this project almost five years ago and I don't want to give the wrong impression, but the objective of this brief visit is simply to be able to fulfil and realise what is possible for me to achieve. Don't presume. I move forward in faith, through faith, and by faith.

11:00 p.m. Well, here I am ensconced, that's a word right enough, in Room 218 at the Real Intercontinental Metrocentral Hotel in Managua, booked into 'this most splendid of the country's international hotels' – so I read in Footprint Nicaragua. Arrived at Air Managua International Airport on flight A598 737 into slight humid warmth, through Immigration and Customs, and collected my suitcase with no bother.

Crowds surround the exit to the terminal building. '*Are you David? I am here from the embassy. Bruce is in the car,*' said this casually dressed man. Now this is more like it! Are you Felix Leiter or James Bond? Neither, just me. We get into the back of the limousine.

'*My name is Alistair. Bruce was telling me about you and your work,*' he said. Oh? Methinks I'll have to play along with this and whatever programme has been laid on for me. The agenda has been set already. You can't afford to go off message and do your own thing – so watch it, chum! '*You have come from the Isle of Bute, I believe,*' he said. He asks me if I know The Butes. I tell

Monday 14/12/2009

him that I do not move in those circles, but I do not tell him that I would never wish to do so. We drove on through this busy, brightly neon-lit city. This is going to be some trip, but I know that I will have to suppress my sense of wonder, enthusiasm, and desire to let it all hang out, as they say.

It was the red-carpet treatment courtesy of Her Majesty's Government, Foreign and Commonwealth Office, British Embassy, San José, Costa Rica, right from the start of my arrival at the airport, being whisked away from that crowd of folk to a warm welcome. But this is going to be, for me, a visit on tramlines keeping my ebullient nature under control. I was driven up to this imposing modern hotel with several doormen, which reminded me of the few infrequent visits to the Hilton Hotel in Port of Spain many years ago. Bruce tells me that he will meet me at 8 a.m. tomorrow. Alastair has told me that he returns to the United Kingdom tomorrow and is doing a PhD on sustainability

Bruce

City view from a window of The Real Intercontinental Metrocentral Hotel.

in the Hebrides, which involves linking communities in the West of Scotland and Nicaragua. He seems interested and keen about the prospect. I told him, should he ever come our way, the Hanschell family would make him welcome.

'*I hope you don't find the air conditioning too cold,*' said Bruce. Me, I'll take whatever comes my way and be thankful: with this luxury accommodation am I going to complain about anything? I am here to take my cues from Bruce, Ambassador Tom Kennedy, and the Nicaraguan Government officials in Bluefields, and to listen to the people they will introduce me to. I am after facts and numbers. From what I learn from this brief visit I will prepare a proposal that will justify any future initiative on my part. One step at a time …

On the flight here I met Dorian, now living in Los Angeles, who tells me that his father had worked for the Somoza government and was kicked out of the country in 1980. His parents now live in Florida. I recall the journeying mercies since I left the Isle

Tuesday 15/12/2009

Bluefields Bay view from a window of The Hotel Oasis.

of Bute yesterday evening: the lady who helped me to call home, and the young couple who had picked up my folder with passport and had followed me up the concourse of Terminal E2 to return it. I had left my glasses and address book at the payphone booth after calling Roland – I have got to learn to be more careful and not get so easily carried away by the immediate novel experience.

Tuesday 15/12/2009

6:21 a.m. The sun is coming up over Managua City as I look out through this wall-to-wall window. A Caribbean West Indies island scene, familiar to me but on a much larger scale. I can see a Hilton Hotel not far away, overlooking the coconut palms, and a massive MacDonald's hamburger sign. Down below me is a swimming pool fringed by palms in large pots. Maybe I shall go for a dip, given that I have been up since 4:15 a.m. I don't think so somehow, as there will be a tension between me wanting to enjoy this experience on the one hand and on the other the need to stay focused on the mission in hand for fear of losing the plot and the purpose of my visit. So, I have shaved, showered, and dressed in a white shirt neatly pressed by Marion. I'm ready for whatever business this day holds. As I look out the other window, across the valley, I can see a range of forested hills in the distance. I am going to vacate the room and go for a stroll around the block. I dare not venture too far, at least there is no harm in walking around the hotel.

6:00 p.m. (almost) The Hotel Oasis which Footprint Nicaragua tells me is …

'150 m from Bluefields Bay. The best hotel in town with spacious modern rooms, comfortable furnishings, and professional service. There's a casino downstairs with a handful of gaming tables should you fancy a low-key punt. Breakfast included.'

Main street, Bluefields, not far from Bluefields Bay. I can just see lights shining on the bay from my bedroom window. Once more I am told that this is the best hotel in town. *'David, we tried to get you the penthouse,'* says Bruce. I can see that there is a big Moravian church several hundred yards away. Night sounds: dogs barking, car horns beeping, people shouting. It sounds like there is an open-air preacher hollering his head off down at the small dock at the end of the street. There is an appetising smell of fish being cooked in the kitchen below this upmarket Costa Caribena hostelry. And here I am alone in Room 6.

I close the window to the balcony that runs the full length of the hotel. Bruce and I booked in here this afternoon after our flight from Managua in a single engine, La Costena Airline, two-piloted prop-driven aircraft. We sat not far behind the cockpit and climbed ever so slowly away beyond the cloud cover. This is a beautiful country. So much of the tropical vegetation; the breeze off the Mer Caribe; the cosmopolitan mix of different peoples and cultures; the horses and carts in the midst of motorised

Tuesday 15/12/2009

traffic; the abject poverty just beyond the confines, and literally cheek by jowl outside my window, has brought me back to the days, months and years I spent living on the islands of Barbados and Trinidad. In my heart, and in my bones, I am a creature of this part of Blue Planet Earth.

When we arrived at Bluefields Airport this morning it reminded immediately of landing up somewhere on a West Indian island. I felt as though I had, at long last after many years, arrived home. This feeling of instant belonging was not to last as I later discovered. Bruce introduced me to Señor Jimmy Henriques, who was there to meet us, and whose title was the Individual Regional Delegate of the Nicaraguan Ministry of the Interior. Señor Jimmy drove us through what easily could have been any small town in Trinidad (where I grew up from the ages of 7 to 18, apart from school terms in Barbados from 1955 to 1961), to the Hotel Oasis, a rather nondescript building on a very crowded pot-holed main street with garbage choking the gutters. I initially took what was to be our new abode to be a large, fairly modern private home surrounded by high walls on one side with huge sheet metal gates. There was what looked like a security guard outside a side entrance doorway, to what later turned out to be a casino, open all day and night. He stood casually with a sub-machine gun. We booked in. I was shown my room with all the mod cons, clean and comfortable, overlooking a side street with views over worse-for-wear, galvanised-roofed buildings, and the small port at the end of the street.

Bruce and I then set off down the main street, crowded with pedestrians and small shops taking up part of the pavement, to the market to find somewhere to eat. The sun was shining brightly. We went into a small café-cum-bar, which back in my Caribbean days was known as a rum shop. There was Country and Western music coming from a small kitchen at the back of a large room. Bruce ordered a beer and I a Coke. Fish and rice sounded good. No sooner had we sat down than we were besieged by several little lads

Homemade, wooden shoeshine boxes.

with their homemade, wooden shoeshine boxes. Unfortunately for them I could give them no custom as I had changed out of my fancy dancing black leather moccasins, which I have worn on special occasions since the day of our wedding, into an old pair of desert boots. But I made up for it by entertaining them with my little Spanglish and Creole patois. Bruce got his shoes shined. Soon another lad, older, of East Indian descent, and with a Guyanese accent, appeared with a bag over his shoulder, and with an assortment of new clothing to sell. I politely declined to purchase his wares, but he persisted and became somewhat aggressive.

Meanwhile, a group of four unsmiling, hard-faced looking men, who sat at a table at the back of the room drinking large bottles of beer, began to take what I thought was an interest in us, which made me feel uncomfortable. I noticed that one of them was more smartly dressed than his companions and was wearing what looked like a bespoke Savile Row striped shirt. As I was about

Tuesday 15/12/2009

to pay the young salesman for several packets of women's white socks, just to get rid of him and away from the scrutiny of the bad vibes coming from across the room, Bruce remarked that the lad was picking his nose as I was paying him. This made me laugh out loud, but it annoyed me at the same time, this contemptuous attitude to an old white man who was being helpful. Here I go again, being the nice guy flaming the sow's arse once more.

At that moment, another visitor, a young man Afro-Caribbean descent, came to our table and sat down. He knew Bruce but declined the offer of something to drink. He had come from Bilwi, a town up the coast (once called Puerto Cabezas) in search of assistance for his small community which had been virtually destroyed by Hurricane Felix two years ago. He told us that he was keen to set up an eco-tourist business whereby tourists could get a tour of his area and gain valuable experience in doing so. He hoped this business would be an economic lifeline for the community in its recovery. This area of Meso-American Nicaragua, as I learned later, is described as Region Autonoma Atlantico (RAAN). He spoke English with a strong Jamaican accent. I liked him right away as he seemed sincere and just wanted a leg up from someone like Bruce, who was here in the town in his capacity as the representative of Her Majesty's Government and had someone with possible access to the distribution of UK Government aid.

We had been waiting some time for our meal to appear and had to ask if it could be taken away with us. An appointment had been made to meet with officials from the local government down at the dock, from where we were to be taken out to Rama Cay, a tiny island in the Bay of Bluefields about half an hour's boat ride away. This island is the home of the remaining Community of the Rama people and Bruce said that he wanted me to meet their leader, Reverend Cleveland McCrea, and other members of the community. Bruce told me that they are desperately poor but resourceful and proud to retain what is left of their unique culture, and that they might be interested in a donation of educational resources from the Surplus Educational Supplies Foundation. Bruce went on to tell me that the British government had recently funded a project to have the Rama First People's tribal records, from a time when the entire Costa Caribena was once a British protectorate, put into a more permanent form. This vital assistance has enabled a small beleaguered community of First People to regain some of their land rights.

So, we set off with our fish and rice take away, up the main street under the gaze of hustlers and watchers, past the security guard with his sub-machine gun at the door of the Hotel Oasis Casino, and down the street that led to the small dock. There is an undefinable atmosphere of menace about this place. We got into an open boat, of which there were about half a dozen similar boats tied up beside each other under a large shed. The boat is what I would have described in Trinidad as a wide-beamed pirogue-type boat, moulded plastic hull with a rounded bough and rows of athwart benches. It had a large outboard motor of Japanese manufacture. We take a seat on one of the benches and don life jackets and proceed to eat our alfresco lunch from plastic trays, swigging bottles of Coca Cola. I am hungry for this grub! Our friend from Bilwi has followed us down to the dock and continues his conversation with Bruce, imploring him to be of some assistance to his community. He looks across hungrily at my tray of food and I move it towards him so he, too, can partake. I would have felt uncomfortable otherwise not to have done so.

No sooner had he began to share the meal with me than four young men, paramilitary types wearing combat fatigues, appeared from nowhere; in fact, I had noticed them squatting with some authority in the sunshine at the entrance to the dock. They grabbed him roughly and frog marched him away in the twinkling of an eye. I am now in a state of slight shock and have lost my appetite for the savoury tray of food before me. A heavy scene and I am now very angry. Bruce tells me to cool it and be careful. A short while before this I was starting to relax a wee bit and enjoy

Tuesday 15/12/2009

the ride. I guess things are not what they appear to be, something I had sensed all along; better to learn the score sooner than later. The engine starts up, some other folk climb aboard, they are better dressed than the other passengers and appear to be movers and shakers in Bluefields. Soon we are doing some rate of knots across the Bay of Bluefields.

This is exciting! I am carefree and the speed of this exit brings to mind the ride I had three years ago, powering out of Grange Dock, Port of Grangemouth, in Eric Adams', of Duncan Adams Transport Ltd, Porsche Carrera. (Eric had kindly offered me a lift to Falkirk High railway station so I could get the train back to Glasgow after I had filled a container with surplus educational resources that I had salvaged that morning from a large Fife Council primary school.) The boat, called a panga, is furiously making its way across the choppy water. I am holding on tightly to my newly purchased baseball cap with Nicaragua embroidered across the front – I would hate to lose it just yet. I wonder if this cracked-looking fibreglass hull will hold up to the strain. The flimsy life jacket I am wearing does nothing to reassure me. No wonder we had to eat our lunch first, for it would have been impossible to do so now. The first lot of fellow travellers had been waiting patiently, saying nothing, while we two finished our meal.

The small Moravian church, which had been built many years ago on Rama Cay Island, soon came into view. Little, smiling-faced nimble-footed youngsters took the painter and tied up the boat for us. They don't give us a second look. There are coconut palms, piles of oyster shells on the shoreline, and outdoor privies perched above the water. Small pigs and mangy skinny dogs wander about everywhere.

A group of older boys who are playing basketball ignore us as we walk through the village up to the McCrea family home to meet Reverend McCrea, Mrs McCrea and their 12 children – not all of whom are living currently under that one roof, at the same time, as they are mostly studying on the mainland. It is a large, one-roomed

At the home of the McCrea family.

wooden building with two doors at the front and one at the back, made from timber planks cut from what appears to be mahogany trees, possibly growing on their diminished ancestral lands in the much-depleted tropical rain forest. There is a fresh breeze blowing in through one of the front doors from the Caribbean Sea off Bluefields Bay, which reminds me once more of my roots. There is a large balcony at the front of the dwelling, roofed with coconut palm thatch. This home is spotlessly tidy. Someone has been doing their college homework. There is no desk – the textbooks are on a bed at the side of the room. The household strikes me as an ordered, happy place of calm, established by folk making the utmost from the very few resources that they have available.

    I am introduced to some of the children who have come home for the Christmas vacation, one of whom is studying medicine at the University of Leon (UNAN), another is studying to become a teacher. My Spanish is not up to scratch, but they all speak

Tuesday 15/12/2009

English. Mrs McCrea is proud of her children's achievements, all of whom are engaged in formal education. Bruce addresses them in Spanish and asks me to tell them a little about myself and why I have come to the Costa Caribena. For me, it is a great privilege to come all this way from Scotland to meet these people. Bruce disappears with Reverend McCrea into the church building next door and the reverend shows him the Rama Tribes transformed precious records, which to some extent have helped preserve their unique history, self-esteem and identity, and perhaps rights to their property. They are a great people: multilingual, and poor, yet managing to remain independent and have somehow survived into the 21st century. I believe UNESCO considers them a unique cultural treasure.

Bruce returns as we have a meeting with the community elders in their village hall further down the muddy track. The older boys are still playing basketball.

Accompanying us, as I later discovered, were the two Bluefields-based officials from the Nicaraguan Ministry of Education who had not been forthcoming about who they were on the boat. I made my pitch to them, taking my cues beforehand from Bruce and Jimmy Henriques, who had met us on our arrival at the airport earlier today. Bruce translated my brief speech into Spanish. There appeared to be no interest in what I had to offer.

We were then taken to another building, to what appeared to be a school classroom. It was empty of school furniture and it looked like someone had had a fire going recently on the classroom floor. They could certainly do with some school furniture and fit-for-purpose educational resources from SESF, but did they want it and if I sent an ocean freight container of it would they get it? At that point, after having had my hopes raised with meeting the McCrea family, it did not appear to me that anyone was making much effort to run what passed for a school. We then walked past another small building where a diesel generator was chugging away, and someone remarked that it had only been recently repaired. We then headed back to shore and before reaching where the panga had been tied up, I saw an elderly gentleman sprawled on the ground. He gave me the impression of having been discarded like a piece of rubbish. He looked up at me appealingly, so I quickly reached into my pocket and gave him some money in American currency. The party ahead were oblivious to it and it was the least that I could have done. One hand doing what the other need knows nothing about.

Back we went across the choppy bay, up to the hotel to chill in the breeze on the hotel verandah with a can of ice-cold beer – the first I'd had in years. It went easily down the back of my throat. Bruce had arranged for us to have a meal later at La Loma, a popular restaurant not far up the road, on a hill overlooking Bluefields in the barrio of San Pedro. At night there was not much to see. Tropical night sounds: cicadas chirruping, little frogs whistling, and dogs barking. There was just a thick fish soup with chunks of lobster and shrimp on the menu, and it was delicious – the best ever. We were the only diners and we had much to talk about and had a good many laughs. It was, for me, a bittersweet day and a memorable evening.

Well, the rest of my brief stay here beckons and I can only try to make the most of this wonderful opportunity to establish in some small way how my Scottish Registered Charity might be able to contribute something of value, even if only to one school. My 40 boxes of library books sent out several months ago have not been received. Wait and see.

Wednesday 16/12/2009

8:55 p.m. Room 6, Hotel Oasis. Heavy beat coming from the boom box across the street. Fan spinning above my head. I have not long returned from having dinner with Bruce at Chez Marcel, where he likes to take his important guests. I smile to myself when he tells me that, because in no way do I feel important.

Wednesday 16/12/2009

This morning I awoke with sunshine beaming in from across the Bay of Bluefields and was up and dressed and away out for a stroll round the block. There were not many folks. I could easily have been back in Tunapuna town in Trinidad, which was not far from where our family lived in the 1950s. I returned to the hotel and knocked on the door of Bruce's room, no response, so I went and had some breakfast of a fried egg with beans and rice, a glass of freshly squeezed orange juice and a mug of coffee. Chilled, listening to sweet bird song that I was unable to identify.

Today we had a meeting with Jimmy, the regional delegate of the Nicaraguan Ministry of Education, in his air-conditioned office along the road. He expressed some interest in the purpose of my visit, but I did not get any commitment of support. From there it was further up the now busy main street to the Bluefields Prison to meet with a prison officer who, for some time now, has supported the Foreign and Commonwealth Office efforts to contribute to prison reform by building cells that would separate young prisoners from seasoned criminals. He told us that recently one of his colleagues had been killed by drug smugglers near the border with Honduras. We had come to deliver a parcel of books that Bruce had brought with him for the prisoners from the Mary Baker School in Costa Rica.

Then it was on to meet with Minerva Forbes, the principal of Santa Rosa School in the barrio of Santa Rosa, where I was dropped off.

We had a long chat in her office along with Elba Blandon, the Asesora de Espanol en Secudaria en el Ministerio de Educacion, who sat beside her and said nothing. Señora Forbes listed some of the needs of her 443-pupil school: whiteboards; desks for teachers, with chairs; doors for classrooms; and repairs for at least three classrooms. The effects of Hurricane Felix, which had passed this way in 2007, were still very much in evidence. Señora Forbes gave me the impression that I, and my supporters back in Scotland, could be of some help. I left that meeting encouraged, feeling

Teachers of Santa Rosa School.

that the long journey and coincidental circumstances that had led to me to coming here, and all the work at personal cost that I had put into SESF four years previously, was now worthwhile. The school's janitor, who did not give me his name, showed me around the school. It could have been a scaled-down, tiny version of Miss Richardson's Private School in Woodbrook, downtown Port of Spain, Trinidad, which my sister Diana and I attended in the 50s.

I was collected later by Bruce and his chauffeur, in a local government ministry vehicle, to attend another meeting across the town of Bluefields with Señor Oscar Aburto the regional delegate to the Nicaraguan Ministry of Education, and Jimmy, who translated for me at what was, I thought, a constructive meeting. Señor Aburto's view was, '*if you and your foundation can deliver those resources no longer required by the Scottish Education system to us here in the Costa Caribena, that would be wonderful.*' He said that he would mention my offer of my charity's delivery of an ocean

Wednesday 16/12/2009

Damage to the Santa Rosa School from Hurricane Felix.

freight container-load of educational resources when he met with his colleagues at the Ministerio de Educacion de Nicaragua headquarters in Managua later that week. I was on a roll and buzzing. From that office I was chauffeured back to the Hotel Oasis to meet with Bruce.

We then walked back up the main street to Bluefields Prison where we were taken into the director's office. From there it was back out into the town to purchase items with funds that Bruce had raised, for such items as toiletries and sweets, to make up Christmas gift parcels for a large number of juvenile prisoners who had been booked in earlier that week, shortly before our arrival in the town.

While walking back up the street, now choked with small Japanese taxis, we were approached by a white American vagrant who looked like a washed-out Big Yin. He told us he was unable to continue his beachcombing sojourn on the Mosquito Coast and that he had had his passport stolen. He asked Bruce if he

Bruce bought gifts for some young prisoners.

could help him and gave him a photocopy of it. At that moment I lost the plot, once again, and being one of the self-appointed patron saints of lost causes and lame ducks, greeted this poor soul in my hail and hearty fashion with a handshake. This move on my part offended him greatly, and he screamed out *'Who do you think you are? You are nothing but a g-d dammed effing egotistical son of a bitch!'* And then threatened, there and then, to stick a knife in me ... Ouch! His response shocked me somewhat. I had never, ever, in all my journeying, especially so in my adopted home city of Glasgow, received such a violent response from an individual in reduced circumstances. Yes, well that's me back again on the straight and narrow highway and keeping my eyes on the road ahead. Bruce found this incident highly amusing.

We headed back to the prison, where we waited a short time until the parcels of gifts, which Bruce had purchased earlier, arrived. In the prison director's office we met with some of the young prisoners who would receive these Christmas gifts, and

Wednesday 16/12/2009

We waited at a small makeshift dock to catch a panga out to El Bluff.

Bruce made a presentation to introduce me. I felt humbled. If only those young folks knew that once upon a time I could have been in their shoes. Someone asked Bruce if I was the new British Ambassador. What a laugh.

Another smart restaurant for lunch. Prawn cocktail and a bowl of fish and lobster soup, which went down a treat. We hung around, chatting away, until the time came for another offshore meeting. We walked back down to the other end of the town and waited at a small makeshift dock to catch a panga out to El Bluff for a meeting with Directora del Instituto Nacional Nueva Puerto and the Directora Primaria Virgen del Carmen. El Bluff sits at the end of a peninsula that separates the Caribbean Sea from the Bay of Bluefields. It was once a small thriving port, but it looked to me as if it had seen better days. There were many big shrimp and lobster boats, with rusting tackle, bobbing about in the harbour. A spanking-new, sleek Nicaraguan Navy and Customs patrol vessel was tied up at the dock and not much else.

Teachers at the Puerto El Bluff school.

Bruce introduced me to the staff at the two schools. They were glad that there might be the prospect of receiving a possible ocean freight container-load shipment of educational resources from the SESF. However, Señora Hansack (Directora del Instituto Nacional Nueva Amanecer, Puerto El Bluff) qualified her colleagues' expectations by saying that after Hurricane Felix there were many foreign visitors who promised assistance, but did not deliver. I was impressed by their dedication and commitment to their students. These teachers were doing their best they could with a paucity of classroom resources. Teachers in the United Kingdom who complain should swap places with them for a salutary sabbatical.

It was dark by the time we made our way back, by panga, across the bay to Bluefields from the Port of El Bluff. As I walked through the town, accompanied by new friends and fellow colleagues in the Nicaraguan education system, who had come to bid us goodbye, I felt assured that I would make every effort on my return to Scotland, providing it was possible to do so, to send them one of my big boxes (see inventory of contents in 40-foot ocean freight container GATU4033193, currently parked at WH Malcolm Transport Ltd, Fould Dubs depot, Grangemouth). Time will tell.

Thursday 17/12/2009

6:41 a.m. I am sitting here on the Hotel Oasis balcony-cum-verandah open-air dining room. The sun is shining brightly now, the dogs are barking, and birds in the nearby mango trees are whistling their once familiar and varied Caribbean tropical song. The city has been awake from early and I am reflecting on the brief time that I have been privileged to spend here in the Costa Caribena. In this short time, I have met a cross-section of the Bluefields community: seen at first hand some of the needs of teachers and their students, and the impoverishment of many, particularly the elderly, who seem to have no visible means of support.

7:30 a.m. I am sitting in the departure lounge of Aeroporto de Bluefields. We are chatting away. Bruce mentions that I should watch The School of Rock and, while telling me why, is summarily interrupted by an immigration official-cum-paramilitary, who has come across the small departure lounge and proceeds to interrogate us both as to what we are doing in Bluefields. Again, it is possibly my fault: perhaps my insouciant, comfortable anywhere on the Blue Planet attitude, which I know irritates some people, and loud laughter may have begun to annoy this individual. Who do you think you are, being so carefree on my patch! Cool it, chum, you are not back home yet. The airport security gentleman was very thorough, removed my shaving kit and emptied it. The spell of pure momentary magic has been broken.

12:40 p.m. I am now back at the Real Intercontinental Metro Centro, Managua. I am sitting outside on the deserted patio beside an aquamarine, shimmering, swimming pool. There at least five different varieties of palm trees in large painted pots beside the pool. The sun is shining brightly. There is a roar of traffic outside the high walls. I consider the opportunity that presents itself to have a splash, but no, this jaunt is not a holiday and I have been grateful so far for journeying mercies. But for a few blunders I have not blotted my copy book. Bruce, bless him, is off to fly back home to San José. He has made sure that this 'Resource,' as he has called me in jest, and who is at the disposal of the Foreign and Commonwealth Office, British Embassy, Costa Rica, has once more been booked into this lap of overflowing luxury. Given its context, for me at any rate, it's embarrassing – for this time I am up several more floors, to Room 511.

Did Howard Hughes once have the entire eighth floor in February 1972, when the Bahamian government told him and his entourage to leave their country and come here at the invitation of then President Anastasio Somoza? Reel it back a few eventful hours …

The hotel is about an hour from Aerpuerto Sandino. We returned from Bluefields this time in a twin-engine aircraft with a plane-load of young holidaymakers from Spain, who had been staying on Corn Island. On the return flight I met Ludovic from Paris, an agriculturalist who has a global vision and who had been working prior to his visit to Nicaragua in Bangladesh. He had been on a short visit to Bluefields and I was able to converse with him in French, and he told me that he was now on his way to Costa Rica, so I introduced him to Bruce when we landed.

As we were being driven into the city the driver, Señor Harold, asked Bruce if I would like to visit the historic Nicaraguan city of Granada, as he would be my guide. I was tempted, momentarily, to accept this offer but reluctantly declined, perhaps another day, should I have the pleasure of returning to this beautiful country. Since I wished to remain on the tramlines, I put his proffered business card into my wallet. Discretion is the better part of valour.

Thursday 17/12/2009

I must continue to gang warily and not go astray, which I could do so easily and would be so much more fun. But I decide to stay on the straight and narrow, thereby limiting the opportunities to come off my bicycle, and think of the wise alternative to chill out in some style and think of those who were awaiting my return.

However, just outside the city limits we got stuck at a set of traffic lights on a four-lane highway when immediately a little girl, no more than eight years old, appeared knocking at the window. I wound it down and, without thinking, handed her some local currency, which to my dismay was the equivalent of a week's wages. Oh dear! Big mistake! Another of my impulsive blunders. One of the mealtime conversations Bruce and I had discussed the Preventive Principle, which he had learned about while watching the Star Trek television series. Point taken. I must stop doing a wrong thing for a good reason. From my perspective, sometimes, it's better to have been too reckless in one's largesse than be calculating and grippit. I only pass this way once. Not to be outdone, at the next set of traffic lights a group of older children had built themselves into a tower, at the top of which one of this team of enterprising acrobats had climbed and proceeded to juggle several balls in the air – another youngster appeared at Bruce's window, which he wound down and made a donation.

I should mention here that this was only one of Her Majesty's government official's many generous acts. Just to mention a few: putting a sticking plaster on an elderly gentleman's badly bruised elbow and buying him a cool drink; making it possible for a group of newly booked young prisoners to receive a Christmas gift, purchased with funds he had raised personally from playing in rock concerts all over Central America and in his home city of Calgary; and bringing me a cup of coffee earlier. What goes round comes round for sure, Bruce.

1:55 p.m. I have been trying to call home. A very helpful hotel receptionist and hotel administrator at the Centro de Negocios, the hotel's business centre, is trying to make a connection. She tells me that the telephone company is having problems. Back in the hotel lobby, Señora Luisa continues to put up with my persistent attempts to call home.

2:30 p.m. I am out of the sunshine and back in Room 511. I am looking out the big floor-to-ceiling window over the tops of the towering cabbage palms, their fronds waving at me in the breeze, which is blowing all the way from the Caribbean coast to the modern Metrocento Mall. I have come up here in this fastness to change into something more casual and collect some laundry to have washed, and then return to the hotel foyer to await a telephone call from Scotland. I decide to step outside and gather a few more of the sun's rays.

4:15 p.m. I have returned to my table beside the pool and there is still just me. Where is everybody? I guess the movers and shakers who can afford the tariff only show up after dark. Señor Miguel has brought me a Chiquito negro coffee and what looks like a pastry of some kind. I have already had a salad and a Coca Cola from the buffet. I have returned through and around Managua's equivalent of Glasgow City's Braehead shopping centre.

5:49 p.m. I return to Centro Negocios and try to make another phone call, and I am still unsuccessful. I have a go at sending an email. Sent! Brilliant! Muchas gracias, Señora, for all your trouble. And I get an abrazo grande. Magic!

6:30 p.m. I am now back in Room 511. I had some trouble calling home, at least they should have got my post and I will try and call again from Miami DV when I get to Roland's office. I had a shower and am staying put. I am watching Nicaraguan Managua News on the widescreen TV. I switch it off and iron my clean clothes, and get my head down.

Friday 18/12/2009

8:35 a.m. I am on Flight 896 American Airlines bound for Miami at a cruising altitude of 36,000 feet and watching the light break over Managua City. Bless them all. I made an early start, up at 3 a.m. with a glimmer of sunrise through the cabbage and coconut palm fronds.

Bruce had booked me a taxi on arrival in Managua yesterday morning. Señor Carlos, the taxi driver, chatted with me on our way to the airport. A large modern terminal with many smart shops. I happen to meet up with Brendan from New York State once more. I am now sitting beside Jack, on his way to his other home in Seattle. He tells me that he is a professor of drama at the University of South Florida. He has travelled throughout the Caribbean archipelago, and on learning that I am a Bajan, he asks me if I knew the actress, Claudette Colbert. Sorry, who she? What an amazing trip this continues to be. I am journeying ever onwards and struggling upwards.

2:27 p.m. I am sitting in the office of Roland Malins-Smith, president of Seafreight Agencies Lines, Miami, Florida, USA.

It was a safe landing at Miami International Airport three hours ago. It was raining heavily. '*What were you doing in Nicaragua?*' asked the uniformed immigration official. '*I was on business,*' I replied. '*What kind of business?*' he asked, forcefully. '*I was on a fact-finding mission on behalf of my Scottish Registered Charity, the Surplus Educational Supplies Foundation,*' I said. An answer which seemed to satisfy him, but I had my doubts. Felix from the Republic of Haiti, who had been living in Miami for 30 years, drove me in his Yellow Cab, of which there were a large queue, bumper-to-bumper, waiting to pick up passengers. I chatted away to him in my Quebecois Creole patois as he drove in on the four-lane highway. Je parle le francais comme un boeuf de la Barbade.

Roland and Mrs Malins-Smith took me out to the Doral Golf

and Country Club for lunch. The latter just looks at me as if to say, what on earth has brought you here? I, between intermittent mouthfuls from a delicious plate of food from the largest, amazing buffet I have ever seen, try to justify my presence in these luxurious surroundings. It's like someone's private residence. Like a huge hacienda with porticos and palms. This is all very impressive, and I wish to revel and enjoy my meal, but no, keep to the programme and don't be distracted. Press on, seize the opportunities presented, and make initial arrangements for sending the next shipment of SESF educational resources to the schools in Bluefields, El Bluff and Rama Cay. I pretend to take it all in my stride. Roland is very welcoming to me and I am in a state of effervescent gratitude.

The offices of Seafreight Agencies.

2:40 p.m. He just introduced me to his entire staff, taking me round to all of the departments, which are linked in an open-plan office, and telling them about my initiative: some of whom handled four of my 40-foot ocean freight container shipments from Kingston Jamaica, to St George's, Grenada. And I was able to thank them personally. Seafreight Agencies Lines have a large warehouse complex on site with loading bays for containers. His corporation has eight ships under charter.

3:40 p.m. We return to Roland's office. He has told me that Seafreight Agencies Lines vessels do not call at any of Nicaragua's Caribbean ports, but their competition does. So, there and then, he's putting through a call to Captain Jordan Monocandilos, the chief executive of Bernuth Lines, whose shipping firm does. He is now making arrangements with him to ship an SESF container to the port of delivery, which is the Port of El Rama on the Rio Escondido, and from where the container can be delivered by road to the final destination of Bluefields city. This shipping firm can also deliver containers to the Port of El Bluff. This connection made on my/SESF's behalf is done and dusted, and all it took was one telephone call. '*Captain Monocondilos owes me a few favours,*' said Roland.

I am now in a state of constant bedazzlement with the pace of events over the hours and days of this week. I am on my own and there is no one to share the burden of responsibility. Well, it has been like that ever since I embarked on this project five years ago. Roland talks with me as if we have known each other for a long time. I ship my next SESF container either to the port of discharge, Port Everglades, or the Port of Miami. Roland, Seafreight Lines Agencies supremo, will clear it, pick it up and deliver it to the Bernuth Lines depot, one of whose ships will deliver to ports on the Costa Caribena. However, there is a problem – this ship can only handle 20-foot containers. Methinks I'll just have to purchase a couple of twenties, or swap one of my forties for two twenties. (It doesn't work that way, as I was to learn later.)

Roland talks easily and freely with me, and I can hardly take in this generous offer of his continuing support. I am greatly privileged. It's no big deal. Nothing is a problem. He is giving me a lot

of sound advice and I am trying, unsuccessfully, to scribble down what I need to do. He makes suggestions:
- I need the approval of the Nicaragua Ministry of Education in Managua. I will get Bruce Callow to work on this.
- Make a film that shows what I am trying to accomplish for the schools to which I will send educational resources.
- Key correspondence 2005–present and audited accounts etc.
- I need to get donations that will sustain this project. From whom? He tells me that I will have to get out there with my hands out. I need to get my Argyll and Bute Member of Parliament to give me a mailing list of potential donors and supporters. Use links of your MP, supporters, and churches.
- Contact the British Council; Freight Forwarders; John Sas at Pantos; Patrick Kilfoyle Warrant Freight, Port of Liverpool; Louise Swanson, Knight Watson Ltd Grangemouth. See if they will cut me some slack and shipping companies likewise.

'If your supporters etc. believe in what you are doing, they should support you, David. Their financial support can be tax deductible, which is an incentive for them to do so. You have seen the need,' said Roland. He goes on to ask me if I have Skype, and if so we can communicate via that means.

8:15 p.m. Room 419, The Baymont Miami Airport West Inn and Suites, Miami. Roland and Mrs Malins-Smith have not long dropped me off at this hotel, where he has booked me in. Another luxurious pile, not the Real Metro Centro Intercontinental Managua, but I am grateful that I have been with him ever since Felix the Haitian cabbie dropped me off at his outfit. Roland insisted that I stay behind and enjoy their annual Christmas party, which was overshadowed by the fact that one of his welders had fallen from the top of one of his containers and was in hospital critically ill.

I had a plateful of sweet Caribbean Cuban food, roast pork, beans and rice, macaroni cheese pie, and a bottle of Coca Cola.

His staff were all friendly and trying to make me feel welcome. I was overwhelmed by the hospitality, not being a partygoer, and having to keep myself in check. Some of his senior executives gave me a body swerve. However, earlier today, David Ross at the staff monthly awards presentation did give the Surplus Educational Supplies Foundation a mention, and the part played by their shipping company in delivering four of its 40-foot ocean freight containers loaded with educational resources for Grenadian Government schools.

Saturday 19/12/2009

8:44 a.m. I am writing this up in the guest laundry room, next to the ice machine of the Baymont Inn and Suites, 4th Floor. I have just met a fellow West Indian, Oswald, barrister, Castries, St Lucia, who tells me he was educated in Canada and at the Hugh Wooding Law School, St Augustine Campus of the University of the West Indies. '*We are doing great things. My wife and I have a shoebox programme. We put good things in them for children and old people and travel roon de island to distribute them. We can do great tings to gedda,*' he said.

I have been up and down in the elevator to have an American breakfast of cereal, coffee and toast. I sat at a table with a Danish beekeeper and his son, who are on holiday and setting off from Miami on a cruise of the Caribbean. He mentions in his chat that Christians from Denmark were the first into slavery at St Thomas, Danish Virgin Islands, Charlotte Amalie. I thought the settlers from Scotland, England, and Ireland were the first slavers, but I let that statement pass. I could also have told him that the Hanschell family forebears had settled in the Danish Virgin Islands, moving later to Barbados in the late 19th century. I was trying to listen to people for a change on this trip and not bum my patter.

I met up with him a little while later on the elevator as I returned from reception having changed a $20 bill for some quarters to get these machines going. Now, at 9:10 a.m. the machines are into a drying cycle. I could go outside and have these clothes dried in a matter of minutes under the bright blue sky, which is cracking with sunshine, and which is a change from yesterday. This establishment appears to be well run, but there are not many staff about.

Okay, what's next? I shall go outside and get some sunshine on my skin and then find a post office and write a few thank you postcards. Stay cool and quiet, dude.

11:55 a.m. I am sitting at a table outside the Easy-Going filling station, mini mart supermarket and post office, Doral, Miami, Florida. I've had a hot dog and Costa Rican banana. This is a land of plenty – treats as the sun shines down and there's a fresh Atlantic Ocean breeze on my back.

'Do you speak English?' I ask this passer-by. *'Ah sure do, where do you want to get to?'* he replies. I am trying to find out where I am. I have not long walked up the main road from Baymont Motel. I was looking for somewhere I could scratch a line on a postcard to a few folks. I had some digital images developed in the big drugstore in the shopping centre complex plaza-cum-mall for those who walk as little as possible and must travel everywhere by automobile. There is a pizza joint on the other side of the post office. I had walked into a restaurant run by some Venezuelans and received directions to come here. I crossed the crossroads of two four-lane highways. Before me is this busy filling station and a constant roar of non-stop traffic heading in opposite directions. There is a row of cabbage palm trees planted along the verge of the highway. I have met no one this morning walking on either side of these busy intersecting highways.

On the other side of the highway there are fields with grazing cattle. The Everglades are way to the south, at my back. This is a busy place. The Latinos and other incomers, like Filipinos and Haitians, work hard to make this state function efficiently. Envian a todos honoraria. Rapid Cargo Transport.

Saturday 19/12/2009

4:55 p.m. I am back at the Baymont, the receptionist tells me that there is no message for me from Roland Malins-Smith. Ah well, I'll just have to get on with it. He did say he would call for me this morning. I go outside and sit by the swimming pool and write some more postcards hoping that he will show up.

5:30 p.m. I am here at Olivos Restaurant at the far end of the mall. I can see the Baymont Motel across the way. I have had three waiters offer me a free bottle of wine courtesy of the Baymont, which I have had to decline graciously. I don't want to take any unnecessary risks in the dark later when crossing the death trap before me. Across the car park I can see no litter under the big Winn Dixie sign itemising all the services that can be found in the mall: body waxing; Horacios Salon Spa; Mexican Grill; Check Cashing; Olivos Argentinian Steak House; Fritango Montimbo; Real Estate Doral Estate, etc.

I can just hear the long-tailed blackbirds singing away above the noise of the traffic. I am looking at the clouds lighted from the sun, which is setting fast. The Stars and Stripes is fluttering in the breeze. The flow of traffic never stops. The soup has just arrived. Get tae wuk. I don't need to eat steak again for a long time.

This is another embarrassing moment. The owner-manager-cum-waiter would not accept my RBS Visa card. Fortunately I had mentioned to him, when he asked me where I had come from and what brought me here, that I was trying to help a community in Central America. In lieu of payment I gave him the last few American dollars in my pocket and my remaining Scottish pin, and slunk off back to my kip for the night. I walked through the empty mall beside the large car park till I got to the hazardous pedestrian intersection of the two four-lane highways. I couldn't live here for long. The blackbirds were now roosting among the cabbage palm fronds.

What can I remember from yesterday's visit to the Seafreight Agencies Lines office? Roland giving me advice. '*Keep it small,*

David. G-D does not expect you to do everything.' David Ross, the company vice president, telling me that they had told their employees at the beginning of the year that none of them would be made redundant and that had all received a rise in salary. '*This was some example to our competitors,*' he said. And telling his staff about my work. I have been humbled to date by the whole experience. I had forgotten what I had wanted to remember, so I do so now and make a note of it here.

7:40 p.m. I am back in Room 419, Baymont Inn. I have ironed two pairs of trousers and the shirt I wore to go out to the Argentinian restaurant.

I recall again, for posterity, how I occupied myself this morning …

Today, for most of the morning, I sat outside the shop of a filling station and wrote about a dozen postcards of Florida views. Then, after posting them at the post office inside the minimart, I went into their 'Rest Room' for a shave and answered a call of nature, which freshened and relieved me somewhat. I then walked back to the Baymont, made myself a coffee and was disappointed why no messages had been left: I was to learn why later. I could have spread my wings and gone sightseeing, but it was just as well I didn't. Everything is plastic and disposable. I went outside and sat by the swimming pool in the rays of the setting sun and sorted the photographs into some order. There was no one about. I'm just chilling out, managing to stay on the straight and narrow. So far so good. I kept 'focused'. For whom, for what?

I am now watching CNN news and Deepak Chopra. Ha cha Babu. I resist switching to any of the other channels. I try to get my head down.

I am later awakened by the phone ringing. It scares the wits out of me. It's Roland, concerned and annoyed, asking me where I had been all day and why I had not got his messages, which unbeknownst to me had been left on my room telephone's answering machine. More embarrassment. I felt miserable. This is not good. I only think later why he had not left a message as well at reception, as I had checked with them throughout the day to see if he had called me. So, I turn on the light and write him an apologetic note explaining what I had done all day while I was waiting to hear from him. Sometimes, no matter how hard I try, I just do not seem to win.

Sunday 20/12/2009

9:31 a.m. I set off shortly after an American breakfast with directions from the Cuban-American receptionist. After several miles up the road (you mean four-lane highway) I arrived at what was a mega condominium gated community situated in parkland. I had to ask directions once more from the gatekeepers' cubicle and headed back down the road from whence I had come, arriving at Seafreight Agencies Lines office and warehouse. A grumpy Latino-American sitting in his car reluctantly told me where the firm's letter box was. I walked on back to the Baymont Inn: sterile hostelry and no fun.

I am going to check myself out and get the Miami International Airport bus. I might as well cool my heels there as it's just as good, if not better, than here. At least I am en route and less likely to miss my flight.

11:30 a.m. I am sitting in the Au Bon Pan Diner. I waited for an hour in the queue to get to the American Airlines desk, to then be told that I had to return in five hours. So, I came here and met a pleasant gentleman who works for Carnival Tours. His job is to welcome folk. He works three days a week, which pays his bills. He has worked all over South America for this American company. I'm cooling my heels right enough. Go with the flow, Davey Boy.

On the way out here, on the Baymont Inn airport shuttle bus, I got into conversation with a family of Venezuelans whose daughter was as keen to speak her little English as I was to speak my even less Spanish, and that was fun.

1:10 p.m. I am still waiting to board my flight back to Heathrow, but at least I have got somewhere to park myself in this terminal at Miami International Airport. I watch the passing scene and try to summarise what I gained from this short trip, which was achieved at no little personal and financial cost.

I can only wait now and see what kind of response I get from the people at the British Embassy in Costa Rica, who represent and better liaise with those in the Republic of Nicaragua whose allegiance is to the Crown. And what kind of feedback will I get from the Nicaraguan Ministry of Education, and specifically the Nicaraguan Ministry of the Interior Region Autonoma Atlantico Sur (RAAS), who have, so far, not delivered my 40 boxes of library books shipped at my expense for the anglophone community in Bluefields. Why the delay in the handover?

Impressions and blessings:
- Bruce's kindness. Thoughtful. He kept me on the tram lines.
- The British Embassy, Foreign and Commonwealth Office, travel arrangements made on my behalf in Nicaragua were without fault. They had prepared a varied and interesting agenda for me, which enabled me to gain some insight into the educational resource needs of the four schools that I had visited – Rama Cay, Bluefields, and El Bluff.
- The contrast between the Haves and the Have Nots – the splendour of the Real Intercontinental Metro Centro Managua and the squalor beyond the confines of its walls, and similarly of Hotel Oasis in in Bluefields.
- The contrast between the Haves and Have Nots here in South Florida, USA, and the poverty stricken mainland of South America. Child beggars on the streets of Bluefields and

Managua, and the elderly and infirm in Nicaragua with no visible means of support.
- Tom Morton and Robert Morton in Bluefields, who both spoke English.
- The friendliness of the many people I met on this brief visit Bluefields, Nicaragua.
- The lush tropical vegetation, which was familiar, and were it not for the languages being spoken and the ever-present subtext of La Violencia I felt at home and not out of place geographically.

What did I gain from this trip?
- Personal contact in Bluefields with local Nicaraguan government officials, who showed a guarded interest in the work of my charity and expressed tentative provisional support. Let us see if the donation of books finally gets to the Costa Caribena, and what they do with them.
- I gained an insight and knowledge of the personal circumstances and the environment of the potential beneficiaries – context which I could have got no other way.
- I received a commitment of assistance to deliver SESF container shipments of educational resources to Bluefields from two of the leading Miami, Florida, shipping companies, Seafreight Agencies Lines and Bernfuth Lines, which operate throughout the Caribbean and Costa Caribena.
- A firm and unequivocal desire to receive at least one 20-foot ocean freight container shipment of educational resources from the Señora Flores Forbes, principal of the Santa Rosa School, Barrio Santa Rosa, Bluefields; Señora Elba Blandon, Asesora de Espanol Secundaria; Señora Grace Paterson Hansack, Directora del Instituto Nacional Nuevo Amanecer, and Directora Primaria Virgen del Carmen, El Bluff.
- A firm expression of interest in the work of SESF from: officials in the local Nicaraguan Ministry of Education, Bluefields

office; the leader of the Rama Cay and Rama Cay High School, Reverend Cleveland McCrea; and Bluefields Indian and Caribbean University.
- My meeting with Señor Oscar Aburto, the Regional Delegate to the Ministry of Education in Managua, who recorded our meeting on Wednesday 16 December (who I was to meet coincidentally prior to our departure from Bluefields on Thursday 17 December). Once again, he thought what I planned was acceptable and expressed his support.
- And finally, and most importantly, the initial interest in my initiative and continuing support for it from Ambassador Tom Kennedy in San José, Costa Rica, which resulted in my visit to see for myself what the needs were. He had come across an account of my SESF initiative in an article by Simon Bain, journalist, in the *Glasgow Herald*. And the support of Bruce Callow representing the Foreign and Commonwealth Office, government of the United Kingdom, who took the trouble to make this visit a success.

12:45 p.m. I am still cooling my heels. I've just visited a spotlessly clean men's washroom.

3:05 p.m. There is some movement in the right direction thanks to the efficient and friendly assistance of Mrs Adams at the American Airlines desk, who pointed me in the direction of E10, the concourse I came in on from the London flight from Heathrow, Monday 14 December.

Not more blunders, surely? When I left my place in the Au Bon Pan Diner, I had forgotten my suitcase. Oops! A family member, who had been sitting nearby on their way back to Saint Maarten, came running after me to tell me that I had left it behind. Whew!

A little while ago I was being rushed through airport security clearance. Belt, shoes off, etc. Another blunder. I had put down my folder with passport, boarding pass etc. Oh no! Where was it?

Sunday 20/12/2009

An immigration official had picked it up. Keep it together, chico. I am now in another departure lounge overlooking a vast runway, with the big sun going down. Mucharse despacho, Señor David.

5:05 p.m. I am sitting here, still waiting. I wandered around, holding tightly onto my belongings. Bought myself a cup of coffee and a hot dog with mustard, eavesdropping on a well-to-do family with distinct Caribbean accents who are sitting here quite close to me. A little lad in the family smiles at me. I say '*hi.*' The little lad's dad, with a solemn face, who had been sitting behind me, appears before me.

'*Where do you come from?*' he asks me sharply. '*I come from Barbados,*' I said. I was going to be polite and truthful, and make this conversation last a wee bit. In another period of my life I would have ignored his rudeness. '*Where do you come from?*' I had staked my claim to this corner of the lounge before this family arrived. '*Are you going to London?*' I asked. '*No,*' he replied. '*Wales?*' I guess. I thought he had what was a Welsh sounding lilt. '*No,*' he said. '*Well then, give me a clue,*' I said. '*It begins with an S,*' he said. Begins with an S, hmmm. Nice little game among grown-ups. I reel off Sweden, Serbia, Spain. Negative. '*Okay then, give me another clue,*' I said. '*St,*' he said. '*Got it, you guys are heading for St Lucia!*' '*Yes,*' he said. And I told him that he was the second St Lucian I had met. '*Oh?*' Quizzical. You're not black, he thinks, you can't be a Barbadian. And he begins to cross-examine me. '*What's your name?*' he asks me in an Englishified Caribbean twang. His interest, or rather his curiosity, has picked up. He has begun to interrogate me now to check out my claim to hail from that island in the West Indies, and he seems keen to invalidate my claim to be a Barbadian. I play along. '*Hanschell? Hanschell Innis, any relation to Hanschell Innis?*' he queries.

'*Hanschell Innis is the title of a merger of two companies in Barbados, which was once Hanschell and Larsen and, before that,*

Hanschell Ltd, which was the firm of ship chandlers and shipping agents that had been founded by my great-grandfather, VH Hanschell. We have nothing to do with the present firm,' I reply. He warms a little to me now, ever so slightly, and he begins to tell me that his family had, until recently, a hardware business in Castries, the capital of St Lucia, for over a hundred years. He travels to Barbados regularly and they have sold their family business to Goddards.

The cross-examination continues. Can he not get off his high horse? *'Did you go to Mapps?'* he asks, pointedly. *'No, I did not,'* I reply. This was a private school started in the early sixties by Graham Wilkes, who was a geography and games master at Lodge School, who had come to the Land of The Flying Fish from England, and was a hero to the boys as he claimed to have played professional football. Everton, I think.

I record here three recollections that come to mind: me clumsily attempting to dribble a football round a row of cricket stumps that had been set out by him on the playing field; him being very annoyed with me in the second form for being unable to write properly with either of my two broken arms, which were in plaster; and him booting a fellow pupil out of the classroom. I am sure the establishment I attended from 1955 to 1961, and his own school, which he founded in the late fifties in the adjacent parish of St Philip, could not, for me, have been worse. Needless to say, none of this was divulged to my interlocutor.

He tells me about the wonderful and privileged life his two boys have sailing, playing squash and rugby. *'We spend three months of the year in England, where I went to school,'* he said. What ho, dear chap, pip, so what? I ask him if he happens to know Oswald W. Larcher, Barrister at Law, the illustrious St Lucian who I met yesterday while I was doing my dhobi at the Baymont Inn laundry room. *'No, I don't him, but I do know a Larcher who is an electrician,'* he replied haughtily. Who are you, dear chap, and where do you rank in my pecking order? A stifling preoccupation and fixation with class and status. Where did I sit in his valuation? He tells me that his family firm were agents for Bernuth Lines.

Ah well, the good folk you meet on the road. Meanwhile his two lads have disappeared, no doubt fed up with two speerin' adults. Our conversation ended with his final remark. He did not tell me his name.

Monday 21/12/2009

12:22 p.m. Terminal One Heathrow, England, United Kingdom. Journeying mercies. I am glad to be off that aircraft and away from the hassle of Miami airport security, who tipped everything before them out of my shoulder bag. I kept my cool. I could hear Marion's words to me on that score. I flew over with Pedro, of Cuban descent, from Tampa, originally from New York. He told me that he was on his way to Kandahar, Afghanistan. An IT communications technician on contract to the US Army. Well, I am looking forward to going home. It has been a long week and an unforgettable one.

3:31 p.m. Aboard BMI Flight 56 to Glasgow. Earlier I met John, who was in my 1991–1992 P3/4/5 composite class at North Bute Primary School, Port Bannatyne. We were both surprised. *'We have been de-iced and are getting ready for take-off.'* Thick grey cloud and sleety rain. Prior to boarding I looked at emails from the family. Welcome home from Marion.

6:04 p.m. I am in the rattling carriage of the train on its way for Wemyss Bay. On arrival at Glasgow Airport I collected my suitcase, put it on a trolley, and went along to the Barrhead Travel Ltd desk to present Elisa, sales executive with a T-shirt from Bluefields, Nicaragua (in lieu of a coconut) for all her efficient and friendly help. I put it on her desk as she was on the telephone. I then continued outside the terminal to get the bus for Paisley. As I pushed the trolley along to the bus, Elisa, bless her, appeared, running after me to give me a hug. What a welcome that was back tae bonita Escocia!

Note to End Volume Two

Over the next eight years, the Surplus Educational Supplies Foundation, in collaboration with the United Kingdom logistics industry and many individuals, were able to deliver welcome shipments of much needed, fit-for-purpose, surplus to requirements educational resources to schools in Ghana, West Africa, Tanzania, East Africa, Nicaragua, Bluefields City, Costa Caribena, Central America, Republic of Liberia, Jamaica and the Republic of Haiti: this was an achievement, I think, of which we could all be proud. I would like to take this opportunity to thank, especially, the following teams of young people from Community Services, Argyll and Bute Council, Fife Council and Edinburgh City Council who assisted me personally in the uplift of resources. And my fellow teacher members of the Educational Institute of Scotland, from the following local associations: Fife, Inverclyde, Aberdeenshire, Aberdeen, East Ayshire, East Dunbartonshire, East Morayshire, Perth and Kinross, and Argyll and Bute – your generosity, defrayed expenses, and solidarity encouraged me greatly.

www.ingramcontent.com/pod-product-compliance
Lightning Source LLC
Chambersburg PA
CBHW071224080526
44587CB00013BA/1487